SEAN O'CASEY
CENTENARY ESSAYS

IRISH LITERARY STUDIES

SEAN O'CASEY
CENTENARY ESSAYS

edited by
David Krause and Robert G. Lowery

Irish Literary Studies 7

COLIN SMYTHE
Gerrards Cross, 1980

First published in 1980 by Colin Smythe Ltd.,
P.O. Box 6, Gerrards Cross, Buckinghamshire

British Library Cataloguing in Publication Data

Sean O'Casey. – (Irish literary studies; 7
    ISSN 0140–895X).
    1. O'Casey, Sean – Criticism and interpretation
    I. Krause, David
    II. Lowery, Robert G.
    III. Series
    822′.9′12   PR6029.C33Z/

ISBN 0–86140–008–9

Printed in Great Britain
Set by Watford Typesetters Ltd.
and printed and bound by Billing & Sons Ltd.,
Guildford, London, Oxford, Worcester

DEDICATION

*To all God's children, the
poor, the unemployed, the
wretched of the earth – Sean's
people.*

Contents

Acknowledgements

The publishers wish to thank the following for permission to publish the extracts from Sean O'Casey's works that are quoted in this volume: –

To Macmillan, London and Basingstoke, for world rights, except for the U.S.A., in all Sean O'Casey's writings.

For the U.S.A. our thanks to Macmillan Publishing Co. Inc., New York for permission to quote from the following works:

I Knock at the Door © 1939 by Macmillan Publishing Co. Inc., renewed 1967 by Eileen O'Casey, Breon O'Casey and Shivaun Kenig;

Pictures in the Hallway © 1942 by Sean O'Casey, renewed 1970 by Eileen O'Casey, Breon O'Casey and Shivaun O'Casey;

Drums Under the Windows © 1945, 1946 by Sean O'Casey, renewed 1973, 1974 by Eileen O'Casey, Breon O'Casey and Shivaun O'Casey;

Inishfallen Fare Thee Well © 1949 by Sean O'Casey, renewed 1977 by Eileen O'Casey, Breon O'Casey and Shivaun O'Casey;

Rose and Crown © 1952 by Sean O'Casey, renewed 1980 by Eileen O'Casey;

Sunset and Evening Star © 1954 by Sean O'Casey;

Purple Dust © 1940 by Sean O'Casey, renewed 1968 by Eileen O'Casey;

Red Roses for Me © 1943, 1944 by Sean O'Casey, renewed 1971, 1972 by Eileen O'Casey, Breon O'Casey and Shivaun Kenig;

Oak Leaves and Lavender © 1946, 1947 by Sean O'Casey, renewed 1974, 1975 by Eileen O'Casey and Breon O'Casey;

The Bishop's Bonfire © 1955 by Sean O'Casey.

To St. Martin's Press Inc., New York, our thanks for permission to quote from *Within the Gates, Windfalls, The Flying Wasp, Juno and the Paycock, The Silver Tassie, The Shadow of a Gunman* and *The Plough and the Stars*.

To Eileen O'Casey for permission to quote from *The Star Turns Red* and *Cock-a-Doodle Dandy*.

SEAN O'CASEY: A CHRONOLOGY

ROBERT G. LOWERY

1880	March 30	Born John Casey at 85 Upper Dorset Street, Dublin, to Michael and Susan Casey.
	July 28	Baptized at St. Mary's Church (Church of Ireland)
1883		Moves to 9 Innisfallen Parade
1885		Attends St. Mary's Infant School, 20 Lower Dominick Street
1886	September 6	Michael Casey, father, dies at the age of forty-nine. Buried at Mount Jerome Cemetery.
1887		Wins a second-class prize for oral proficiency in Holy Scripture and Church Formularies at St. Mary's Sunday School.
1888		Moves to St. Mary's School, 20 Lower Dominick Street, where his sister, Isabella Casey, works as a teacher.
	April	Attends St. Mary's National School through February 1889.
1889		Moves to 22 Hawthorne Terrace, St. Barnabas Parish.
	March 7	Isabella Casey marries Nicholas Benson.
1890		Attends St. Barnabas National School for a brief time.
1894		Employed as a stock boy at Leedom, Hampton and Co. wholesale chandlers, 22 Henry Street, where he works for about eighteen months.
1895		Acts as Father Dolan in Dion Boucicault's play, *The Shaughraun*, at the Mechanics Theatre, Abbey Street. In 1904 the Mechanics became the Abbey Theatre.
1896		Employed as a van boy for one week at Eason and Son, wholesale newsagents, Lower Abbey Street. Dismissed for disobedience.

1

1897		Moves to 18 Abercorn Road near St. Barnabas Church.
1898	March 29	Confirmation in the Church of Ireland at Clontarf Parish Church.
1900		Teaching Sunday School at St. Barnabas Church until 1903.
1902		Begins employment as a laborer on the Great Northern Railway of Ireland where he remains for nine years.
1906		Learns Irish language and Gaelicizes his name to Sean O Cathasaigh. Joins the Drumcondra Branch of the Gaelic League where he becomes secretary. Recruits Ernest Blythe into the Irish Republican Brotherhood.
1907		Joins the St. Laurence O'Toole Club and writes stories and articles for the club journal.
	May 25	Publishes first article, 'Sound the Loud Trumpet,' in *The Peasant and Irish Ireland*, edited by William Patrick Ryan.
1910		Founder-member and secretary of the St. Laurence O'Toole Pipers' Band.
1911		Joins the Irish Transport and General Workers' Union.
	December	Dismissed from his job at the Great Northern Railway of Ireland for refusing to sign a pledge not to resign from the union.
1912		Reads the Home Rule Edition of George Bernard Shaw's *John Bull's Other Island* and gives up nationalism.
1913	July	Secretary of the Wolfe Tone Memorial Committee.
	August	Secretary of the Women and Children's Relief Fund during the six-month Dublin Lockout.
	October	Joins the Irish Citizen Army.
1914	February 6	Tom Casey, brother, dies at age forty-four
	March	Secretary and member of the Army Council of the Irish Citizen Army through October. Writes their constitution and recruiting leaflets.

	Writes a regular column, 'By the Camp Fire,' for the Irish Citizen Army in the *Irish Worker*.
June	Helps to organize march to Bodenstown to honor the memory of Wolfe Tone.
October	Resigns from the Irish Citizen Army after dispute over Constance Markiewicz.
1915 August 15	Enters St. Vincent's Hospital, Dublin, for an operation on his neck for tubercular glands which had troubled him since his youth.
1916 January	Publishes 'The Grand Oul' Dame Britannia', one of the greatest of anti-war ballads.
1917	Meets Maura Keating, his first steady girlfriend, at the St. Laurence O'Toole Dramatic Club.
September	Publishes *Lament for Thomas Ashe*, a moving tribute to his friend and Irish patriot.
November 25	Acts in the St. Laurence O'Toole Dramatic Club production of Thomas K. Moylan's *Naboclish* at the Empire (now Olympia) Theatre.
1918 January 1	Isabella Casey Beaver, sister, dies at the age of fifty-two.
February-May	Publication of The Story of Thomas Ashe; The Sacrifice of Thomas Ashe; *Songs of the Wren No. 1; Songs of Wren No. 2;* and *More Songs of the Wren*.
November 9	Susan Casey, mother, dies at the age of eighty-one.
1919 March	Publication of *The Story of the Irish Citizen Army* under the name 'P. O Cathasaigh,' typographical error.
1920 January 26	Abbey Theatre rejects his first two plays, *The Harvest Festival* and *The Frost in the Flower*.
	Moves to a tenement at 35 Mountjoy Square where he shares a room with Micheal O Maolain.
	Works as a janitor at the Old Forester's Hall, 10 Langrishe Place, Summerhill.
1921	Moves into a room at 422 North Circular Road where he writes his three major Dublin

		plays : *The Shadow of a Gunman, Juno and the Paycock*, and *The Plough and the Stars.*
	November	Secretary of the Release Jim Larkin Committee and the Jim Larkin Correspondence Committee.
1922	April 15	Abbey Theatre rejects *The Seamless Coat of Kathleen.*
	September 28	Abbey Theatre rejects *The Crimson in the Tri-colour.*
	November 17	Abbey Theatre accepts *The Shadow of a Gunman.*
1923	April 12	World premiere of *The Shadow of a Gunman* at the Abbey Theatre.
	October 1	World premiere of *Cathleen Listens In* at the Abbey Theatre.
1924	March 3	World premiere of *Juno and the Paycock* at the Abbey Theatre.
	June 7	Visit to Lady Gregory's house at Coole Park, Galway.
	June	Joins Society of Authors and Playwrights.
	September 29	World premiere of *Nannie's Night Out* at the Abbey Theatre.
1925		Lady Gregory urges him to take position of registrar of National Gallery of Ireland, but he declines.
	February 10	Publication of *Two Plays* (*Juno* and *Gunman*), dedicated 'To Maura and to the Abbey Theatre.'
	November 16	British premiere of *Juno and the Paycock*, Royalty Theatre, London.
1926		Translation of *Juno and the Paycock* into Swedish, probably the first foreign translation of his works.
	February 8	World premiere of *The Plough and the Stars* at the Abbey Theatre.
	February 10	Nationalist riots in the Abbey Theatre against the *Plough and the Stars.* Disturbances continue for several days. He publicly debates the nationalists.
	March 15	American premiere of *Juno and the Paycock*, Mayfair Theatre, New York.
	March 23	Receives the Hawthornden Literary Prize of £100 in London for *Juno and the Paycock.*

	April	Publication of *The Plough and the Stars*, dedicated 'To the Gay Laugh of my Mother at the gate of the grave.'
1926		Lives at 7 Lansdowne Terrace, Guildford Street, London.
		Moves to 2 Trafalgar Chambers, Chelsea Square, Chelsea.
	May	Has his portrait painted by Augustus John which is used in later published editions of the *Plough*.
	May 12	British premiere of *The Plough and the Stars*, Fortune Theatre, London.
	July	Moves to 32 Clareville Street, South Kensington, S.W.7.
1927	May 27	British premiere of *The Shadow of a Gunman*, Court Theatre, London.
	September 23	Marries Eileen Reynolds Carey in the Roman Catholic Church of Our Most Holy Redeemer and St. Thomas More, Chelsea.
	November 27	American premiere of *The Plough and the Stars*, Hudson Theatre, New York.
1928	January	Moves to 19 Woronzow Road, St. Johns Wood, N.W.8.
	April 20	Abbey Theatre rejects *The Silver Tassie*.
	April 30	Birth of his son Breon.
	June 12	Publication of *The Silver Tassie*, dedicated 'To Eileen with the yellow daffodils in the green vase.'
1929	October 11	World premiere of *The Silver Tassie* at the Apollo Theatre, London, directed by Raymond Massey.
	October 24	American premiere of *The Silver Tassie*, Irish Theatre, New York.
1930	September 22	Film of *Juno and the Paycock* is released, directed by Alfred Hitchcock.
	November 10	Film of *Juno and the Paycock* is burned in the streets of Limerick by Irish nationalists.
1931	September	Moves to 2 Misbourne Cottages, Chalfont St. Giles, Buckinghamshire.
	October	Moves to Hillcrest, Chalfont St. Giles, Buckinghamshire.
	November	Writes first autobiographical sketch, 'A Child is Born,' which becomes the opening

	chapter of *I Knock at the Door* (1939).
1932 July	Writes *A Pound on Demand*, a one-act play.
1933 May	His short story, 'I Wanna Woman,' is censored by the printer of *Time and Tide*.
November 24	Publication of *Within the Gates*, full-length play.
1934 February 7	World premiere of *Within the Gates* at the Royalty Theatre, London.
September 13	Leaves Southampton on the *Majestic* and arrives in New York on September 19 for the American premiere of *Within the Gates*.
October 16	Publication of *Windfalls*, a collection of early poems, four short stories, and two one-act plays (*A Pound on Demand* and *The End of the Beginning*).
October 22	American premiere of *Within the Gates*, National Theatre, New York.
November 16	Gives the Morris Gray Poetry Talk at Harvard University on 'The Old Drama and the New.'
December 4	*Windfalls* is banned by the Irish Censorship of Publications Board.
December 12	Leaves New York on the *Britannic* and arrives in Liverpool on December 23.
1935 January 11	Birth of his son Niall.
January 15	*Within the Gates* is banned by Mayor Frederick Mansfield of Boston, forcing the cancellation of a scheduled thirteen-city tour.
August 12	Irish premiere of *The Silver Tassie*, Abbey Theatre.
September	Visits Wales with his family for a vacation. Returns to Dublin for the last time on a two-week visit, and meets Yeats on friendly terms.
October	Publication of *Five Irish Plays* (*Gunman, Juno, Plough, End of the Beginning, Pound on Demand*).
1936 February	Gives a talk, 'The Holy Ghost Leaves England,' to the Shirley Society of St. Catharine's College, Cambridge.
1937 February 8	World premiere of *The End of the Beginning* at the Abbey Theatre.

	March 5	Publication of *The Flying Wasp*, a collection of essays, articles, and reviews.
	March 15	Film of *The Plough and the Stars* is released, directed by John Ford.
	August	Spends six weeks in Wales with his family on vacation and speaks at a rally in support of imprisoned Welsh political activists.
1938	September	Moves to Tingrith, Totnes, Devon.
1939	March 3	Publication of *I Knock at the Door*, first volume of autobiography.
	May 16	*I Knock at the Door* is banned by the Irish Censorship of Publications Board.
	September 28	Birth of his daughter Shivaun.
1940	January	Barry Fitzgerald and Sara Allgood appear together for the last time in a revival of *Juno and the Paycock* at the Mansfield Theatre, New York.
	February 15	Publication of *The Star Turns Red* in London. Not published in the United States for fear of alienating British opinion.
	March 12	World premiere of *The Star Turns Red* at the Unity Theatre, London, directed by John Allen.
	June 10	Becomes a member of the Advisory Board, *Daily Worker*, London.
	November 19	Publication of *Purple Dust*, dedicated 'To Shivaun.'
1941	July	Finishes writing *Pictures in the Hallway*.
1942	February 17	Publication of *Pictures in the Hallway*, volume two of his autobiography.
	November 17	Publication of *Red Roses for Me*. dedicated 'To Dr. J. D. Cummins in memory of the grand chats around his surgery fire.'
1943	March 15	World premiere of *Red Roses for Me* at the Olympia Theatre, Dublin.
	December 16	World premiere of *Purple Dust* at the People's Theatre, Newcastle-upon-Tyne, England.
1945	January 17	Turns down offer of $100,000 to write the screenplay for Thomas Wolfe's *Look Homeward Angel*.
	October 16	Publishes *Drums Under the Windows*, volume three of his autobiography.

October 31	*Purple Dust* opens in Liverpool, performed by the Liverpool Old Vic Company.
1946 February 26	*Red Roses for Me* opens in London at the Embassy Theatre.
April 30	Publication of *Oak Leaves and Lavender*.
November 28	World premiere of *Oak Leaves and Lavender* at the Helsingborgs Stadtteatre, Sweden.
1947 January 11	Michael Casey, brother, dies in Dublin at the age of eighty-one.
January 30	Long-time friend, James Larkin, dies in Dublin at the age of sixty-nine.
May 13	English premiere, *Oak Leaves and Lavender*, Lyric Theatre Hammersmith, presented by Bronson Albery.
May 26	*The Silver Tassie* opens at the Gaiety Theatre, Dublin.
December 16	Ban against *I Knock at the Door* and *Pictures in the Hallway* removed by the Irish Censorship of Publications Board.
1949 January 28	Publication of *Inishfallen, Fare Thee Well*, volume four of his autobiography. Given the 'Page One Award' by the Newspaper Guild of New York for *Inishfallen, Fare Thee Well*.
April 8	Publication of *Cock-a-Doodle Dandy*, dedicated to James Stephens, Irish poet.
July 21	*The Silver Tassie* opens at Carnegie Hall, New York, presented by the 'Interplayers' for eighty performances.
November 11	Publication of volumes one and two of *Collected Plays* (*Juno, Gunman, Plough, End of the Beginning* – I. *Tassie, Gates, Star Turns Red* – II.)
December 10	World premiere of *Cock-a-Doodle Dandy* at the People's Theatre, Newcastle-upon-Tyne, England.
1950	Signs the Stockholm Appeal for the elimination of nuclear weapons.
January 30	American premiere, *Cock-a-Doodle Dandy*, Theatre '50, Dallas, Texas, directed by Margo Jones.
1951 April 25	American premiere, *Red Roses for Me*, Playhouse, Houston, Texas, directed by

		John O'Shaughnessy.
	July 17	Publication of volumes three and four of *Collected Plays* (*Purple Dust, Red Roses, Hall of Healing* – III. *Oak Leaves and Lavender, Cock-a-Doodle Dandy, Bedtime Story, Time to Go* – IV.)
	September 24	*The Silver Tassie* opens at the Abbey Theatre, directed by Ria Mooney.
1952	May 7	World premiere of *Bedtime Story, Time to Go*, and *Hall of Healing* at Yugoslav-American Hall, New York.
	July 4	Publication of *Rose and Crown*, volume five of his autobiography.
	November 8	German-language premiere of *The Silver Tassie*, Schauspielhaus, Switzerland.
1953	June 20	*The Silver Tassie*, in a German translation by Elisabeth Freundlich and Gunter Anders, is performed in Berlin, three days after an uprising in the German Democratic Republic. Disturbances break out in the theatre.
	September 15	*Juno and the Paycock* opens in Berlin, translated by G. Goyert and E. Kalser, directed by Peter Thomas.
1954	May 26	German premiere of *The Shadow of a Gunman*, Berlin, translated by A. M. Jokl, directed by Rudolf Wessely.
	June 9	Moves to 3 Villa Rosa Flats, 40 Trumlands Road, St. Marychurch, Torquay, Devon.
	October 29	Publication of *Sunset and Evening Star*, volume six and the last instalment of his autobiography.
1955	February 28	World premiere of *The Bishop's Bonfire*, Gaiety Theatre, starring Cyril Cusack, directed by Tyrone Gutherie.
	June 24	Publication of *The Bishop's Bonfire*.
	December 28	*Red Roses for Me* opens in New York at the Booth Theatre, directed by John O'Shaughnessy.
1956	February	Undergoes a prostrate operation at the Tor Bay hospital, followed by a kidney stone operation a month later.
	March	Publication of *The Green Crow*, a collection of essays.

	October	Publication of *Mirror in my House*, a two-volume edition of his autobiographies.
	December 27	*Purple Dust* opens in New York at the Cherry Lane Theatre and runs until January 5, 1958: the longest run of any O'Casey play.
	December 29	Youngest son, Niall, dies of leukaemia.
1957	January 3	Niall O'Casey's ashes are scattered in the Garden of Remembrance, Golders Green Crematorium, London.
	February 15	*The Green Crow* seized by Irish Customs office and unofficially banned for a year.
	May	Russian translation and publication of *Gunman, Juno, I Knock at the Door*, and *Pictures in the Hallway*.
	September	Translation of *The Bishop's Bonfire*, published in *Zvezda*, organ of Union of Soviet Writers.
	October 10	Dublin Tostal Council accepts *The Drums of Father Ned* for the International Theatre Festival in 1958.
1958	January	Archbishop of Dublin disapproves of *The Drums of Father Ned* and a dramatisation of Joyce's *Ulysses* at the Theatre Festival.
	February	The Archbishop's attitude leads indirectly to the censorship of O'Casey, Joyce, and Beckett, whose works are withdrawn from the Tostal Theatre Festival.
	July	In retaliation for the banning of *Drums* of *Father Ned*, he bans all professional productions of his plays in Ireland, which he maintains until 1964.
	November 12	New York premiere of *Cock-a-Doodle Dandy*, Carnegie Hall Playhouse.
	November 20	*The Shadow of a Gunman* opens in New York at the Bijou Theatre, presented by the Actors' Studio, directed by Jack Garfein.
1959	January	Appears in a reunion scene with Barry Fitzgerald in the documentry film, 'Salute to the Abbey Theatre: Cradle of Genius,' directed by Paul Rotha.
	February	Translation and publication of *The Star Turns Red* in China.
	March 9	*Juno*, a musical based on *Juno and the*

	Paycock opens in New York at the Winter Garden Theatre. Book by Joseph Stein, music and lyrics by Marc Blitzstein.
April 25	World premiere of *The Drums of Father Ned*, Lafayette, Indiana.
September 17	London premiere, *Cock-a-Doodle Dandy*, Royal Court Theatre.
1960 March 30	A celebration of his eightieth birthday during which a group of eighteen writers and theatre people from Dublin send him a silver tankard or 'tassie' in appreciation. Samuel Beckett in Paris sends a message: 'To my great compatriot Sean O'Casey, from France where he is honoured, I send my enduring gratitude and homage.'
May	Translation of *Cock-a-Doodle Dandy* into Polish by Cecylia Wojewoda for *Dialog*.
June 16	Publication of *The Drums of Father Ned*.
November 8	European premiere, *The Drums of Father Ned*, Queen's Theatre, Hornchurch.
1961 January 29	'Sean O'Casey Pipe Night' celebrated at the Players Club in New York.
February 4	Refuses to accept honorary degree of Doctor of Letters from Trinity College, Dublin.
June 1	Publication of *Behind the Green Curtains, Figuro in the Night*, and *The Moon Shines on Kylenamoe*.
July 26	English premiere, *The Bishop's Bonfire*, Mermaid Theatre, London.
October	Translation of *Red Roses for Me* into Polish by Cecylia Wojewoda for *Dialog*.
1962 May 4	World premiere of *Figuro in the Night*, Hofstra University, Hempstead, New York.
August 16	*Purple Dust* opens in London at the Mermaid Theatre O'Casey Festival, directed by Frank Dunlop.
September 5	*Red Roses for Me* opens in London at the Mermaid Theatre O'Casey Festival, directed by Julius Gellner.
September 26	*The Plough and the Stars* opens in London at the Mermaid Theatre O'Casey Festival, directed by Joss Ackland.

October 23   Publication of *Feathers from a Green Crow*,
              a collection of his early political writings,
              edited by Robert Hogan.

October 30   A double bill of *Figuro in the Night* and *The
              Moon Shines on Kylenamoe* opens in New
              York at the off-Broadway Theatre de Lys,
              presented by ANTA Matinee Theatre,
              directed by John O'Shaughnessy.

December 5   World premiere of *Behind the Green
              Curtains* at the University of Rochester, New
              York.

1963 January 3   Publication of *Under a Colored Cap*,
                  'Articles Merry and Mournful, with Com-
                  ments and a Song.'

March   *Red Roses for Me* performed at the
              Deutsches Theatre, German Democratic
              Republic, in a German translation.

March 27   Theatre section of Union of Soviet Writers
              in Moscow pay tribute to him on Inter-
              national Theatre Day.

July   The Lord Chamberlain bans a performance
              of *Figuro in the Night* at a Festival of Irish
              comedy in London.

1964 January Lifts his seven-year ban on professional pro-
              ductions of his plays in Ireland so that the
              Abbey Theatre can present his works in
              London at the World Theatre Festival
              honouring the 400th anniversary of Shake-
              speare's birth.

April 20   *Juno and the Paycock* is presented by the
              Abbey Theatre in London at the World
              Theatre Festival.

April 27   *The Plough and the Stars* is presented by
              the Abbey Theatre in London at the World
              Theatre Festival.

August   Suffers a heart attack and spends two weeks
              at Tor Bay Clinic.

September 18   Dies of a second heart attack at the Tor
               Bay Clinic.

September 22   His body is cremated in Torquay.

October 3   His ashes are scattered in the Garden of
              Remembrance at the Golders Green
              Crematorium, London, in an area between
              the Shelley and Tennyson rose beds.

SEAN O'CASEY AND
THE ABBEY THEATRE, DUBLIN

RONALD AYLING

I

I have just re-read your *Irish Theatre*, and have harboured
a feeling of regret that I wasn't with the Abbey in the great
fight that did so much for Ireland's soul, and Ireland's body.
I have been thinking of Synge, Hugh Lane, Robert Gregory . . .
and Ledwidge . . . all now of the dead; and you, Yeats, Stephens
and Shaw, still, happily, of the living. . . . When one remembers
those that have died; and these that still live, one, when thinking of Ireland, can still murmur: blessed is the womb that bore
them, and the paps that they have sucked.
Letter from O'Casey to Lady Gregory, October 1924.
All art is a collaboration.
J. M. Synge: Preface to The Playboy of the Western World.

Irish critics and commentators, possibly begrudging Sean
O'Casey's exceptional popularity, have claimed that much of this
success in his native city can be attributed to the acting of the
Abbey company and the active collaboration of the theatre's
directors in writing and revising his plays. I remember vividly, on
one of my first visits to Dublin in the early 1950s, being assured by
Professor David Greene – a fine critic, distinguished Gaelic scholar
and, at that time, Professor of Irish at Trinity College Dublin –
that the 'difference in quality' between O'Casey's Abbey dramas
and his later ones was that Lady Gregory and other unacknow-
ledged 'collaborators' had helped to reshape the earlier writings.
Subsequently, I discovered that this astounding view was then
widely held in literary and critical circles in Dublin. Yet many
other authors have written for the same company – before, during,
and since O'Casey came into prominence – without achieving either
the popular or the critical success that he obtained. Why could not
the same combination of Abbey players and writer-directors

13

do for young playwrights what it is claimed was done for O'Casey? And how can the inimitable flavour of O'Casey's characters and their dialogue be explained? None of the Abbey directors, writers, or players of that time or since have shown any comparable ability in the creation of the characters and environment of the Dublin slums; and no Irish writer in any literary sphere has created an idiom anything like that of O'Casey. In his writings there are linguistic traits which occasionally sound like Carleton one minute or Joyce the next, or even (as Denis Johnston is never tired of saying) like Amanda McKittrick Ros at times, but the total impact is peculiarly his own. It is an idiosyncratic idiom that, whether we like it or not, can only be described as O'Caseyan.

If a writer as sensitive as David Greene could believe that O'Casey's most successful early plays were heavily indebted to the editorial work of others, then it is not difficult to envisage how and why the playwright's detractors have seized hold of similar arguments in order to minimize his achievements. One should not be surprised, perhaps: indeed, his left-wing political views and occasional anti-clerical sentiments may not necessarily be the main reasons for such denigration. Throughout the years a number of critics and scholars have fairly consistently attempted to prove that Shakespeare could not possibly have written the plays generally attributed to him; the primary grounds for their dissatisfaction appear to be those very qualities which, to some extent, he shared with the Irish writer: his humble origins and relative lack of formal education. (Shakespeare almost certainly had less deprived domestic circumstances and his schooling was longer and better but, nonetheless, those seeking an alternative authorship have usually argued for candidates whose social origins were considerably more exalted and their education – on paper, at least – usually much better.) A good deal of misleading information and gossip about O'Casey's early and apprentice plays has been accepted as factually accurate while some details have yet to be disclosed. His working relationship with the Abbey Theatre directorate and its acting company is in itself a significant subject for revaluation, and his much discussed friendship with Lady Gregory warrants reassessment.

One of the most striking features of the quarrel over *The Silver Tassie* in 1928 between the Abbey Theatre directorate and O'Casey was the reaction of the three senior board members to O'Casey's refusal to accept meekly their adverse opinions on his play. In answer to their criticisms, O'Casey turned round on each of them from Yeats to Lennox Robinson, tearing their objections to pieces

in a series of letters remarkable for their sustained ferocity. Today
it is difficult to understand how Yeats and, in particular, Lady
Gregory could have so completely misunderstood the contentious
side to O'Casey's character. I am not arguing that they needs
must have accepted the play, but that their rejection should really
have been more tactfully and straightforwardly conducted. Yeats
was, to my mind, only trying to help one whom he still regarded
as an apprentice writer when he suggested that the playwright
should publicly evade the Abbey's decision by telling the press,
not that it had been rejected but that he (O'Casey) had withdrawn
the play for 'revision.'[1] Instead, the playwright scorned excuses
and explanations and told the public that the Abbey had refused
his play because its directors considered it a bad play whereas he,
the author, still thought it a fine one. From then on, the battle
lines were drawn: O'Casey never submitted another play to the
theatre and no later play by him was given its première there.

Lady Gregory was his best friend on the theatre's board. She had
personally befriended the author from the time his *The Shadow of
a Gunman* was accepted by her little theatre in 1923. Yet, although
he stayed with her at Coole Park and though she recorded in her
Journals many conversations with O'Casey in which he related
experiences from his early life and work as a building labourer, she
obviously had little real understanding of his way of thinking or
even his literary activities before the Abbey advent. Several of his
early songs and ballads, including his *Songs of the Wren*, were very
popular among all classes of Dublin society particularly during the
later years of the First World War, but most were published
anonymously or under his Gaelicised name of Sean O'Cathasaigh.
On the title page of *Songs of the Wren*, published in 1918, was the
inscription, 'By Sean O'Cathasaigh, author of "The Grand Oul"
Dame Britannia" ', which shows how popular was that particular
anti-recruiting song, written most probably late in 1915. Copies of
the ballad circulated widely in Dublin without providing the
author's name on the one page broadsheet. It was published by
James Connolly in his journal, *The Workers' Republic*, on 15
January 1916 under one of O'Casey's pseudonyms 'An Gall Fada'
('The Tall Stranger'). When Lady Gregory printed a version of
the song in her *Kiltartan History Book* in 1926 it appeared
anonymously and it is apparent that she did not initially relate its
author with her new literary 'find' and friend, the creator of *Juno
and the Paycock*.

Moreover, for all her sympathy with O'Casey's struggle for
self-expression, she obviously had little understanding of his views

about proletarian art. We remember, for instance, that when he
was staying with her at Coole she began to read aloud to him – as
he recollects in *Inishfallen, Fare Thee Well* – Upton Sinclair's
Singing Jail Birds, to him 'the worst play ever written signifying
sympathy with the workers.' Since its author was on the side of
the proletariat, Lady Gregory expected this propaganda play to
interest O'Casey. Instead, as we might expect from the kind of man
and writer who we now know from his early journalism and from
six volumes of autobiography, he angrily denounced Sinclair's play
in aesthetic as well as political terms – 'The Labour Movement isn't
a mourning march to a jail-house' – and resolutely refused to hear
any more of the wailing birds.[2]

Lady Gregory did not really comprehend the playwright; little
wonder then that the other Abbey directors, Yeats and Robinson,
misjudged him completely, both adopting somewhat patronising
attitudes towards him. Yeats, in particular, exhibits a condescending
patrician air in the correspondence that has survived. Since
O'Casey had seemed to accept (and *seemed* is the operative word)
the Abbey's verdicts on his apprentice plays the directors thought
that they could for ever dictate their views to him on such matters.
This attitude is perhaps most sympathetically expressed by Lady
Gregory in one of the hurt and bewildered notes she wrote after
O'Casey had reacted so belligerently to the theatre's rejection of
The Silver Tassie. In her *Journals* (entry for 10 June 1928) she
records writing of O'Casey to Walter Starkie, a new director on
the theatre's board:

> He had stayed here [at her home in Coole] and I looked on him
> and treated him as a friend I could speak or write openly to.
> He had accepted our criticisms in other cases, had rewritten one
> of the scenes of *The Plough and the Stars* at Yeats's suggestion,
> and I did not think he would have refused to consider this.[3]

More information is now available regarding O'Casey's working
relationship with the Abbey directorate before, as well as after, his
first play was accepted for production. In the published criticism,
however, there is a good deal that is inaccurate; lack of knowledge
has led to supposition and guesses by O'Casey's commentators
and even the best of them have been misled by inadequate information. Of *The Harvest Festival*, O'Casey's second apprentice work,
David Krause writes that Lady Gregory had praised 'several scenes
and particularly the characterisation of a clergyman.'[4] There is no
evidence whatsoever that Lady Gregory ever read *The Harvest*

Festival. It is true that she praised several scenes in his following
play, *The Crimson in the Tricolour*, and that Lennox Robinson (as
O'Casey acknowledged in his autobiography) liked the portrait of
the Reverend J. Jennings in *The Harvest Festival*. Perhaps Dr.
Krause compounded these two facts. Lady Gregory's own account
of O'Casey's apprenticeship, 'How Great Plays are Born: The
Coming of Mr. O'Casey' (published in *The Daily News* on 27
March 1926), certainly gives the impression that the very first
play by him that she saw was his third one, *The Crimson in the
Tricolour*, and this impression is confirmed by the recent publication of her voluminous *Journals* in full (their earlier appearance in
print in 1946 was in a rigorously pruned edition selected by
Robinson). On 5 November 1921 she jotted down her criticisms of
The Crimson, adding (in a postscript written in April 1928): 'This
was the first play I had seen by Sean O'Casey.'[5] Such retrospective
information is corroborated by an entry for 8 March 1924 – jotted
down in the first week that *Juno and the Paycock* was staged in
Dublin – in which she recorded a conversation with the dramatist
during which she said to him (obviously thinking that *The Crimson*
was the first play that he had submitted to her tiny theatre, though
we know that both of the two earlier efforts in playwriting had
been received and rejected by the Abbey): 'You must feel now that
we were right in not putting on that first one you sent in *The
Crimson in the Tricolour*.'[6]

Of the theatre's three directors, only Robinson is likely to have
read the first two works; like Lady Gregory, W. B. Yeats's first
acquaintance was with the third one (we have first-hand accounts
of their immediate impressions in each case). In a letter to O'Casey
dated 13 May 1921 Lennox Robinson wrote about *The Crimson*
(long before his fellow directors had seen the longhand script):

> Although I read your play some time ago it has puzzled me just
> as much as your other plays did. I must have another opinion on
> it. There is a great deal in it that attracts me and I shall get it
> typed and read, and then I should like to meet you and talk
> about your work.

This note and other hitherto unpublished correspondence from
Robinson shows his early interest in, and undoubted liking for,
the writings of the unfledged playwright – as well as the striking
difference between his favourable view, which coincided with Lady
Gregory's subsequent verdict that she was 'inclined to put it on
[the stage] because some of it was so good', and the wholly hostile

reactions of W. B. Yeats to the same work. It is no exaggeration to say, in fact, that O'Casey as an aspiring dramatist first received a helping hand from Robinson and, at the time, fully appreciated this fact. In his letter of 9 October 1922, strongly defending *The Crimson* against Yeats's criticisms at the time the play was finally turned down by the Abbey, O'Casey told Robinson: 'Many, many thanks for your own kind expression of appreciation. I shall certainly take advantage of your generous invitation to go to see you and talk of my work.'

In later years, particularly after *The Tassie* had been repudiated (for which decision its creator thought Robinson chiefly responsible[7]), the playwright often spoke contemptuously of Robinson as a dramatist as well as a judge of drama, declaring in letters to Lady Gregory and Gabriel Fallon that Robinson would 'never add one jot or tittle to life or literature.'[8] He thought that the latter had become jealous of his own new-found box-office and critical successes in London as well as Dublin and, indeed, there is some evidence to support this belief. Even on personal grounds there were reasons for such feelings: Robinson knew that, for all the kind words Lady Gregory expended upon his work for the Abbey, she never really liked him as a man and she actively distrusted him as the theatre's manager (a post he occupied for a time in the early 1920s), especially as his drinking bouts increased over the years. He had never managed to get close to her, personally, and, by the mid-1920s, he must have been resentful that, though he had worked with her for nearly twenty years, she was not nearly as friendly with him as she was, so transparently, with O'Casey whom she had known for a relatively short time; moreover, her admiration for the latter's writings quite clearly far surpassed her liking for Robinson's plays. Something of this ill-concealed jealousy leaked to the surface when Robinson answered Lady Gregory's letter telling him that she did not like *The Silver Tassie* (her missive has not survived, so far as I know); his undated letter, presumably written in April 1928, candidly admitted:

> I was very relieved to get your letter today and to find that you agreed with me about O'Casey's play. If you had disagreed with me I should have suspected myself of all sorts of horrid subconscious feelings.

However, Robinson's subsequent envy should not obscure his initial kindnesses and encouragement when the insecure O'Casey most needed such support.

While we are now perhaps too much inclined to disregard Robinson's early assistance it is possible that, in recompense, too much reverential attention is paid to Lady Gregory's part in the proletarian author's success story. In recent years several books have largely been concerned with his genius for character creation, using as a starting point Lady Gregory's oft-quoted advice, as recorded in her *Journal's* entry for 15 April 1923:

[O'Casey] says how grateful he was to me because when we had to refuse the Labour [play] *The Crimson in the Tricolour* I had said, 'I believe there is something in you' and your 'strong point is characterisation.'[9]

I do not see any reason why he would not have discovered this particular strength for himself as he progressed further in his writing career but Lady Gregory made sure that she staked the claim for herself. On 8 March 1924 she noted another conversation with him during which he thanked her for having had *The Crimson in the Tricolour* typed at the theatre's expense (though Robinson had proposed the self same aid months before Lady Gregory had read the play):

And he said 'I owe a great deal to you and Mr Yeats and Mr Robinson, but to you above all. You gave me encouragement. And it was you who said to me upstairs in the office – I could show you the very spot where you stood – "Mr O'Casey, your gift is characterisation." And so I threw over my theories, and this [*Juno and the Paycock*] is the result.'[10]

The advice that obviously meant so much to him (and he never denied the validity of these remarks after they were in print) was given in an interview in the Abbey, but we did not know until 1978, when the first unabridged volume of Lady Gregory's *Journals* was published, that the date on which the authoress first met him was 10 November 1921, the season before a play by him was first accepted for production by her theatre.[11]

Twice in her *Journals* she speaks of herself as having wanted the Abbey to stage *The Crimson* ('I had wanted to pull that play together and put it on to give him experience'[12]. . . 'I was inclined to put it on because some of it was so good'[13]) but Yeats was adamant in opposing this. Her view that 'Yeats was down on it' is abundantly confirmed by the poet's vehement comments, especially the following aside implying a sharp disagreement with Robinson on the matter:

[*The Crimson in the Tricolour*] is so constructed that in every
scene there is something for pit and stalls to cheer or boo. In
fact it is the old Irish idea of a good play – Queens Melodrama
brought up to date would no doubt make a sensation – especially
as everybody is as ill mannered as possible, and all truth considered as inseparable from spite and hatred. If Robinson wants
to produce it let him do so by all means and be damned to him.
My fashion has gone out.[14]

W. B. Yeats sent these comments to Robinson – their forcefulness
undoubtedly influenced him and Lady Gregory against mounting a
production of the work – and Robinson passed them on to O'Casey
with the returned playscript. Like Lady Gregory, Robinson
remained interested in staging the play and he told its author that,
though he himself had to agree with certain of Yeat's criticisms,

I persist in finding the play very interesting. I have felt an
attraction to all your work. If you are still interested in the
subject of this play we might be able to make it over again and
make a play of it. I think you have got the scenario – the shape
of the play wrong, or if you have another play in your mind will
you come over and talk over the idea and we will work out a
scenario together?

These remarks were sufficiently encouraging to allow O'Casey,
in a letter written to Robinson eleven days later, to make radical
proposals for revising the drama (changing it into a comedy and
having a different character take the leading role). However, he had
by this time already written more than three quarters of a new
play, *The Shadow of a Gunman*, which by reason of its fairly
prompt acceptance, made him abandon the scheme to revise old
material, though he did maintain sufficient interest in *The Crimson*
to try to have it staged in Dublin in its original version after *The
Shadow of a Gunman* had become a distinct popular success at
the Abbey.

An astonishing fact regarding the theatre's acceptance of *The
Shadow of a Gunman* (submitted in manuscript under its original
title 'On the Run') has remained unrecorded. We are by now so
used to the oft reiterated truth that Lady Gregory was the playwright's best friend on the Abbey board that it comes as a great
surprise to discover that she had no voice in the acceptance of
The Shadow of a Gunman as O'Casey's first contribution to the
Abbey repertoire – and, indeed, to learn that she had not even

seen the typescript of that play when its author received the following letter (dated 25 February 1923) from the then manager of the Abbey, typed on the theatre's stationery:

Dear Mr. O'Casey,
 I am very glad to say that Mr Yeats likes your play 'On the Run' very much and we shall try and put it on before the end of our season. Lady Gregory hasn't read it yet but I am sure her opinion of the play will be the same as Mr Yeats. The play will need a little cutting here and there. I like it very much myself.
The letter was signed 'Yours sincerely, Lennox Robinson.'

Looking back, in conclusion, one sees that the break with the Abbey, though regrettable, was inevitable. Although the Abbey directors gave O'Casey help it was, necessarily, only of a very limited kind. They were incapable of understanding him or truly appreciating how talented a dramatist he was and they did not see how much potential for future development there was in him. They were totally unprepared for the formal and linguistic innovations in *The Silver Tassie* because they had, from early in their dealings with him, pigeon-holed him as a slum realist, first and last, though one with a brilliant talent for realising topical Dublin events and memorable tenement characters and with a remarkable ear for working class speech and mannerisms. An analogous mistake was commonly made, at least initially, with regard to Harold Pinter's alleged tape recorder fidelity to English speech patterns when it should have been apparent that at his best his language is, similarly, as carefully stylised as any mannered Restoration prose. As we can now perceive, the experiments in *The Tassie* were not at variance with previous work but part of a developing pattern. Were the Abbey directors as completely oblivious to the ambitious growth in dramaturgy in each of O'Casey's four full-length works submitted to them subsequent to *The Crimson in the Tricolour* as the relevant documents suggest? It is impossible to be sure but I tend to think that they were. Yet the steadily expanding scope in theme, characterisation (both individual and collective) and linguistic devices – let alone in stage settings, where it is most obvious – makes the technical experimentation in *The Tassie* in no way surprising or unpremeditated, though it is more ambitious and varied than might have been expected. There is still a realistic bedrock to theme and character but the fantastic elements always dear to O'Casey's imagination are now more freely and surrealistically handled. He had always shown contempt for straightforward

narrative plot as such, together with a propensity for a loose, fluid
and not necessarily linear dramatic form (both anticipated
Brechtian Epic Theatre) so that his later occasional forays in
parallel scenes and montage, choric group drama and multi-media
effects were in accord with earlier less accomplished attempts in a
similar direction.

Instead of recognising the consistency of purpose (though not
necessarily of artistic success) in his playwriting, the Abbey directors
believed that he should stick to the subject matter, characters and
environment which distinguished his earlier dramas. Looseness of
form in those works appeared to them a symptom of incidental
failures, probably resulting from inexperience or theatrical naivety
rather than the product of conscious design. At no time do they
appear to have looked upon O'Casey as a well read and discriminat-
ing artist who was also — as his manuscripts reveal — a deliberate
and painstaking literary craftsman. To them, he was a naive and
spontaneous, if clever, recorder of a limited segment of Irish
working-class life and behaviour; more than a quarter of a century
later, in Brendan Behan, the Dublin proletariat spawned very much
the kind of man and writer the directors had expected O'Casey to
be, but, in both respects, the two were poles apart.

O'Casey's abiding concern with visual, musical and balletic
possibilities in drama, while it was evident from early in his career,
became increasingly insistent long before he left Dublin. He never
downplayed the role of language in his plays, as so many of his
contemporaries and younger writers have done, but from *The
Plough* onwards he sought more and more diversified means of
dramatic expression. Accordingly, it was inevitable that he would
eventually have to look beyond the imaginative as well as physical
resources of the Abbey Theatre, which was never renowned in the
first fifty years of its existence for scenery, lighting, costumes or
choreographic effects.[15] Indeed, it was not until quite recent times
that Abbey programmes even deigned to acknowledge the names
of stage designers in productions there. Perhaps the reason was
shame and not modesty or neglect. The poverty of sets, costumes
and stage properties generally in the years up to (and long after) the
advent of O'Casey can be confirmed by consulting any representative
collection of photographs – see, for example, the comprehensive
sample provided in James W. Flannery's book on *W. B. Yeats and
the Idea of a Theatre* (1976), a study most favourably disposed
towards the early Abbey and the work of its chief begetter.

The old Abbey even at its very best could never have done full
justice to the staging of theatrically challenging dramas like *The*

Tassie, Within the Gates, Purple Dust and *Cock-a-Doodle Dandy*,
had the theatre accepted them for performance in those years from
1928 to 1949 when they first appeared in print; one can be quite
sure that O'Casey would have had to look well outside the narrow
confines of the Abbey for the mounting of productions worthy of
their varied and often difficult (let alone expensive) imaginative
effects. In plain words, O'Casey soon outgrew the playwriting
possibilities of the Abbey directorate, the practical as well as
artistic resources of the theatre's production team and the physical
limitations of what was, before 1966, a tiny theatre. From 1928,
indeed, he needed to find a bold and enterprising stage producer/
director conversant with contemporary *avant-garde* movements in
world theatre, such as Expressionism, as well as being alert to the
serious uses to which popular elements like pantomime clowning
and music hall routines could still be put. This was easier said
than done, then or now. A difficult task was made virtually
impossible by O'Casey's failure to interest those theatre men of
the time – Reinhardt, Piscator and Gordon Craig come most
immediately to mind – who might have been able to do justice to
the full potential of such plays; subsequently, a stage director like
Peter Brook, who I should dearly have liked to have staged
The Tassie and *Cock*, seems to be uninterested in this body of
work.

In the fifty-two years since *The Tassie* was completed it has
been next to impossible to find the financial and artistic resources
for mounting the major later plays (so much so that the revised
Within the Gates – virtually a new play, if compared with the
original text – has yet to receive an adequate professional production). These works require a large, well balanced and well trained
company, which, like the Berliner Ensemble or the (British)
National Theatre, is used to skilled and unselfish ensemble playing
as well as lengthy rehearsal periods for such variedly experimental
scripts. O'Casey was satisfied, aesthetically, by stage representations
of only two of his later plays: the London production of *The
Tassie* in 1929 and the 1934 New York presentation of *Within the
Gates*. Since his death in 1964 there have been very few exciting
productions in the English-speaking world, though there are hopes
that the centenary year may help revive interest in O'Casey's
writings in those companies – like the National Theatre and the
Royal Shakespeare Company – which are best equipped to inherit
the mantle of the Irish National Theatre. To date, however, the
mournful fact remains that, while the Abbey Theatre eventually
failed its most gifted native son when most he needed its creative

co-operation, no other theatre group has even come close to fulfilling such a necessary role.

II

I hope, however, that when your justifiable anger has subsided, you will remember that you are an Irish dramatist, and that the life of the Abbey is more important to Ireland than the life of you or me or Yeats or any other individual.

Letter from St John Ervine to Sean O'Casey, 6 June 1928

O'Casey's alleged debt to the influence and practical playwriting experience of the Abbey directors was, then, always more apparent than real. The same claim is equally true insofar as concrete editorial work on his plays staged at the Abbey is concerned. Detailed and comprehensive examination of the extensive collection of manuscript and typescript material among the papers left behind by the dramatist at his death gives no support whatsoever to the theory that any other person helped write, revise, or shape O'Casey's work. On the contrary, these papers show how, from the beginning, O'Casey continually revised and reshaped his own dramas. We know from various letters by him that he took advice from the Abbey board of directors and from Abbey producers of his plays in making minor alterations (mostly cuts[16]) to his early work; but there is no evidence whatsoever of any creative help or collaboration worthy of the name in O'Casey's drama.

Joseph Holloway wrote in his *Diaries*, presumably on the basis of Abbey 'Green Room' gossip, that Lady Gregory had helped with the revisions made to the one-act work *Kathleen Listens In*.[17] Yet it is clear from an aside in one of O'Casey's letters to the grand old woman of Coole that he was himself responsible for the changes, which were no doubt prompted by requests from the Abbey board and helped by a conversation with Lady Gregory: 'I sent in to the Theatre the beginning of the week the Revised Version of *Kathleen Listens In*, and am again working slowly at *The Plough and the Stars*.' This extract is taken from a letter dated 22 February 1925, and refers to plans for the only revival (so far as I know) of the play to take place after its initial production on 1 October 1923, that is, the production which opened on 3 March 1925. It is my guess, for which there is no evidence whatsoever, that in this case the playwright was asked to add some up-to-the-moment dialogue to what was in any case a highly topical allegory. The changes must have been very slight ones.

In discussing *Juno and the Paycock* both David Krause and
Gabriel Fallon have emphasised the indebtedness of its author to
the Abbey Theatre. Arguing that he was 'still learning his craft,'
Professor Krause writes:

> In the original version of the play he had written an extra scene
> for the third act in which he described the actual shooting of
> Johnny Boyle by the I.R.A.; however, it was wisely cut out by
> the Abbey directors during rehearsals. The visualization of
> Johnny's death is not so important as its impact upon Juno, and
> it is enough that she hears the tragic news for at that point she
> has become the central figure in the play.[18]

Here, again, the debt is more apparent than real: the shooting of
Johnny is a case in point that can be substantiated by reference to
the text. If we compare the scene as it was first submitted in
typescript to the theatre management with the equivalent scene
in the printed play, we see that there is hardly a word of dialogue
changed (the final text merely gave an extra sentence to the third
speech of the Irregular to Johnny Boyle, 'Poor Tancred was an
oul' comrade o' yours, but you didn't think o' that when you gave
him away to the gang that sent him to his grave'); instead, part of
it is merely transferred from the murder spot in the Dublin
Mountains to the 'removal scene' in the Boyle's tenement room.
Here is the full episode in the typescript draft, starting in the
tenement:

Irregular:	(*to Johnny*): Come on Sean Boyle; you're wanted; some of us have a word to say to you.
Johnny:	I'm sick; I can't – what do you want with me?
Irregular:	Come on, come on; we've a distance to go, an' haven't much time – come on.
Johnny:	I'm an oul' comrade – yous wouldn't shoot an oul' comrade.
Irregular:	We've no time to waste; come on – here Dermot, ketch his arm. (*to Johnny*) Have you your beads?
Johnny:	Me beads! Why do you ass me that, why do you ass me that?
Irregular:	Go on, go on, march!
	(*They go out leading Johnny*)

*During the last few sentences, the room has been growing darker,
and darker, till it disappears, to give place to a lonely, narrow
boreen on the hip of one of the Dublin mountains. It is pitch*

dark; the hedge is scarcely perceptible, except for its darker silhouette. A few stars are faintly showing in a clouded sky. An hour has gone by. A motor is heard coming rapidly along, stopping some distance away. After a pause, some figures emerge from the darkness on left, and slowly cross to the right.
Voice of Johnny: Are yous goin' to do in a comrade – look at me arm, I lost it for Ireland.
Voice of Irregular: Commandant Tancred lost his life for Ireland.
Voice of Johnny: Sacred heart of Jesus, have mercy on me! Mother o' God, pray for me – be with me now in the agonies o' death! . . . Hail, Mary, full o' grace . . . the Lord is . . . with Thee.
(They pass out of sight)
A pause; then several shots are heard, followed by a cry; then silence again. Figures cross the stage from right to left; the motor is heard starting, and moving away, the sound growing fainter in the distance. The scene gradually brightens, till the room of the Boyles is again revealed. The most of the furniture is gone. Mary and Mrs Boyle, one on each side, are sitting in a darkened room, by the fire: it is an hour later.

Of course one agrees with Krause and Fallon that the actual shooting is best left to the audience's imagination; the extent of the revision, however, is not sufficient to warrant references to any debt to the Abbey directors or Fallon's assumption that O'Casey would have been 'aggrieved' by the change of location, a belief that leads the critic to add: 'Again it was borne in on me that the artist is not always the best judge of his work.'[19] It should be noticed that Johnny's death is not concretely visualized in the original version (it takes place off-stage) nor is there any attempt to supplant Juno from her central position at this stage in the drama. O'Casey's instinctive theatrical flair is as marked here as it is elsewhere in the play. There is little doubt that from early in the work's inception the author had a very clear idea of what he wanted to do and say. The various drafts and revisions show these intentions increasingly clarified and refined but they do not reveal any startling departures from the final shape and themes with which we are all familiar – and they show, beyond any question, that the dramatist could make all the necessary changes without any help from the Abbey directorate.

As I have said, most of the alterations made in staged performances at the Abbey were cuts in dialogue. So far as his own attitude to this practice was concerned, we have evidence once again from the dramatist's correspondence with Lady Gregory. The following excerpt is taken from a letter of 11 September 1925 (as background, we must bear in mind that, long before the public riots over *The Plough* and, indeed, even before the work had been put into rehearsal, various members of the Abbey company had demanded changes in the play):

> I am going up on Sunday to Mr. Yeats to speak about some cuts in my play – he asked me to come – and, of course, I've no objection to cuts made by him, or you or Mr. Robinson. My little song, I think, has to go.

And later, on 1 November 1925, he wrote again to her (note that it is O'Casey, and not the Theatre's directors, who did the rewriting): 'I have altered the love scene in the first act of *The Plough*, and the alteration has eliminated any possibly objectionable passage.' At no time, however, did O'Casey allow anyone else to revise his work (in old age he told me that he did not wish his plays to be produced at Miss Joan Littlewood's then highly regarded Stratford East Theatre Workshop because he had heard of her reputation for altering and adapting playscripts, adding that he could not understand why a good playwright like Behan would allow any director to take the considerable liberties that she took with his writings) and, in his early days as an Abbey author, cuts were restricted to the discretion of the three Abbey board members, all of whom were practising dramatists, of course.

Moreover, while he accepted constructive criticism from the Abbey directorate, O'Casey maintained a firmly independent critical stance at all stages of his relationship with the theatre's board. For one thing he retained a good number of the Abbey cuts in the published texts of his work – the 'little song' at the end of Act II of *The Plough* is an obvious example among many others in that play alone. And for another, there is his clearly stated opposition to the board's judgements at various times. His fierce and courageous defence of *The Silver Tassie* against W. B. Yeats in 1928 is well known; but some critics have argued that his attitude in that situation was an arrogant one made by a writer whose head by this time had been turned by public applause. What was not so well known, until the recent publication of the first volume of *The Letters of Sean O'Casey*, was the fact that even before a single one of his plays had been accepted for performance at the Abbey, O'Casey had freely expressed certain significant disagreements with the directors' dramatic values. When his full-length

The Crimson in the Tricolour was rejected in 1922, after various hints that it might be accepted, Lennox Robinson sent to O'Casey a letter from W. B. Yeats (without naming the poet) containing criticisms of the play. O'Casey's response was determined, unequivocal, and prophetically consonant with his subsequent action over *The Silver Tassie* six years later. Here is part of his reply to Robinson, dated 9 October 1922, (the 'reader' is Yeats):

> I was terribly disappointed at its final rejection, and felt at first as if, like Lucifer, I had fallen never to hope again. I have re-read the work and find it as interesting as ever, in no way deserving the contemptuous dismissal it has received from the reader you have quoted. Let me say that I do not agree with his criticism. . . . What could be more loose and vague than life itself? Are we to write plays on the framework of the first of Genesis; and God said let there be light and there was light; and he separated the light from the darkness and he called the light day, and the darkness night; and the morning and evening were the first Act. It is the subtle vagueness in such writers as Shaw and Ibsen that – in my opinion – constitute their most potent charm.[20]

One could hardly call this respectful timidity! Yet, written by a manual labourer who had never had a play staged or published and who had seldom seen a play performed (he had only been to the Abbey itself twice or, at the most, thrice before any of his own works were staged there), it was addressed to an author whose writings had had considerable success in performance as well as in print and who had been responsible for numerous stage productions at the Abbey since he had served a practical apprenticeship under Bernard Shaw at the Court Theatre, London. At no time in his life, in fact, did O'Casey show any undue regard for or deference to anyone's reputation.

Subsequently, once he had become an 'Abbey playwright', he saw little to make him change his earlier independent outlook. Indeed, increased theatrical experience served to confirm his views, and he came to believe that, in some cases, the judgement and advice of the Abbey directors regarding certain of his plays had been misleading if not harmful so far as he was concerned. One particular example, to O'Casey's mind, was when Lennox Robinson made him delete the death scene near the end of *Nannie's Night Out*. The playwright substituted for it a short incident in which Nannie is arrested by the police, but to the end of his life he insisted (I think rightly) that the original version was the better one.

In any case, right or wrong, he went his own way: when his one-act *The Cooing of Doves* was rejected outright by the Abbey, the dramatist built the play into *The Plough and the Stars*, virtually as it stood, as the second (and very effective) act of that drama. This use of material decisively rejected by O'Casey's supposed mentors and the way in which he re-submitted it to them in an even more ambitious work shows his critical as well as artistic independence and his growing confidence in his own writings. Lady Gregory herself acknowledged how fine *The Cooing of Doves* showed itself to be within the much admired larger structure – she recognised the earlier rejected play, as she admitted in conversation to the playwright – and Yeats, too, was of the same opinion about the second act, though whether he recollected that that particular act comprised an earlier repudiated play is uncertain. We do know that Yeats fought hard within the board of directors to protect *The Plough and the Stars* (and especially the second act) from cuts demanded by George O'Brien and some of the actors in the play; and the poet's opinion of the second act was given in one of his letters quoted by Lady Gregory in a journal entry for 20 September 1925 (while the pre-production censorship fight was in progress): 'The scene as a whole is admirable, one of the finest O'Casey has written.'

III

[O'Casey] said, 'All the thought in Ireland for years past has come through the Abbey. You have no idea what an education it has been to the country.'
Entry in Lady Gregory's Journals for 15 April 1923.

While there is no doubt that O'Casey during the 1920s was fortunate in having a talented ensemble like the Abbey Theatre company to interpret his work, it is equally true to .say that seldom has a theatrical group in the finest flowering of its genius had so gifted and responsive a playwright to write for it. Ernest Blythe, for many years managing director of the Abbey Theatre, has, in the course of defending the theatre from its many detractors, put this point in a succinct manner:

The existence of a permanent company of trained and talented players is an aid to certain dramatists. The members of a standing group whose personalities and whose range and powers of variation are well known, can help an author to draw vivid and convincing characters, somewhat as a model helps a painter. And some dramatists, including the very greatest, have had individual players in mind even when they were in part depicting characters known to them in real life.[21]

Though Blythe makes this claim without reference to any specific playwright, he may well have been thinking of O'Casey when he wrote it; the observation is certainly correct in his case. While, throughout O'Casey's writing career, he drew upon actual people he knew, situations he had experienced, and snatches of dialogue he overheard or had had reported to him (his notebooks bear overwhelming testimony to this), he also wrote with specific members of the Abbey company in mind. Of course he had already evolved a highly personal, even idiosyncratic style of dramatic expression by the time he came to compose *The Shadow of a Gunman*, and this style (only intermittently apparent in the sole surviving play of his early period of apprenticeship, *The Harvest Festival*) was, naturally, maintained for the rest of his working life. Even so, once he had seen *The Shadow of a Gunman* on the Abbey stage and had come to know the company personally as well as professionally, he did definitely identify certain players with particular character parts in his work.

Before *The Shadow of a Gunman* was staged in April 1923 at the Abbey, O'Casey had not been able to afford playgoing there: according to his own testimony, he had attended no more than three performances up to this time and he knew none of the performers there. Afterwards, when he could always slip into a spare seat or pay out of forthcoming royalties without having to have the cash in his pocket (for he was still hard-up before the London run of *Juno and the Paycock* started in November 1925) O'Casey witnessed virtually every production at the theatre until he left Ireland in March 1926. Indeed, his constant presence at the theatre gave rise to the myth that he had learned playwriting from attendance there. Moreover, he often visited the Green Room in the evenings even when he did not watch the performance; it became for him, as it were, his 'club' where he could chat about literature and drama and everything under the sun with interested and knowledgeable people. In particular, he made friends with Barry Fitzgerald, F. J. McCormick (for a short while), and Gabriel Fallon, three younger actors at the Abbey, and saw a certain amount of them outside the theatre.

Thus we may say that, although *The Shadow of a Gunman* owed nothing to personal or professional knowledge of a particular theatrical company, each of the subsequent four plays (*Kathleen Listens In, Juno, Nannie's Night Out,* and *The Plough*) was assuredly influenced by this consideration, as, indeed, was *The Silver Tassie,* which was written with the Abbey company in mind, though it was not performed by that company until seven years had elapsed after the play's publication. We may take that last fact for granted since, though O'Casey wrote *The Tassie* in London, he intended it for production by the Abbey. The supposition is borne out by the following aside in a personal letter written to Ivor Brown in reply to the latter's review of *The Silver Tassie* when it was first published in 1928:

> By the way, the part of Sylvester Heegan was written for Barry Fitzgerald of Dublin who, I think, could play Arthur Sinclair off the stage. How I wish you could see him play a Demon in Yeats's *Countess Kathleen,* Bloomfield Bonnington in *The Doctor's Dilemma* or Boyle in *Juno.*[22]

There is evidence that, from an early stage in the composition of *Juno,* O'Casey envisaged Barry Fitzgerald as 'Captain' Boyle, Sara Allgood as the heroine, and F. J. McCormick as 'Joxer', and this circumstance, while possibly making little difference to the scope and purpose of the work as a whole, no doubt accounted for certain details in its characterisation and, perhaps, even its shape and dramatic proportions to some extent. It is most likely that the existence in the theatre company of a magnificent full-blooded comedian like Barry Fitzgerald encouraged the dramatist to give full expression to his love of idiosyncratic characters and speech (both grievously missing from his sole surviving apprentice play, *The Harvest Festival*) and to make Boyle's role as prominent as it is. McCormick's adaptability as a 'character' actor may account for the creation of a parasitical person who has little dramatic justification other than as the foil to, and 'feed' for, the Captain and yet acts as a splendid support for the leading male figure and, indeed, becomes a distinct personality in his own right. Certainly, the scenes between Boyle and Joxer are invariably characterised by exuberant idiomatic language of a high order and provide the comic highlights of the play; such writing, together with a muting of overtly didactic oratory, distinguishes the early plays staged by the Abbey from the earlier unstaged one, *The Harvest Festival.*

Shortly before *Juno and the Paycock* was first staged, W. B. Yeats – the managing director of the Abbey – wrote a short public tribute to the theatre's leading lady, Sara Allgood, in which he urged Irish playwrights to provide her with dramatic material commensurate with her talent. At the same time he disclosed that Sean O'Casey had written a rewarding part for her in his latest play, which was then in rehearsal:

> Miss Sara Allgood is a great folk-actress. As so often happens with a great actor or actress, she rose into fame with a school of drama [early in the twentieth century, at the beginning of the Abbey's history]. . . . It has been more difficult in recent years to supply her with adequate parts, for Dublin is a little tired of its admirable folk-arts, political events having turned our minds elsewhere. Perhaps the Spaniard, Sierra, who in his plays expounds a psychological and modern purpose through sharply defined characters, themselves as little psychological and modern as Mrs Broderick [the actress's early creation in Lady Gregory's *Spreading the News*, 1904] herself, may give her the opportunity she needs. I am looking forward with great curiosity to seeing her in his *Two Shepherds*, which is just now going into rehearsal, and one of our Irish dramatists, Mr Casey [sic], has in his new play, *Juno and the Paycock*, given her an excellent part.[23]

Miss Allgood, who, as Yeats reminded his readers, was the dominant female personality in the early years of the little theatre in Marlborough Street, had returned to Dublin and to the Abbey Theatre only a few months before this article was written. She had been many years abroad, in the course of which she had married, been tragically widowed, and virtually stranded in Australia for some time afterwards. She was not with the Abbey when O'Casey's first play was staged there in April 1923, and, though she was in the company shortly before his second one, *Kathleen Listens In*, was performed in October of the same year, she was not cast for it nor was there in it a part written for her. Her work must soon have come to the attention of the writer, however, and with some force because the female leads in each one of his next three plays – *Juno and the Paycock*, *Nannie's Night Out*, and *The Plough and the Stars* – were definitely written with her in mind. Moreover, it can be argued that, although *Kathleen Listens In* bears a woman's name in the title, neither that drama nor the preceding one contains any really important women's parts, at least from an acting point of view. O'Casey realises the women's standpoint with great sympathy and understanding in *The Shadow of a Gunman*, but it is the men who have the most rewarding stage roles. In the three plays that followed *Kathleen*, though, the leading women's parts are arguably the best in each work. Certainly, Juno Boyle, 'Irish' Nannie, and Bessie Burgess (all three written with Sara Allgood in mind) possess a depth and stature unapproached by any of the author's earlier female figures, and it is assuredly not an accident that this new dimension in his writing makes its appearance at the moment that this actress returns to the company.

One cannot say that the character of Juno would never have been written had not Miss Allgood re-emerged on the Dublin theatrical scene – clearly, O'Casey was certain to have attempted such a role at some stage in his career, if for no other reason than as a tribute to his mother. Indeed, an earlier sketch is found in the mother of the hero in *The Harvest Festival* and a much later one in *Red Roses for Me*, both written without Sara Allgood in mind. But it is surely no exaggeration to claim that the knowledge that a mature actress of her stature was available to play such a part must have helped encourage the change of emphasis in O'Casey's characterisation at this particular time. In both *Juno and the Paycock* and *The Plough and the Stars* there are several other fine women's parts, too. Mrs Maisie Madigan, though her role is a brief one, provides something of a tour de force for an actress for the period she is on-stage in Act II of *Juno*. Mrs Jinnie Gogan is designed as a very effective foil to Bessie Burgess in the following play. The actress Maureen Delany, who took the part of Mrs Madigan in the Dublin première of *Juno*, was no doubt originally intended by the playwright to create Jinnie Gogan. With Sara Allgood away in London, playing Juno in the English première of the work, the way was clear for the younger woman to take over the role intended for the Abbey's leading lady. Miss Delany played Bessie in the world première of *The Plough*, went on to re-create the role on many future occasions in and outside Ireland, and also regularly took the part of Juno Boyle in subsequent revivals of the earlier work. Bessie, like Juno, had been originally intended for realisation by Sara Allgood and, sure enough, she first enacted both roles in London and often re-created them in England, Ireland and the United States in the 1920s and 1930s.

It is perhaps significant that, in the article quoted earlier, Yeats should emphasise Miss Allgood's genius in comedy as well as tragedy; he spoke of her as 'not only a great actress, but that rarest of all things, a woman comedian; for stage humour is almost a male prerogative.'[24] Knowledge of her ability in both spheres allowed O'Casey in *Juno* to create a difficult part for a leading lady which requires her to hold the serious balance of the play –

and to 'lift' it at the appropriate moment into stylised tragedy –
despite the presence in the play of two consummate comedians with
splendid comic parts. At the same time, while her major task,
technically, is to prevent the play toppling into farce, she must also
portray, in a sympathetic way, a wife who nags her husband and
who is neither irritating nor boring to the audience. O'Casey makes
considerable demands on the actress playing his heroine; knowledge
of Sara Allgood's presence in the company gave him confidence
that these demands could be more than adequately fulfilled.

I am not saying that *Juno and the Paycock*, say, would never
have been written had not the author a definite and talented cast
in mind – clearly, it would have been – or even that Boyle and Juno
(and perhaps Joxer) would have been very different characters if
O'Casey had not written them for realisation by Fitzgerald, Miss
Allgood, and McCormick. But I do suggest that the proportioning
of the play was almost certainly influenced by this consideration.
The great strength of the Abbey at the time was the large number
of good male actors that it contained – all of them capable of doing
meaty 'character' parts – and its assured playing in comedy. In
each successive full-length play that O'Casey wrote for this company there is a marked increase in the number of rounded character
parts for men, and, as James Agate noticed, the larger part of
each of the plays that he entitled 'tragedies' was in fact taken up
with his unique kind of comedy. The English drama critic wrote of
Juno and the Paycock, when it first appeared on the London stage:
'The tragic element in it occupies at the most twenty minutes,
and . . . for the remaining two hours and a half the piece is given
up to gorgeous and incredible fooling.'[25] It should be added,
though, that in each of these Abbey plays – from *The Shadow of a
Gunman* to *The Silver Tassie*, inclusive – this fooling, though it
usually starts as light-hearted fun or fantasy (sometimes both, as in
Boyle's descriptions of his life as a 'deep-sea sailor'), gradually
becomes tinged with more and more serious overtones in the course
of the action. In each case, by the end of the drama, the most
absurdly farcical speeches and actions are also – *at the same time* –
deeply poignant in relation to the total dramatic situation. There
is most of the time a sharply serious critical purpose behind the
comic action: Ireland is in grave peril and yet many Dublin slum
dwellers seek escape in alcoholic or patriotic fantasies (and sometimes in both).

In his book *Sean O'Casey: The Man I Knew*, Gabriel Fallon has
testified that when O'Casey first mentioned that he was writing a
play about the Irish Civil War the theme that preoccupied the

playwright in conversation at this time was the tragic story of the young Republican Irregular who had betrayed a comrade in the movement to his death.[26] There is no reason to suppose that this account is inaccurate as a recollection of the playwright's reminiscences at this time because, though the early longhand manuscript version of the play (clearly the first draft, too) keeps Johnny Boyle's role as subservient to the main action as does the final printed version, the playwright, with his mind full of the play's characters, may well have spoken about the originals of some of them and have dwelt on the betrayal theme in particular. His autobiographies show how strongly he felt about the murders and reprisals among former comrades,[27] and betrayal is a significant element in *Juno and the Paycock* itself. Be that as it may, in the play as it evolved this tragic theme and the character of Johnny Boyle who realises it in his person, though vitally important, are given much less prominence than are the actions and antics of 'Captain' Boyle and Joxer Daly. The rich comic talents of Fitzgerald and McCormick, and the ability of many others in the Abbey company, too, to play Dublin 'character parts' indubitably influenced O'Casey in this direction. The playwright's dramatic genius, it seems to me, is most fully realised in his comic writing, and the Abbey company, in encouraging and exploiting this aspect of his work, afforded him a creative partnership in the very best sense. That the same company in later years tended to overplay the comedy and make the Dublin characterisation a good deal broader than originally envisaged is neither here nor there. It is the creative response and interaction of O'Casey and the tiny group he initially wrote for that remains of enduring interest.

Notes

1 Other interpretations are less favourably disposed to W. B. Yeats's advice. Anthony Butler sees it as a devious strategy proceeding from personal jealousy of an experimental poetic drama that offered a challenge to Yeats's reputation as a poet-playwright (see his essay in *The World of Sean O'Casey*, ed. S. McCann, 1966); Eileen O'Casey puts forward a similar viewpoint in her memoir *Sean* (1971). Richard F. Peterson writes of 'Yeats's duplicity' in this incident, see pages 121 of an article that provides further background material to O'Casey's relationship with the Abbey directorate: 'Polishing Up *The Silver Tassie* Controversy: Some Lady Gregory and W. B. Yeats Letters to Lennox Robinson', *Sean O'Casey Review*, IV, 2 (Spring 1978).

2 See O'Casey's excellent critique of the play in his October 1924 letter to Lady Gregory ('to me the play is to Labour what street preaching is to religion'), collected in *The Letters of Sean O'Casey*, ed. D. Krause New York: Macmillan Co. Ltd., 1975), pp. 118–119.

3 *Lady Gregory's Journals 1916–1930*, ed. L. Robinson (London: Putnam and Co. Ltd., 1946), p. 110. Hereafter referred to as *Journals* ed. Robinson. The question here is: consider *what*? It sounds as though Lady Gregory thought that, in answer to the criticisms of the three directors in their initial letters rejecting *The Tassie*, O'Casey could somehow revise the work as he had done in some earlier cases. But Yeats's letter, foremost among those sent to O'Casey by Lady Gregory, rejected the play out of hand. It is true that he liked the first two acts (Act I was 'the best first act you had written', Yeats telling a friend that O'Casey had 'surpassed' himself) but, otherwise, there were no concrete suggestions about alterations or improvements by any of the Abbey writers. Indeed, Yeats clearly wanted a new play altogether. His letter of 25 April 1928 concludes: 'This is a hateful letter to write . . . and all the more so because I cannot advise you to amend the play. It is all too abstract, after the first act; the second act is an interesting technical experiment but it is too long for the material; and after that there is nothing. . . . I see nothing for it but a new theme . . .' Lady Gregory writes to Starkie: 'I did not think [O'Casey] would have refused to consider this', but what choice had he other than the two extremes of either accepting the refusal and thereby abandoning *The Tassie* or repudiating the rejection and telling the Abbey so? Even though the script had not yet been returned when he first received the Abbey letters there was no hint whatsoever that any of the directors thought the play could be salvaged, though a letter from Robinson to Lady Gregory, not seen by O'Casey, indicates that he thought the last two acts could have been amended. Writing before Yeats had read the script Robinson said: 'If W.B. agrees with you and me Sean will have time to think over the last acts before July

and August. It looks to me as if he had put very careful work into Acts I and II, and finished the other two acts haphazard because everyone was beginning to say he would never write a play again and he wanted to show that he could.' He then tells Lady Gregory how he would have written the last two acts! However impertinent this may appear, it does show that he did not think the Abbey's initial refusal was as absolute as Yeats later made it appear.

4 D. Krause, *Sean O'Casey, the Man and his Work* (New York: Macmillan Co.. 1975), p. 34.

5 D. J. Murphy (ed.), *Lady Gregory's Journals: Volume One, Books One to Twenty-nine, 1916–1925.* (Gerrards Cross: Colin Smythe, 1978). p. 307. Hereafter referred to as *Journals*, ed. Murphy. See also *Journals* ed. Robinson. p. 68.

6 *Journals*, ed. Murphy, p. 512; *Journals*, ed. Robinson, p. 74.

7 O'Casey was both right and wrong about this. W. B. Yeats, returning after illness with renewed vigour to reading scripts submitted to his little theatre, was vehemently opposed to *The Tassie* and. as with *The Crimson in the Tricolour* some six years previously, his views were decisive insofar as the initial rejection of the play was concerned. However, the typescript had not been returned nor had any rejection slip been sent though Yeats's letter is surely resolute enough on this point. After receiving O'Casey's indignant replies to each of their letters and in the light of press reports about the (as yet unpublished) controversy, three of the five directors on the newly enlarged board met unofficially to discuss the matter further; the other two had not seen the play and had, accordingly, taken no part in the correspondence about it. At the meeting Yeats and Lady Gregory were prepared to have *The Tassie* staged at the Abbey (if only to show its author the error of his ways, perhaps) but Robinson's negative vote carried the day so that the script was returned to O'Casey. In a journal entry for 10 June 1928 Lady Gregory copied parts of a letter she had written to Walter Starkie, one of the directors not present at the meeting: 'In spite of [O'Casey's] letters I asked Yeats and Lennox Robinson, when we went up to the office on one of the last nights of *The Plough and the Stars.* if we might consider putting it on. Yeats inclined to it, but L.R. said 'No. It is a bad play.' No doubt we ought to have had a regular [board] meeting then, with you.' (*Lady Gregory's Journals.* ed. L. Robinson (London: Putnam and Co. Ltd., 1946), p. 110.) A later entry (written in London on 23 October 1929, after she had witnessed the premiere of *The Silver Tassie* there) records her strong belief that the Abbey's final decision had been governed by Robinson's veto: 'But my mind goes back to *The Tassie* – we ought not to have rejected it. We should have held out against Lennox Robinson that last evening the order to return it was given.' (*Ibid.,* p. 124.)

8 *The Letters of Sean O'Casey,* (New York: Macmillan, 1975), see p. 320 and p. 321.

9 *Journals*, ed. Murphy. p. 446; *Journals.* ed. Robinson, p. 73.

10 *Journals*, ed. Murphy, p. 512; *Journals.* ed. Robinson. p. 75.

11 *Journals*, ed. Murphy. pp. 308–309.

12 *Journals*, ed. Murphy, p. 446; *Journals.* ed. Robinson, p. 73.

13 *Journals*, ed. Murphy, p. 512; *Journals*, ed. Robinson, p. 74.

14   Yeats's critique, written in June 1922, is quoted in full in *The Letters of Sean O'Casey*, pp. 102–103.

15   The constant financial difficulties experienced by the Abbey from its inception hampered creativity in these matters and so, too, did the lack of stage depth in the old building used from 1904 to 1951. Yeats had many good ideas about lighting, scene painting and the use of screens (those designed by Gordon Craig were done in collaboration with the poet); Robert Gregory made several early experiments in lighting at the theatre; and even Miss Horniman was constrained to contribute costume designs on at least one occasion. However, these were but sporadic and shortlived gestures towards new visual experiences on stage. In the 1930s Yeats hired Ninette de Valois to create a school of ballet at the Abbey, seeking to place new emphasis on movement and choreography in general, but his own highly stylised Dance Plays were seldom performed there and it is a measure of his disillusionment with Abbey standards in such matters that all his more imaginative later dramas were composed for a theatre other than his own.

O'Casey was well aware, from early in his relations with the Abbey, of these limitations. A fragmentary series of typescript notes found among his private papers give details to substantiate this claim. Entitled 'Abbey Theatre,' the notes appear to date from 1930 to 1932, judging from internal evidence. Among criticisms that are listed of the theatre's failings is the charge that 'very little was done to bring colour and a new vision to the decoration of the plays.' O'Casey's typescript also says: 'The scenic interpretation of the plays, with a few exceptions, never reached the originality and brilliance of the acting. Kitchen scenes and country scenes were all the same. Of course there never was much money to do these things, but there was usually enough to do better than was done there. The box screens made by Gordon Craig, the scenes for *Kincora* and *Shadowy Waters*, conceived by Robert Gregory, the Old Lady's son, were perhaps, as far as my experience went the only imaginative things in the way of scenery in the Theatre. In fact the scenic and costume [department] of the Abbey Theatre was a very poor one, and, I fear, is a very poor one still, and the lighting leaves a lot to be done. So that, from the points of view of lighting and scenic effects the Abbey Theatre is rarely, if ever, able to display any picturesque and decorative effects upon the stage, so that the Theatre in these respects is limping miles behind the newly-established Gate Theatre.' (Extracts from hitherto unpublished manuscripts and letters by O'Casey are printed by kind permission of Mrs Eileen O'Casey, whose unfailing generosity over many years is much appreciated. The copyright in all the playwright's writings remains invested in her name.)

16   The stage version of *The Plough and the Stars*, for example, prepared for the press by O'Casey and published by Samuel French in 1932, shows a good deal of dialogue for Nora Clitheroe cut in Act III: such deletions undoubtedly help director and actress in staging the play, but the playwright retained the speeches in subsequent Macmillan editions (including the *Collected Plays* text of 1949), presumably because they make the viewpoint of Nora clear on certain points.

17 In an entry for 1 March 1925 (not recorded in any of the published extracts from his Journal in the National Library of Ireland entitled 'Impressions of a Dublin Playgoer'): Holloway writes: 'In speaking to Perrin, he said that some time ago Lady Gregory and Sean O'Casey got together for an hour and revised *Cathleen Listens In.* with good and topical results.'

18 D. Krause, *Sean O'Casey: The Man and his Work* (New York: Macmillan Co. Ltd., 1975), p. 92.

19 G. Fallon, *Sean O'Casey, the Man I Knew* (London: Routledge and Kegan Paul, 1965), pp. 24–25.

20 The original of this letter is now in Southern Illinois University Library. It is a reply to Robinson's letter of 28 September 1922, which quoted Yeats's criticisms of *The Crimson in the Tricolour.* Among Yeats's comments appears the folowing passage which is startlingly prophetic so far as the poet's bewilderment when confronted by *The Silver Tassie* is concerned: 'I find this discursive play very hard to judge for it is a type of play I do not understand. The drama of it is loose and vague. . . . It is a story without meaning – a story where nothing happens except that a wife runs away from a husband to whom we had not the least idea that she was married, and the Mansion House lights are turned out because of some wrong to a man who never appears in the story' (handwritten notes, dated 19 June 1922. also in Southern Illinois University Library). Robinson answered O'Casey's defence of *The Crimson* in the following letter of 18 October 1922: 'I should have answered your letter before but I have been rather busy and away in England for a few days. I am sorry you were so disappointed about the Crimson etc. There is something to be said for vague drama – the drama of Tchekov – but surely Ibsen and Shaw are both as hard and clear as possible – except perhaps Heartbreak House – however this is mere literary controversy and what I want to say is that you should come along with your new play as soon as ever you like. I wish you had come before you started to write it and talked over the scenario with me.'

21 E. Blythe, *The Abbey Theatre* [1963], p. 13.

22 Unpublished letter dated 24 June 1928 in the possession of Ivor Brown.

23 W. B. Yeats, 'Sara Allgood,' *Irish Times,* 19 January 1924.

24 In *Daughters of Erin* Elizabeth Coxhead points out that, in 'harping on her Mrs Broderick, Yeats was wide of the mark, for she had lost the comic touch; it is generally admitted that her comedy in the latter half of her career was heavy and bumbling. But her astonishing gain in tragic power was more than compensation, as the audience acknowledged on that legendary first night of *Juno and the Paycock.* when the players were recalled so often that in the end the exhausted stage-hands left the curtain up for good.' (p. 211). It is not generally known that O'Casey preferred the playing of Juno by Sara's sister, Molly O'Neill, probably because her handling of the comic business was lighter and better integrated with the more poignant action. The playwright told me that, while Sara was magnificent in ritualistic action and formal tragic speech, Molly gave the part a deeper humanity.

25 *The Sunday Times.* 16 November 1925.

26 *Sean O'Casey: The Man I Knew* (London, 1965), p. 19 and p. 24.
27 There are many examples but I would particularly emphasize the chapter 'Comrades', in *Inishfallen, Fare Thee Well* (London, 1949).

SEAN O'CASEY AND/OR JAMES JOYCE

BERNARD BENSTOCK

IF THEY HADN'T BEEN SO DIFFERENT, YOU COULDN'T TELL THEM APART, commented a Dublin wag about Sean O'Casey and James Joyce. Born less than two years apart at opposite ends of Dublin, they spent their formative years in that city and, although they may well have passed each other on a major thoroughfare, there is no evidence that they ever met. Each went from Ireland into a self-imposed exile that lasted the best part of the last forty years of their lives, Joyce on the continent and O'Casey in England: during their exile years they were scheduled to meet when Joyce visited Britain, but the plan fell through (years later O'Casey commented with a sigh that they would have got along fine). Both developed something akin to paranoia about Ireland, or at least shared a paranoia that went a long way toward corroborating the justice of their jaundiced views. When *Finnegans Wake* was published in 1939 the *Irish Times* announced the event and credited O'Casey with having written it. In what was probably their only exchange of letters, they quickly communicated with each other on the subject (Joyce: 'I wonder whether you have seen already the Dublin paper I sent you with its curious misprint – if it is a misprint. . . . Anyhow I hope you will take the printer's error, as I do, for a happy and amusing omen'; O'Casey: 'I was very glad to get a letter from you, and to find that you weren't annoyed at "Finnegans Wake" being put against my name. . . . I don't think the reference was a misprint. I know many of Dublin's Literary Clique dislike me, and they hate you (why, God only knows), so that "misprint" was a bit of a joke').[1]

Half-a-century earlier they were children growing up in Dublin: Joyce was the first of what became a houseful of surviving children, O'Casey the last of a handful of survivors in the Casey household. Both their fathers had transplanted to Dublin, John Joyce from Cork and Michael Casey from Limerick, and in neither case did their Dublin lives bring either success to them or advantages for their sons. John Joyce was a 'gentleman' who eventually sold off his remaining properties and, eminently unemployable, gingerly carried his growing family down the economic ladder; Michael Casey, as serious as his counterpart was frivolous, died before his son was of school age, leaving a family that descended rapidly into poverty. The deaths of O'Casey's father and Joyce's mother had profound repercussions for their sons, while in each instance the surviving parent lived into their eighties, Mrs. Casey in constant companionship with Sean, Mr. Joyce abandoned but ambivalently remembered by Jim. By the end of the 1880s Johnny Casey was at the beginning of what would prove to be a very scant education at the hands of Protestant teachers, serious eye ailments eventually terminating formal education, while James Joyce was an underaged pupil at the highly respectable Jesuit institution, Clongowes Wood College, a child with 'weak and watery eyes' not much unlike Stephen Dedalus. The pandybat of Father Daly (alias Dolan) and the ruler of Mr. Hogan (alias Slogan) were primed as instruments of their instruction, which neither student would quickly forget.

Religion quite obviously accounts for one of the major differences between Joyce and O'Casey, as well as evolving into an important correspondence: each had at some point in adolescence or young manhood fervently embraced the Church in which he had been baptized. Joyce at Belvedere College had even contemplated the possibility of a vocation as a Jesuit priest, while O'Casey displayed preaching talents as a young parishioner at St. Barnabas' of the Church of Ireland. The latter emulated two of the dynamic clergymen at his church, later warmly depicting them in his plays and autobiographies, but for Joyce the kindest portrait of a Jesuit was that of the benign Father Conmee, with attendant ambiguities in both *A Portrait* and *Ulysses*. It would be insufficient to say that each merely found something as a surrogate for the abandoned faith (Joyce his art, O'Casey his socialism and allied causes), since both proved to be strong and loud in their apostasies, though neither became a professional atheist. They carried powerful aspects of their religions with them throughout their artistic lifetimes, Joyce consciously retaining a supersaturation of Catholicism as fundamental to the mystique of his art, O'Casey adding Catholicism both as part of his basic Irish culture and as an existing force against which he was constantly embroiled. As Irishmen they had felt the social impact of their religions in their years of maturation. The Joyce family had a firm investment of their social standing in the vaults of the

Catholic Church, and gentleman John Joyce sent his sons to be
educated by the Society of Jesus, disdaining the lower levels of
the Christian Brothers schools (yet Joyce *did* spend several months
with the Micky Muds and Paddy Stinks, keeping the fact from his
authorized biographer, an indication of the decline of the family
fortunes and a retention of his father's shame at the lowering of
family standards). Michael Casey devoted his life to Church
missionary work (and probably limited his financial possibilities
because of his religious dedication), attempting to veer his children
into educational vocations, leaving a widow to fight the battle of
Protestant shabby-genteel against the mass of Catholic poor that
were her lifelong neighbors. The young Joyce devolved into near-
poverty without ever becoming proletarian, adopting a quasi-
bohemian veneer as a convenient cover and divorcing himself
essentially from the facts of his father and siblings. The young
O'Casey became proletarianized by age fourteen, continued to live
at home, was often unemployed, and survived as the sole means of
support for his mother. His 'glances back' in the autobiographies
describe unmistakable tenement life, and it was Protestant pride
apparently that made the marginal difference from the slum
existences of their Catholic neighbours.

Although the diametrics of their faiths are counterbalanced by
both the intensity of their early religious experiences and the
exalted positions within their Churches as Jesuitical Catholic and
High Church Anglican, their divergent paths within the confines of
Dublin indicate important differences in their directions. Joyce and
O'Casey co-existed for over twenty years as coincidental Dubliners:
they might just as well have started out as far apart as Paris and
Devon. O'Casey's entire Dublin existence remained in residences
north of the Liffey, while the economic straits of the Joyce family
brought them from the middle-class areas of south Dublin and the
fashionable suburbs to more squalid dwellings to the north, so that
there were times in the 1890s that the two youngsters were within
a large stone's throw of each other. The topographical game was
one that Joyce enjoyed, especially in the Wandering Rocks chapter
of *Ulysses* where Church and State, personified by Father Conmee
and the Viceroy, traverse large sections of Dublin without crossing
paths with each other. Joyce's directions from Fairview and Lower
Drumcondra took him centripetally toward the heart of the city.
It was the city itself that was his adventure of discovery, as he
records in *Stephen Hero* and *A Portrait of the Artist*; along the
way he notes certain locations to which he attaches associations
from his other adventures of discovery, his reading. His terminus

is University College on Stephen's Green, once he has successfully
skirted the Protestant counterpart, the more prestigious Trinity
College, and the Green itself is the centre of Self for him
('Stephen's, that is, my green'). The intellectual life directly or
indirectly engendered by the university kept the center of focus
in the general confines of central Dublin (University College in *A
Portrait*, the National Library in *Ulysses*); for O'Casey the
centripetal force remained his neighbourhood in northeast Dublin,
for a while the nearby church, and his work at the Great Northern
Railway. His intellectual life brought him into central Dublin,
but to such places as the Gaelic League (where Joyce had only
looked in before decamping in disgust) and Liberty Hall (where
Joyce would have had no business). By the time O'Casey was a
familiar at the Transport Workers' Union and the meeting rooms
of the Irish Citizen Army, Joyce was already a familiar on the
streets of Trieste. If there was any place in Dublin that they might
momentarily have rubbed shoulders, it would have been the
second-hand book stalls along Crampton Quay or Bachelor's Walk,
Joyce either buying or pawning, O'Casey either buying or appro-
priating.

Neither one would likely have been seen too often inside Dublin's
Abbey Theatre; by 1901 Joyce had leveled a blast at the Irish
Literary Theatre in 'The Day of the Rabblement' which should
have granted him lifetime persona non gratis status at the Abbey
('I smell the public sweat of monks,' quipped Buck Mulligan),
while O'Casey admits that until his own play was staged there he
was rarely inside the theatre, rarely able to afford the price of
admission. For decades the Irish Literary Theatre survived without
the critical approval of James Joyce or the plays or patronage of
Sean O'Casey, but Joyce had once had hopes of gracing its
hoardings (permanently dashed when the 'popular devil' of Irish
nationalism took possession), and O'Casey of course had a forty-
year relationship there of marital engagements and ruptures. An
important but tangential link, consequently, between Joyce and
O'Casey was the personage of William Butler Yeats, target of
Joyce's attack for surrendering to the rabblement, then defender
of O'Casey against the rabble during the 1926 riots over *The
Plough and the Stars*, then vilified by O'Casey for his cavalier
dismissal of *The Silver Tassie*. Both Joyce and O'Casey frequently
voiced their admiration of Yeats's stories and poems, and both
made their peace with him eventually. Yet in 1932, when from the
stage of the Abbey's Peacock Theatre Yeats inaugurated the Irish
Academy of Letters, he found that he would have to do without the

membership of either James Joyce or Sean O'Casey, who independently from their coigns of vantage in Paris and London refused to join. Joyce's refusal came in a polite letter to Yeats indicating that he felt dissociated from such a venture, but O'Casey's letter went to the *Irish Times* and denounced the Academy for condoning censorship in Ireland and seeking to be the arbiter of Irish literature.

The relationship between Joyce and O'Casey, which on a personal basis began and ended with an exchange of letters during the last week of May 1939 (O'Casey's contained a parting shot at 'Them and their Academy of Letters'), was primarily a one-way street. James Joyce's literary career began almost immediately (if not sooner – there is no reason to assume that eleven-year-old John Casey ever saw a copy of 'Et tu, Healy,' nine-year-old Joyce's political broadside); at least from the publication of *Ulysses* on, O'Casey was an avid reader and re-reader of Joyce's work. He would probably qualify as Joyce's 'ideal reader' for *Finnegans Wake*, having attempted to discourage at least one American student from writing a thesis on the *Wake* because only a Dubliner could really understand it ('Stick to *Ulysses* – it's easier').[2] Eventually he found himself reading and advocating all of Joyce's works, almost indifferent to occasional critical commentary that found elements of imitation in his own. In a letter to Brooks Atkinson within a month of exchanging letters with Joyce, O'Casey explains that his earliest literary efforts were in fantasy: 'I led off with fantasy – having then heard nothing of the bould & (to me) great James Joyce. It was in my blood.' He goes on to quote a review by Austin Clarke of *I Knock at the Door*, in which the poet notes with approval the analogy with Joyce: ' All this in its savage satire is set down in a rhythmical deludhering extravagance of vernacular that recalls the masterful blarney & gab of Joyce, but has a lyrical spontaneity of its own.'[3] And a few months later O'Casey is responding to a request that he nominate the writer of the most distinguished books since 1918, and he names *Ulysses* and *Finnegans Wake*, adding: 'They are unique and, I think, tremendous. There can be no question of the artistry of this man, of his strange originality, and of the rich tragic and comic poetry that blossoms in all that he has written.'[4] Earlier he had signed petitions protesting the misuse of Joyce's name for a story in a German newspaper and the pirating of Joyce's work by Samuel Roth, and there can be no doubt that he must have identified with his fellow Irish writer in exile; but from the *Wake* on, and the death of Joyce in 1941, O'Casey became one of the strongest

champions of Joyce's greatness and one of the angriest voices
against official neglect of James Joyce, especially his having been
overlooked for the Nobel Prize.

There was no reciprocal adulation or advocacy, much less imitation, of O'Casey by James Joyce. O'Casey's career had of course
begun late and sustained several years of rejection before he
attained his goal of writing for the Abbey. He was 43-years-old by
then, and a year or so older before he could permanently ditch
his pick and shovel: by that time Joyce was the world-known author
of *Ulysses* and determined to keep well away from his native
Ireland in the throes of civil war. He probably did consider himself
significantly remote from Ireland for the reasons given to Yeats
regarding the Academy of Letters to be partially accurate
(although he might also have shrunk from the public sweat of
aesthetes at the Abbey's Peacock Theatre). He kept in touch with
Ireland in individual ways and for idiosyncratic purposes, mostly
having to do with materials necessary for his Work in Progress and
the people he knew personally. The changes in the program at the
Abbey probably passed him by most of the time, although he does
mention in a letter to Harriet Weaver in 1926 that he read *Juno
and the Paycock*.[5] By a nice coincidence, in the letter to O'Casey
he adds that he and Nora were planning to see *Juno* in Paris at
the Theatre de l'Oeuvre. It is characteristic of the exilic condition
that the Irish novelist should be writing from France to the Irish
playwright in England indicating that, although someone in
Dublin had blundered, he was going to see a French translation of
the latter's play.

When O'Casey first became aware of Joyce is not easy to
determine, but the ways in which that awareness manifested itself
are not unimportant. There is little evidence that he was an early
reader of *Dubliners* and *A Portrait of the Artist*, although they
were later incorporated into his pantheon. Occasionally a critic
comments that one or another of O'Casey's handful of stories
resembles a story in *Dubliners* (the comparisons are marginal at
best: O'Casey made no effort to inaugurate a style of 'scrupulous
meanness, a vital factor in the Joycean short story). Eventually,
comparisons arose between Joyce's novel of childhood and adolescence in Dublin with *I Knock at the Door* (Marvin Magalaner has
skilfully extended the parallel to *Stephen Hero* as well, although
there is no possibility of O'Casey having read it before writing his
own Portrait of the Artist as a Young Chiselur, and Magalaner's
analysis of O'Casey's first volume of autobiography, varying
between the two Joycean attempts at quasi-autobiography, works

well).[6] Particularly relevant is the total ambience omf the Stephen Dedaluses and the Johnny Cassides in Dublin, and the ways in which the two Dublin artists fashioned their works around the world of the Dubliners and the inner worlds of the Stephens and Johnnys. For Joyce the dual facets of his subject matter were simultaneously perceived from the very beginning, the stories that became *Dubliners* recorded the society in which he lived, while the novel that became *A Portrait* concentrated on the self, the privacy of the artistic soul. O'Casey maintained almost an exclusive focus on the external scene until his late fifties, when he not only embarked on his 'Swift Glances Back at Things That Made Me,' but later on the drama *Red Roses for Me*. That there were tempting elements of his own life which were fit materials for dramatic literature must have been present in his creative consciousness fairly early, since *Red Roses* proves to be a reconstruction of one of the plays that the Abbey rejected before *The Shadow of a Gunman*, the play called *The Harvest Festival*.

'Oh, be God, I ferreted out a copy of "Ullyses" [sic] at last.' announces O'Casey in a letter from London dated 12 April 1926.[7] Yet there is little direct evidence that even *Ulysses* made a significant impact on O'Casey or in any important manner influenced his own creative work. He calls it 'that great and amazing work' in his 1939 letter to its author, also commenting, 'I've had constant contact with you in "Dubliners" and "Portrait of the Artist," ' but it is evident that it was *Finnegans Wake* that captivated O'Casey. Until then Joyce for him was a celebrity and a cause (and a *cause célèbre*) with whom he could identify as an Irishman, a Dubliner, an exile, an enemy of the Literary Clique. The quick succession of certain events (the publication of the completed *Wake*, the letter from Joyce, and Joyce's death) brought Joyce into O'Casey's consciousness as never before, as a force driving O'Casey's own creative energies forward and in somewhat newer directions. The act of invincible journalistic ignorance or of Irish humor (wet and dry) which coupled Joyce's title with O'Casey's name inadvertently resulted in magnetic magic, a crystalization for O'Casey of the Joycean mystique in direct relation to his own campaigns as an exiled Irish writer. Joyce the Martyr became his consistent theme, and the relatively harmless but nonetheless brainless award by Cambridge University of a D. Litt. for P. G. Wodehouse exacerbated his indignation and broadened the perspective from a strictly Irish to a British (and consequently international) injustice; O'Casey received very little

more from Cambridge than a student invitation to speak and a
cold bed to sleep in. This trival episode also finds its way into the
letter to Joyce: 'Well, Oxford's (or Cambridge) going to hang the
coloured gown of a D. Litt. over the shoulders of Wodehouse,
whom, [sic] Belloc says, is the greatest living writer in English. So
"Finnegans Wake" will, I fear, be a wake in earnest.'[8] Two decades
later another act of parochial Irish imbecility served to link the
names and works of Joyce and O'Casey together: the Archbishop
of Dublin refused to offer an opening mass for the 1958 Tostal's
Dublin International Theatre Festival because of the presence of
O'Casey's *The Drums of Father Ned* and a dramatized version of
Joyce's *Ulysses*. The Tostal Council capitulated and O'Casey
retaliated: neither of the plays was performed, and Samuel Beckett,
with his unerring integrity in such matters, withdrew his works
as well. With Joyce now long dead, it was left for O'Casey and
Beckett to represent him in battles against censorship and
ecclesiastical encroachment.

The equestrian knight in armor with lance is hardly an appropriate image for either of the two near-blind writers, but David
Krause has aptly suggested that the mythic figures of Daedalus and
Prometheus correspond to Joyce and O'Casey respectively, and
have been adopted by them as totem personages in their 'autobiographic' self-treatments.[9] For Joyce major emphasis was on
Daedalian craftsmanship and craftiness: every aspect of his
defiance related directly to his art or indirectly to Art (as when he
championed the tenor John Sullivan in Paris in the twenties). As
soon as he dissociated himself from the self-image as Jesuit Father,
he assumed the pose as 'priest of eternal imagination', and the
rebellion against the Church began in earnest once he had stature
as a young artist. (The childish act of defiance against the pandy-
batting priest, so vital to the Daedalian calling, was actually a
demand for rectification rather than open rebellion, and did not
limit his view of himself as a potential priest). Daedalus was an
acknowledged transgressor, and Joyce defined himself in various
ways as 'guilty' rather than 'innocent' (Stephen quietly admits well
after his Clongoweys days that although he was twice punished
unfairly, there were many instances in which he escaped justifiable
punishment). Joyce accepted the view of the artist as somewhat
divorced from and even antithetical to society (MacCann very
accurately comments, 'Minor poets, I suppose, are above such
trival questions as the question of universal peace'). Joyce had no
intention of becoming a minor poet (there is nothing in the
Daedalian creed to sustain anyone other than a consummate

artificer); the only justification for certain anti-social stances was true genius, and the literary achievements commensurate with true genius. In embracing Daedalus as his guide, Joyce was also accepting the role of Icarus (his Stephen vacillates between the artificer Daedalus and the rebel Icarus), and the possibility that his rebelliousness will lead to his own destruction.

O'Casey's role as Prometheus preceded and often existed outside his position as an artist. His identification was with the Promethean figure of Jim Larkin and his campaign was primarily social, a political stance that often allowed for his plays and polemics as weapons. There evolved as well highly 'political' objections to his works of art (the riots against *The Plough* in Dublin, the rejection of *The Tassie* by the Abbey, the banning of *Within the Gates* in Boston, the snubbing of *Father Ned* by the archbishop), but these served to corroborate rather than initiate his sense of injustice. Even within political organizations O'Casey found himself to be in disfavor, often in the minority and occasionally a minority unto himself. Had Larkin not left Ireland for America leaving Connolly in charge, had the Irish Citizens Army not chosen to ally itself with the Irish Volunteers, had the Easter rising been a proletariat revolution rather than a bourgeois rebellion, socialist rather than nationalist, O'Casey might have lived out his days in Dublin as a political activist, although his chances for success at carrying the day would hardly have been any greater. Finding himself progressively more isolated from Irish public opinion and at crosspurposes with the society in which he lived, O'Casey eventually arrived at a position similar to Joyce's. But it was not for himself that the modest man fashioned the image of a Prometheus Hibernica but for James Larkin; for himself he chose less grandiose totems, flying wasps and green crows. Nonetheless, he inherited the stature of the defiant humanitarian, condemned by those in power against whom he rebelled in the name of the greater mass of humanity.

Class identification, if not class consciousness, continued to govern the artistic perceptions of Joyce and O'Casey throughout their work. To an important extent they both accepted the position of chronicler of their social class, Joyce essentially limiting himself to the petit bourgeoisie of Dublin and O'Casey espousing the cause of the Dublin worker. An examination of *Dubliners*, a collection of stories that has as its aim the writing of 'a chapter in the moral history' of Ireland, reveals a wide cross-section of the middle class, from the harassed shop girl Eveline to the merchant prince of butchers, Mr. Doyle. Yet the spectrum remains exclusively with

the middle class: no semblance of the Anglo-Irish Ascendancy
living in the Big Houses of Merrion Square is discernible, nor do we
find a laborer or a navvy as a central character. There are indica-
tions in *Dubliners* that Joyce sought to provide intimations of the
total spectrum of Dublin life, introducing Mr. Browne as a lone
Protestant among the Catholics of the Morkans' soirée in 'The
Dead,' and even hinting at the presence of a Jewish Mr. Goldberg
in 'Grace,' but essentially the world of his Dubliners is Irish Catholic
– as it is Irish bourgeois. The professional common denominator
in the book is the clerk (Farrington, Chandler, Donnelly, Doran,
Duffy), the white collar worker with eminent claims of
respectability but often with only a tenuous hold on economic
survival. James Duffy's bank job seems particularly secure and his
position somewhat elevated, while Farrington is obviously unsuited
to office work and in imminent danger of dismissal. His grasp on
class privilege is slipping, yet as he steals away for a quick drink,
his ploy is to secrete a cap in his pocket so that the chief clerk,
seeing his hat still on the rack, will assume that he is still in the
building, while he remains sufficiently respectable wearing a cap
while crossing the street to the pub. With a large family to support
Farrington can hardly afford to lose his job, while Duffy has only
himself to provide for with his decidedly better salary. Farrington
is physically and temperamentally unsuited to the confining work
and would be better equipped for manual labor, but his class status
seems sufficiently important to him for desperate acts of subterfuge. Even if this particular clerk deserves the sack for his
inefficiency, someone like Thomas Chandler apparently does not:
there is every reason to believe that he is competent at his work
(although as a would-be poet he may think himself superior to it),
but there is also the hint that he too may be vulnerable. Farrington
remembers that someone called 'little Peake' was 'hounded' out
of his job so that the boss could give the position to his own nephew
– what job security then for 'little Chandler'?

Eveline Hill, on the other hand, seems willing to give up her
demeaning job at the Stores (salary: seven shillings a week), and
knows that she would be quickly replaced, but security, respectability, and her sense of responsibility conspire to paralyze her in
the act of escape. Other Dubliners have managed to shake off
bourgeois responsibilities and prefer living lives of precarious
freedom: John Corley is perfecting his talents as a gigolo, while his
crony Lenehan cadges drinks by wit and subterfuge (and 'his name
was vaguely associated with racing tissues'). 'Two Gallants' tracks
the ascendant line of Corley's movement toward the attainment of

a 'small gold coin' (apparently ten shillings, far more than Eveline earns in a week), while Lenehan's arc is apparently descending. He finds himself hungry and tired, and condescends to eating a plate of peas in a 'poor-looking shop' where the other customers, a mechanic and two work-girls, eye him suspiciously. Lenehan has to attempt to 'belie his air of gentility' in order to pass in this proletarian ambience, and in a moment of weakness even yearns for respectability ('He was tired of knocking about, of pulling the devil by the tail, of shifts and intrigues. He would be thirty-one in November. Would he never get a good job? Would he never have a home of his own? He thought how pleasant it would be to have a warm fire to sit by and a good dinner to sit down to. . . . He might yet be able to settle down in some snug corner and live happily if he could only come across some good simple-minded girl with a little of the ready'). The shift from real concern to an exalted variation of his usual 'shifts and intrigues' is occasioned by the satisfaction derived from having eaten his plate of peas. Lenehan remains incorrigible, a segment of the middle class that sees itself as kicking over the traces, but in actuality is being summarily dumped by the middle class to make room for those who better embody the class mores. In *Ulysses* both 'gallants' return for an ironic encore. Corley's ascent proved shortlived, and late at night he is seen alone, friendless, homeless, and penniless, panhandling from Stephen Dedalus, while Lenehan has temporarily persevered (his association with racing tissues has strengthened) and is still living by his wits. But his newfound status may also be on the wane, since his touting of Sceptre for the Gold Cup has backfired and earned him the enmity of swells like Blazes Boylan.

Joyce is not only the chronicler of his class but also its severest critic. He scrutinizes every precept of the bourgeoisie: hard working, honest, religious, temperate, and secure. Those who succeed best do so with the hard work of others or with finagling of lucrative contracts; their honesty nonetheless allows shady business practices, and their religiosity consolidates social and economic control. Mr. Alleyne can play gallant to Miss Delacour, while the Farringtons are copying out the correspondence under the watchful eye of the chief clerk, Mr. Shelley. Mrs. Mooney is assured that Bob Doran will marry her Polly since his employer, the Catholic wine merchant Mr. Leonard, will sack Doran if there is any scandal. Mr. Fitzpatrick can shortchange Kathleen Kearney since he has only a girl and her mother to deal with. And Mr. Duffy, who apparently does his job well as a cashier in a private bank, is dissuaded from stealing from his bank only because of

the inadvisability of doing so: 'He allowed himself to think that
in certain circumstances he would rob his bank but, as these
circumstances never arose . . .' Even the firm rock of economic
stability shows itself to be vulnerable. If Jimmy Doyle's father is
the epitome of a butcher who has attained great wealth ('He had
also been fortunate enough to secure some of the police contracts
and in the end he had become rich enough to be alluded to in the
Dublin newspapers as a merchant prince'), then his declining
counterpart is Mr. Mooney, the defunct butcher who now 'was
obliged to enlist himself as a sheriff's man.' Mooney's weakness was
drink: 'He drank, plundered the till, ran headlong into debt. It
was no use making him take the pledge: he was sure to break out
again a few days after. By fighting with his wife in the presence of
customers and by buying bad meat he ruined his business.' Mr.
Doyle had modified his strong nationalist views in order to gain
success (the police contracts), but Mr. Mooney could not modify
his drinking, and ruined not just himself, but his business. Not that
Doyle is perpetually invulnerable: during the events of 'After the
Race' his son drunkenly gambles away what must be assumed to
be a large segment of his patrimony. In contrast to the intemperate
Mooney, there is Mr. Kearney, successful bootmaker on Ormond
Quay, who can afford to send his family away on holiday at the
fashionable resorts, but for all his solid masculine presence, he can
do little to prevent Mr. Fitzpatrick and the 'Committee' from
denying his daughter her contracted fee.

The precariousness of even the most staunchly comfortable of
the middle class is always intimated throughout *Dubliners*, and in
'The Dead' the Morkans display the full panoply of their solid
position: the impressive array of food, the goose and the ham and
the spiced beef, the jellies and jams, the nuts and fruit and
chocolates and sweets, the port and sherry, and in particular the
controlled and orderly arrangement of the drinks on the piano
('three squads of stout and ale and minerals, drawn up according
to the colours of their uniforms, the first two black, with brown
and red labels, the third and smallest squad white, with traverse
green sashes'). They have maintained the full measure of their
genteel position, their Christmas party the exhibition of their
sustained success ('For years and years it had gone off in splendid
style as long as anyone could remember'), but Mary Jane is giving
music lessons, and the Morkan sisters are very careful to see
that her pupils 'got the best slices,' since they come from prominent and wealthy families. The death of Pat Morkan had meant
that they had to sell their house in Stoney Batter, and although

'they believed in eating well; the best of everything: diamond-bone sirloins, three-shilling tea and the best of bottled stout,' they now live in a 'dark gaunt house on Usher's Island, the upper part of which they rented from Mr Fulham, the cornfactor on the ground floor.'

The perimeters of Joyce's sociographic portrayal of Dublin are within the elements of that society in which he had his own roots and personal experiences, but his attitudes and conclusions derive from his analytical perspective. Sean O'Casey's people (at least for the early plays of Dublin life, several later plays that return to that setting, and the initial volumes of the autobiographies) were the residents of those tenements north of the Liffey. Charges have occasionally been brought against O'Casey, particularly in journalistic circles in his native city, that he over-represented the case for his own tenement existence, that his autobiographies fabricate a poverty that was not really the case for himself and his family. The argument parallels the 'insult to Ireland' conten-tions which were heard during the *Plough* riots, although no one has as yet insisted that There Are No Slums in Ireland, as they once insisted that there are no prostitutes. The assumption seems to be that O'Casey, as a self-professed lifelong Communist, has claimed for himself a greater identification with the urban poor by misrepresenting the shabby but genteel buildings in which he lived as *tenements*. O'Casey's mother and sister and brothers must certainly have clung desperately to their slight edge as declassé Protestants, but their degree of success was marginal at best. O'Casey saw what members of his family might not have wanted to see, that they were being ground down into the poverty that presumably God had intended only for their Catholic neighbors, a view that he depicted so graphically in *Pictures in the Hallway* and *Drums under the Windows* that it managed to offend the fear-less journalists of the established press. They might just as well argue that someone else must have written *Juno and the Paycock*, since no Protestant bourgeois like Sean O'Casey could possibly have had the first-hand knowledge of tenement life!

Not that O'Casey was unaware of bourgeois life in Dublin, or the bourgeois aspirations of many of the working class families in the tenements. *Juno* is a comic document of such aspirations and a tragic reminder of the dangers of the illusion. On one side there is Boyle himself, a lumpen proletariat with no vestige of the work ethic to compel him to take a job, even when one is miraculously available, and on the other there is Juno herself arguing for bourgeois proprieties and against Mary going out on strike. The

instrument of their illusions and their destruction is the bourgeois
school teacher Charles Bentham, who, once the will proves to be
banjaxed and Mary pregnant, takes off for England. The Boyles
have no particular identification with the working class and accept
the concept of an unexpected windfall as a natural result of the
good bourgeois life that they have innately assumed was theirs by
right, but had somehow been mysteriously denied them. Juno and
Mary had once believed that jobs were necessary realities for
survival, so that although they too have been lured into unreal
expectations by bourgeois Benthamism, their awakening returns
them to reality (a fate Captain Boyle is spared). In a plot situation
that depends on familiar devices, the Paycock is as easily deceived
as Molière's *bourgeois gentilhomme*, and in the same direction.
That such level-headed women as Juno and Mary should be as
easily won over to the fantasy indicates just how deeply ingrained
is the desire for middle-class conveniences and position in the
dreams of the depressed lower classes.

Despite O'Casey's particular sympathies with women as the
most victimized members of society, he avoided idealizing them
inordinately. Even Mrs. Breydon, so carefully modeled after his
own mother, retains the ethos of her genteel origins, and
campaigns against so many of her son's proletarian ideals. It takes
the death of her son for her to understand the reality of her social
situation, and, as in *Juno and the Paycock*, the important indicator
of change resides in the ultimate realizations by the older and
younger women of the play. There is every indication in *Red Roses
for Me* that it was only the accident of widowhood that caused the
economic decline of the Breydons, as it had for the Casey family.
The sudden loss of the principal male wage earner in a society in
which economic power resides almost exclusively in masculine
hands occasions the kinds of disruptions visible in Mrs. Breydon's
condition. Had Michael Casey lived his full span of years, had
his serious interests in his sons' education been enforced, keeping
them out of the British Army, the family might have resided in
dwellings that would have delighted the denizens of the Dublin
press. Joyce also was keenly aware that the economic forces of
capitalist society operated along male-dominated lines, as is seen
in his subtle portrait of the Morkans at their best (and probably
entertaining in grand fashion for the last time, if we read the
indicators at the end of 'The Dead' prophetically). Kate and Julia
are fatherless and brotherless, and with their niece Mary Jane
live in isolation from those factors which generate new wealth.
Their talents are peripheral in the financial scheme of things;

they have not been educated to replace the males who made and sustained the family's fortunes, any more than Kathleen Kearney's mother had been educated. Music and French were her particular scholastic attainments, but only when she allied herself in marriage to a successful bootmaker could she hold on to bourgeois advantages; and not having been taught the rules by which such men as Fitzpatrick and Holohan play will cost her daughter her career in Dublin.

For a committed aesthete Joyce nonetheless proved himself to be an observant sociologist and politically astute in comprehending his society. Nor was Sean O'Casey so thoroughly enmeshed in the embroilments of the class struggle not to stand above the battle on occasion: his Donal Davoren is a odd creation for O'Casey, for as much as Donal is one of the butts of O'Casey's satirical thrusts, he is also the artist-as-a-young-man identifiable with his creator. There is every reason to wonder what he is doing there sharing a tenement room with Seumas Shields. He certainly does not identify himself with the lower-class dwellers in the building, nor does he indicate where his own roots lie. His exclusive identity is as an aesthete, an intrusive element in the environment hoping for a quiet room in which to write his poetry. Again, as so often happens in these early plays, O'Casey contents himself with a traditional device, in this case the uninvolved intruder, for comic juxtaposition and ironic commentary; but Donal is unmistakably quasi-autobiographic, although O'Casey's intentions were apparently self-satiric. Nor is Seumas Shields a member of the working class: as shiftless as Captain Boyle he is nonetheless bourgeois, a peddler of small household items who earns his living by selling, but proletarianized at least as far as his insufficient finances are concerned mainly by his own laziness. The real proletarian in *The Shadow of a Gunman* is Minnie Powell, whom Shields denigrates from his prejudiced bourgeois viewpoint. The play purposely displays the three variant approaches – the romantic working girl, the hypocritical failed bourgeois, and the detached and classless intellectual – with the real heroism the revealed factor in Minnie Powell alone.

Neither *The Shadow of a Gunman* nor *Juno and the Paycock* is a drama of photographic realism, although it was proverbial for a long time to consider them so (Irish newspaper reviewers in the 1920s actually tarred O'Casey, Joyce, and Liam O'Flaherty with the same 'naturalistic' brush, a tendency that may be on the decline) – O'Casey's early plays were exercises in functioning theatrical conventions, heightened by his fine ear for Dublin

talk and deepened by his individual perspectives. Throughout his
career O'Casey continued to add new theatre techniques, usually
known techniques, and some, like the expressionistic ones, relatively
new, always depending on the blend and balance for unique com-
binations. Once he settled in England he also extended the canvas
to areas beyond the north Dublin tenements, to English locales he
was becoming familiar with, back to Dublin on various occasions
as Irish political changes were making effects upon the country
that he could profitably comment on, and into rural Irish settings
as well. He jotted down scraps of conversation in Hyde Park, as
he had done in Dublin, and *Within the Gates* resounds with the
products of his notations. Some Irish critics prefer to believe that
O'Casey lost his touch once he divorced himself physically from
his native land, but that James Joyce retained his Dublin background for his later work while he existed abroad *in vacuo*. That
Joyce carried away with him enough Irish material to last him a
creative lifetime is indisputable, but not that time stopped for
him when he left. There are important changes in his Dublin
material as he continued writing, and in particular his perspective
on the class from which he evolved altered significantly from his
dealing with it in *Dubliners* to his handling of the same group in
Ulysses. Lenehan and Corley are carried over and redeployed, as
has been seen. Their fortunes have been reversed, but by midnight
of 16 June 1904 neither one is in an enviable position. We never
learn what has happened to 'Lord' John Corley's hold over women
that could once net him a half sovereign just for the asking, nor
what became of Lenehan's occasional yearning for a job and a
home.

What is determinable from *Ulysses* is that few of the bourgeois
'survivors' of *Dubliners* fare particularly well in their return
appearances. Bob Doran is a perennial drunk now that he is
married to Polly Mooney, and James Duffy may well be the
deranged Man in the Macintosh ('once a prosperous cit.'); and
Bantam Lyons, having been talked out of betting on Throwaway
by Lenehan, has gone off the wagon and is wobbling drunk. Tom
Kernan has survived: he is back at his profession selling tea,
wearing his secondhand clothes with dignity, but probably none
the better for the retreat at the Jesuit church, since he still displays
elements of backsliding into Protestantism ('The service of the
Irish church, used in Mount Jerome, is simpler, more impressive,
I must say'). The chances are that Bloom is right, and Kernan
has been given a hand up by the Freemasons, but he is also the
butt of the joke at the Ormond bar because of his inflated rhetoric:

'Most trenchant rendition of that ballad, upon my soul and honour it is.' And the gin is still hot in his mouth.

The important carryover from *A Portrait of the Artist* is the most diagnostic of the degraded bourgeois condition: Simon Dedalus, already described by his son as 'a bankrupt and at present a praiser of his own past', is a parody of the gentleman of leisure, pawning the household items for drink money, but refusing to give much of it to his daughter for food for his children. Simon is at the nucleus of a band of middle-class failures who gab on endlessly at the newspaper office and sing and drink at the Ormond. He and Ned Lambert and J. J. O'Molloy and Ben Dollard and Bob Cowley waltz around each other trying to borrow money or get off jury duty or keep from being distrained by landlords for their rent or creditors for their goods. It is expected to be of some solace to Cowley that the moneylender Reuben J. Dodd is considered not to be able to reclaim because the landlord, Rev. Love, has the prior claim. They sing themselves into sentimentality and drink them-selves into camaraderie under the watchful eyes of Bloom and Richie Goulding, Dedalus's despised brother-in-law, who also is seriously in debt, although at least still employed. The new variable in their midst is Leopold Bloom, who observes them from a distance and is hardly accepted within their inner circle (only Kernan and Goulding make overtures to him, since the former assumes that he too is a backslider, and the latter has been banished from his brother-in-law's company and joins him as a fellow outcast). Bloom's difference becomes apparent when he and Dedalus and Power and Cunningham are riding in a carriage together during the funeral procession, and see Reuben J. Dodd, the moneylender. The others deride and curse him, but Cunningham comments, 'We have all been there', until he notices Bloom and corrects himself: 'Well, nearly all of us'. Bloom is too prudent to have been trapped in their dependence on moneylenders, nor is he a part of their consolidated group. In the creation of Leopold Bloom, Joyce evolved from within the ethos of his own class an alternative to the self-destructiveness of the Irish bourgeoisie, just as he had earlier experimented with the beginnings of an alternate daemon to the anti-intellectualism of that class. To his mythic Daedalus-Icarus, Joyce had added a polytropic Ulysses.

The dead Joyce became for O'Casey an important identification: at times he stood alone as the prophet unhonored in Ireland (and by the Swedish Academy); at others he was a member of a small pantheon that included Yeats and Shaw and O'Casey, and at rare

moments he was exclusively an alter ego for O'Casey – one who
had taken the high road. As early as 1945 Joyce was 'perhaps the
bravest and proudest artist of them all' – in an O'Casey blast
against censorship in Ireland: 'Joyce, the bravest and finest soul in
literature that Ireland has had for many years; who made of Dublin
a dancing Hecuba, and, at the last, wrote the most extraordinary
and wonderful Everyman the mind of man could conceive. . . .
the stars themselves move over the Dublin sky to figure out the
name of Joyce there.'[10] The fulsomeness of praise is nonetheless
qualified ('perhaps'/'has had for many years'); idolatry did not
come easily to Sean O'Casey, and he strove to stay this side of it.
The association with his own work is also carefully concealed
in the descriptive content, for it was surely O'Casey who consciously made Dublin a dancing Hecuba only a few years before
in the third act of *Red Roses for Me*. And once again it is the
difficult *Finnegans Wake* on which O'Casey focuses for the
Joycean Everyman, the mythic Earwicker rather than the ordinary
Leopold Bloom of *Ulysses*. How the *Wake* must have teased
O'Casey's imagination as no other work had, to have engaged him
so intimately and kept him involved so consistently. It created a
mythic Ireland, more than the prosaic one that is found in *Ulysses*
and the early O'Casey plays, and he could pair off the disappoint-
ing homeland of censorship and philistinism with the Ireland that
he felt both he and Joyce believed in. 'For her size, Ireland has
done more than well in the world of literature', O'Casey wrote in a
1939 article for *International Literature*, echoing a sentiment
found in Joyce's lectures three decades earlier in Trieste that he
could hardly have known; 'and the daddy of all those who write, a
genius standing alone on a high and lonely peak [compare Joyce's
youthful identification with Henrik Ibsen: 'the mountain-ridges
where/ I flash my antlers on the air'] is undoubtedly him who is
called James Joyce with his *Dubliners*, *Ulysses*, and, now,
Finnegans Wake lying at his feet; the last a judgement on the
world's life as it was and is; a Sinai spouting flames of scorn, with
the thunder changed to peals of laughter.'[11] At work on his own
autobiographic 'novels' O'Casey conflated Joyce's work with
Joyce's life, and apparently a reading of the posthumous *Stephen
Hero* caused him to assume that it was as autobiographic as *I
Knock at the Door*: 'fighting to save a child even when the child
is drawing out his last long sigh, as James Joyce's mother battled
for the life of her poor and beloved Isabel.'[12] 'Isabel Daedalus'
was of course a fictional representation of Joyce's young brother

George, but for O'Casey the poignant scene had the dynamic significance of real life.

With the publication of *Drums under the Windows* it became apparent to reviewers and critics that O'Casey's admiration for Joyce was affecting his own writing style, and he was particularly ruffled that the accusation of sedulous aping came from George Orwell; he retaliated in *Sunset and Evening Star* against the 'low note about cogging from Joyce'. His dander up O'Casey declared that 'bad or good; right or wrong; O'Casey's always himself', and counterattacked immediately: 'Orwell has as much chance of reaching the stature of Joyce as a tit has of reaching that of an eagle.'[13] The intimation of imitation has of course persisted, and even an avowed admirer like David Krause has on occasion found a 'laboured passage in which he attempts to play with some Joycean puns'.[14] The technique in question is certainly Joycean: it builds a series of mock-saint names for various industries (the source here is more the catalogues in the Cyclops chapter of *Ulysses* than anything in the *Wake*), leading toward an all-inclusive Prayerman, St. Preservius. The puns are rather good ones, consistent with each other, nicely Latin-looking but baldly colloquial, and winding up with a reference to Joyce's *Ulysses* within the context – quite a Joycean way of signing the acknowledgment. St. Scinful for brewers and distillers is archly apt, Spudadoremus for Irish Agriculture perfect in welding the verbally profane and sacred, St. Ironicomus nicely tripartite in Iron-ironic-Comus, but best of all the direct thrust in St. Banaway for Book-making. If these puns are laboured, it is only in the sense that they are well worked out. A far more sanguine view and ably argued is Hubert Nicholson's defense:

He has been accused lately of imitating (I suppose 'imitating badly' is meant) James Joyce. He is certainly no Daedalus, no maze-maker, as Joyce is; but to me he seems the one completely natural inheritor of some of the Joyce techniques: some of the methods of word-minting, the punning and portmanteauing into multiple meanings, and that melting from place to place, as the emotion roused by a scene seems to dissolve the outer appearances and show something else underneath. Joyce did not patent his methods; when they were invented they were available at once, for all. . . . (Personally, I like his neologisms, his 'soulos' and 'insectarianism' and 'chasubulleros bullen a laws'.)[15]

And Nicholson is not the only appreciator of O'Casey's fiddling with

language, twisting it by its tail, winking at the reader while nodding
to Joyce. What no one seems to have noticed in the process,
however, is that O'Casey probably learned from Joyce how to
disguise a tendency toward sentimentality that both were somewhat
addicted to, how to hide it quickly behind irony and humor and
mock-pathos.

Perhaps the most important factor that unites Joyce and O'Casey
is that throughout their literary careers both writers worked
primarily in the dramatic mode, that all of their efforts aspired to
the mode that Stephen Dedalus described as the ultimate achievement for the writer. In *A Portrait of the Artist as a Young Man*
Stephen Dedalus explains:

> The dramatic form is reached when the vitality which has flowed
> and eddied round each person fills every person with such vital
> force that he or she assumes a proper and intangible esthetic
> life. The personality of the artist, at first a cry or a cadence
> or a mood and then a fluid and lambent narrative, finally refines
> itself out of existence, impersonalises itself, so to speak. The
> esthetic image in the dramatic form is life purified in and
> reprojected from the human imagination. The mystery of
> esthetic like that of material creation is accomplished. The
> artist, like the God of the creation, remains within or behind or
> beyond or above his handiwork, invisible, refined out of exist-
> ence, indifferent, paring his fingernails.[16]

Both Joyce and O'Casey began with the writing of songs and lyrics
(the cry and the cadence), but were quickly lured into the writing
of drama. Joyce, however, abandoned theatrical drama for narrative prose in comic and ironic form, attaining the dramatic mode
within prose fiction, while O'Casey's drama was eventually supple-
mented by his experiments in autobiography. Yet *Ulysses* and
Finnegans Wake and all six volumes of *Mirror in My House*
sustain their unique qualities as innovations in the dramatic mode:
for Joyce the dismissal of the author's intrusive presence and the
suspension of the narrator's license shifted the central focus to
dramatic interexchange between characters, within characters,
and between characters and the objects of their perceivable
universe. For the autobiographies O'Casey created a central
character to operate and exist in the third person, and set him in
dramatic tension with his evolving and changing world. It is hardly
surprising that literal-minded critics have found fault with these
works, insisting as they do that novels behave as externally narrated

pieces of prose fiction and that autobiography present itself
factually and chronologically in the first-person singular. What they
would easily allow in a piece of theatrical drama they shy away
from in their Joycean and O'Caseyan formats.

Stephen differentiates between the lyrical, the epical, and the
dramatic forms as he fashions his aesthetic, viewing the progression
as characteristic of the developing literary artist. He defines the
three as 'the lyrical form, the form wherein the artist presents his
image in immediate relation to himself; the epical form, the form
wherein he presents his image in immediate relation to himself and to
others; the dramatic form, the form wherein he presents his image in
immediate relation to others.'[17] *Mirror in My House* certainly
contains and retains all three. By its very nature as autobiography
it begins with the lyrical solipsism of the self, but whereas other
autobiographies end there as well, O'Casey's strives for an epical
containment of Ireland and the world surrounding Johnny/Sean
Casside, and refines the author out of his solipsistic involvement. His
image is constantly presented in immediate relation to others,
much as that of Bloom or Stephen is in *Ulysses*. Joyce boasted to
Frank Budgen, ' "I want,' said Joyce, as we were walking down the
Universitätstrasse, 'to give a picture of Dublin so complete that
if the city one day suddenly disappeared from the earth it could
be reconstructed out of my book." '[18] Joyce's efforts as such were
primarily confined in *Ulysses* to a spatial reconstruction (and even
Budgen has fallen into the Joycean habit, as he describes the
conversation in terms of spatial locale, 'walking down the Universitätstrasse'), while in his plays and autobiographies O'Casey is
guided more in terms of time than space. But both techniques
derive essentially from the recreation of a facet of reality through
the dramatic presentation of a world of others, specifically the
inhabitants of the vocal scene of Dublin.

The evolution of their shared talent for recording the speech
of that Dublin world runs along parallel lines, from the poetic
recapturing of real speech overheard to the fantastic-poetic reconstruction of the 'unheard music' that became the epitome of that
collective speech. In a Dublin tenement a denizen of the city is
overheard saying:

– That's my principle, too, said my uncle. Let him learn to box
his corner. That's what I'm always saying to that Rosicrucian
there: take exercise. Why, when I was a nipper every morning
of my life I had a cold bath, winter and summer. And that's
what stands to me now. Education is all very fine and large. . . .

Mr Cotter might take a pick of that leg of mutton, he added to my aunt.[19]

And in another such dwelling, not a mile away, another of his ilk is overheard saying:

Chiselurs don't care a damn now about their parents, they're bringin' their fathers' grey hairs down with sorra to the grave, an' laughin' at it, laughin' at it. Ah, I suppose it's just the same everywhere – the worl's in a state o' chassis. . . . Breakfast! Well, they can keep their breakfast for me. Not if they were down on their bended knees would I take it – I'll show them I've a little spirit in me still! . . . Sassige! Well, let her keep her sassige. . . . The tea's wet right enough.[20]

There is enough in these Joycean and O'Caseyan speeches to satisfy John Millington Synge's demand that dramatic speech be as rich as nuts and apples, and perhaps as sour, bitter, and acidic as lemons, wormwood, and olives. What Joyce and O'Casey understood about the talk of Dublin is that its excellence has nothing whatever to do with factual truth, that its poetry is in its inventive imagination and not in logical coherence. 'Mollycewells an' atoms!' shouts Fluther Good; 'D'ye think I'm goin' to listen to you thryin' to juggle Fluther's mind with complicated cunundhrums of mollycewels an' atoms?'[21] And in a calmer voice Martin Cunningham defies facts with just as resonant a contention:

– There they were at it, all the cardinals and bishops and archbishops from all the ends of the earth and these two fighting dog and devil until at last the Pope himself stood up and declared infallibility a dogma of the Church *ex cathedra*. On the very moment John MacHale, who had been arguing and arguing against it, stood up and shouted with the voice of a lion: *Credo!*[22]

Whether it is Simon Dedalus pronouncing *ex cathedra* his meteorological observation ('It's as uncertain as a child's bottom') or deriding his wife's relations ('the Goulding faction, the drunken little cost-drawer and Crissie, papa's little lump of dung, the wise child that knows her own father'),[23] or Captain Boyle denouncing Joxer as a 'prognosticator an' a procrastinator' and the world as 'in a terr . . . ible state o' . . . chassis!' and his daughter ('I lived before I seen yous, an' I can live when yous are gone. Isn't this a

nice thing to come rollin' in on top o' me afther all your prayin' to
St. Anthony an' The Little Flower! An' she's a Child o' Mary, too
– I wonder what'll the nuns think of her now?'),[24] it is the spit and
spice of Dublin gab that reverberates through the dramatic
language of James Joyce and Sean O'Casey. How much more
potent is that language when a heightened sense of fantasy invades
it as well, as when the washerwoman in *Finnegans Wake* complains:

> And sure he was the quare old buntz too, Dear Dirty Dumpling,
> foostherfather of fingalls and dotthergills. Gammer and gaffer
> we're all their gangsters. Hadn't he seven dams to wive him?
> And every dam had her seven crutches. And every crutch had
> its seven hues. And each hue had a differing cry. Sudds for me
> and supper for you and the doctor's bill for Joe John.[25]

Or when an enraged Dubliner in *I Knock at the Door* complains:

> – Looka them pulling down the Royal Standard, moaned the
> man of the wide watery mouth. His mouth slavered with rage,
> and he could hardly speak. Where's the polish! Why don't
> the polish do somethin' – the gang of well-clad, well-fed, lazy,
> useless bastards! If I was bether dhressed than I am, I be down
> in a jiffy to show them how to jue their job.[26]

Joyce has of course tampered with language in the *Wake* to an
extraordinary degree, while O'Casey has merely extended the
colloquial to include the illogic of anger and the wild words of
provocation. With the later volumes of *Mirror* O'Casey instituted
his own narrative voice in an official capacity as a dramatic entity,
and although some critics (and victims) have complained that it
was at times strident or petulant or haughty or even contemptuous,
no one would deny that it was whimsical and taunting and
colorful. Not just in passages of punning and fantasy and
neologistic byplay, but in every mood and change of tone – the
voice became stronger and more distinctive as the autobiographies
grew. Every chapter of the later volumes contains its rise and fall
of dramatic action in that characteristic voice, its feints and thrusts
and narrative jabs, and even when fairly subdued, it is individual
and sharp, as when he discusses G. B. Shaw:

> A great man, but not great enough for the closed shop of
> saintship in the Christian church. Indeed, a name to be

mentioned with great caution; and so the churchmen slip down to the hell of mediocrity. No, no; not Shaw. What a scandal it would have aroused had Shaw been allowed to climb into a pulpit! Bernard Shaw in the pulpit of Westmonaster Cathedral. Monastrous! Do stop him from playing such fantastic tricks before high heaven as make the angels laugh. Church in danger! The gates of hello are prevailing against her! Even the figures in the stained-glass windows are climbing out to go. Mention a more suitable name.[27]

This mild passage is characteristic of the general play of techniques in _Sunset and Evening Star_: the language always borders on the familiar, quotations are being wrenched to fit new shapes, puns are anticipated with their unpunned versions first (hell of mediocrity, gates of hello) or are relayed into echoes of themselves (Westmonaster Cathedral, Monastrous), but far more prevalent and consistent is the blending of voices, the assuming of the voice of indignation assigned to the Churchmen, that makes _Sunset_ a delightful narrative and sustains its dramatic interaction. And on those occasions when O'Casey pulls out all the stops and allows his monologue outrageous prerogatives (enough to bring down charges of Joycean imitation – usually from those who do not much like Joyce even in the original), there are dramatic hijinks galore in what was usually employed as a staid expository form. No sooner is Shaw presumably eliminated from consideration for sainthood ('saintship' in O'Casey's language) than others are presented instead, and the fun goes on and on in a many-voiced dramatic monologue that displays O'Casey's skill in handling his form and material:

Hiawatha's a name, sirs, I mention with glee, for the way to make honey he taught to the bee; to Red Men, he gave agriculture, and more – he cur'd them whene'er they felt sick or felt sore. A pagan chief he must have been, and we've no room for pagans here; we drink no wine, but sit and sip the sober excellence of beer. No dionysiac thought or laughter can enter here, now or hereafter. So get you gone, you brazen smarty, and lecture to life's cocktail party!

If not saints, then bishops! What a grand bunch they'd be on the bench – Shaw, Joyce, and Yeats! Stop them! Rerum novarum oram pro noram. Maanooth is in an unpsoar. O, catholic herald, come blow your horn, before a wild oak comes from the little acorn. St. Patrick's coming down on a winged horse. Was there ever such a one as the Bull from Shaw; was there ever such a one as the pastoral from Yeats; was there ever such another as the encyclical from Joyce! They'll ruin and maruin us.[28]

Like Joyce, Sean O'Casey had the unerring instincts of dramatic situation regardless of the restrictions of genre, and added to it a tendency to lilt and pun and play wildly with language, conjuring up a host of characters, like the multitudes in Joyce's *Wake*, and doing the police in many voices.

Notes

1 David Krause, ed., *The Letters of Sean O'Casey*, Vol. I (New York: Macmillan, 1975), 799–800.
2 Conversation with O'Casey in St. Marychurch, Devon, 29 June 1955.
3 *Letters*, pp. 792–93.
4 *Letters*, p. 810.
5 Richard Ellmann, ed., *Letters of James Joyce*, Vol. III (New York: Viking, 1966), 139.
6 Marvin Magalaner, 'O'Casey's Autobiography,' *Sean O'Casey: Modern Judgements*, ed. Ronald Ayling (London: Macmillan, 1969), pp. 228–31.
7 *Letters of Sean O'Casey*, p. 190.
8 *Ibid.*, p. 800.
9 Krause, *Sean O'Casey: The Man and His Work* (New York: Macmillan, 1960), p. 279.
10 Sean O'Casey, 'Censorship,' *Blasts and Benedictions*, ed. Ronald Ayling (London: Macmillan, 1967), pp. 168, 167.
11 'Literature in Ireland,' *Blasts*, pp. 180–81. See 'Ireland, Island of Saints and Sages', *The Critical Writings of James Joyce*, eds. Ellsworth Mason and Richard Ellmann (New York: Viking, 1959), pp. 153–74.
12 'Immanuel,' *Under a Colored Cap* (New York: St. Martin's Press, 1963), p. 145.
13 'Rebel Orwell,' *Sunset and Evening Star* (New York: Macmillan, 1955), pp. 144, 146.
14 Krause, *Sean O'Casey*, p. 276.
15 'O'Casey's Horn of Plenty,' reprinted in Ayling, *Sean O'Casey*, pp. 210–11.
16 *A Portrait of the Artist as a Young Man* (New York: Viking, 1964), p. 215.
17 *Portrait*, p. 214.
18 Frank Budgen, *James Joyce and the Making of Ulysses* (New York: Harrison Smith and Robert Haas, 1934), pp. 67–68.
19 *Dubliners* (New York: Viking, 1967), p. 11.
20 *Juno and the Paycock, Collected Plays*, Vol. I (London: Macmillan, 1952), p. 20.
21 *The Plough and the Stars, Collected Plays*, p. 170.
22 *Dubliners*, p. 169.
23 *Ulysses* (New York: Random House, 1961), pp. 90, 88.
24 *Juno*, pp. 72, 89, 75.
25 *Finnegans Wake* (New York: Viking, 1939), p. 215.
26 *I Knock at the Door* (New York: Macmillan, 1939), p. 283.
27 *Sunset*, p. 250.
28 *Sunset*, p. 251.

SEAN O'CASEY AND LADY GREGORY: THE RECORD OF A FRIENDSHIP

MARY FITZGERALD

Although it lasted less than seven years, Sean O'Casey's friendship with Isabella Augusta Persse, Lady Gregory (1852–1932), was clearly one of the most crucial relationships of his professional life, and one of the happiest of hers. It began with her reader's report on *The Crimson in the Tri-Colour* for the Abbey Theatre in 1921, and ended, for all practical purposes and despite her periodic efforts to revive it, over her handling of the readers' reports for *The Silver Tassie* in 1928. While it lasted, however, it was warm, affectionate, intellectual, and intense, enriching both writers, enlivening the Abbey Theatre, and endowing dramatic literature with an energy and zest it had not known for ages and may not soon see again.

What has been written to date of their friendship has depended heavily on O'Casey's telling of it in his autobiographies. so it is instructive to recall that the autobiographies postdate the break over the *Tassie* and are more than a little tinged with retrospective bitterness. The clarity of hindsight clouds even his first Abbey success and follows directly upon his introduction of Lady Gregory as Blessed Bridget O'Coole:

> He felt, though, as he stood quiet in the [Abbey] vestibule, that he had crossed the border of a little, but a great, new kingdom of life, and so another illusion was born in his poor susceptible soul. He didn't know enough then that it was no great thing to be an Abbey playwright; and afterwards, when he knew a lot more, he was glad he had suffered himself to feel no jubilation to mar his future by thinking too much of a tiny success: life remained a mystery to him. He thought, not of what he had done. but of what he had to do in the form and substance of his second play; realizing, though unaware of it at the time, that to be a great playwright was a very different thing from merely being

the one who had had one, two, or even three plays produced by
the Abbey Theatre.[1]

There is pain and even venom in that passage, and O'Casey follows
it by deftly preparing his readers for the ultimate Abbey outrage
against him. He notes that of his next two submissions to the
theatre, *Cathleen Listens In* and *The Cooing of Doves*, one was
arbitrarily rejected and the other accepted. This establishes Abbey
criticism as fallible and quixotic:

> This was the first shock given to Sean by the selective committee
> of the theatre, for the second work was definitely better as a
> play than the first. This was the first jolt he got, but he was to
> get many more before he was much older, and from the same
> source, too. [*IFTW*, 164–165]

What follows these passages is touched with their spirit, and while
it adds poignancy to what he writes of Lady Gregory, it robs the
story of some verisimilitude – a sense of events gradually unfolding
as they really seemed to the participants at the time. For this
quality, David Krause's edition of *The Letters of Sean O'Casey*[2]
is especially valuable, as it supplies not only the give and take
of both sides of the O'Casey–Gregory correspondence, but also
enough ancillary letters to amplify meanings beyond the literal
level of what each wrote the other. The letters, however, were not
available until 1975, and Lady Gregory's *Journals* are only now
coming fully into print.[3] As a result, even Lady Gregory's biographer, Elizabeth Coxhead, has told their story primarily from
O'Casey's perspective.[4] Lady Gregory herself did not write an
autobiographical account of the friendship: she was seventy-six,
handicapped by rheumatism, and already stricken with the cancer
that would eventually take her life, when the quarrel over the
Tassie occurred, and besides, she continued to hope that the final
chapter about O'Casey – seeing him with his wife and child – had
yet to be written. She was not too ill to write letters and journal
entries, fortunately, and these, now in the Berg Collection of the
New York Public Library together with O'Casey's papers, help
round out the record of their friendship.

It began even before either had met the other, when, on 5
November, 1921, she singled O'Casey's energetic voice out of the
dreary background hum of terrible-to-mediocre-plays she had been
reading for the Abbey and wrote with some excitement in her
journal: 'I read, and wrote a long note on, an interesting play

The Crimson in the Tri-Colour, the antagonism sure to break out between Labour and Sinn Fein, and sent it to [Lennox] Robinson.' (*J*: 307). The reference is sandwiched between two other notes marking turning points in her life: her daughter-in-law's change of heart over keeping Coole – leaving Lady Gregory with sole financial responsibility for the house and estate – and her own first attempts to write her memoirs. Burdened with writing (and rewriting) letters and drafts for both of these preoccupations, she nonetheless spent a good part of the day reading O'Casey's hand-written manuscript and composing a detailed analysis of it:

> The Crimson in the Tricolour – (a very good name) This a puzzling play – extremely interesting – Mrs. Budrose is a jewel, & her husband a good setting for her – I don't see any plot in it, unless the Labour unrest culminating in the turning off of the lights at the meeting may be considered one. It is the expression of ideas that makes it interesting (besides feeling that the writer has something in him) & no doubt the point of interest for Dublin audiences. But we could not put it on while the Revolution is still unaccomplished – it might hasten the Labour attack on Sinn Fein, which ought to be kept back till the fight with England is over, & the new Government has had time to show what it can do.
>
> I think Eileen's rather disagreeable flirtation with O'Regan shd. be cut – their first entrance – or rather exit (or both) seems to be leading to something that doesn't come. In Act II a good deal of O'Regan & Nora shd be cut.
>
> In Act III almost all the O'Malley and Eileen part shd. be cut. The end is I think good, the entry of the Workmen, & Fagan & Tim Tracy.
>
> I feel that there is no personal interest worth developing, but that with as much as possible of those barren parts cut, we might find a possible play of ideas in it.
>
> I suggest that (with the author's leave) it shd. be worth typing the play at theatre's expense – with or without those parts – For it is impossible to go through it again – or show it – or have a reading of it – while in handwriting. A.G. (*L*: 96).

Copying the journals at the typewriter in 1928 she added the note: 'This was the first play I had seen by Sean O'Casey.' (*J*: 307). It was not; the Abbey had previously rejected his two earlier efforts,[5] and she might well have been asked to read them. If she had, she had not noticed any distinctive voice of the caliber she now found in *The Crimson in the Tri-Colour*.

Her evaluation of the play is worth noticing for several reasons. It is uncharacteristically long, unusually enthusiastic, and uncommonly thorough for any readers' reports for the Abbey. The customary style for such things among Yeats, Lennox Robinson and Lady Gregory was flat, succinct analysis, frequently no more than two or three sentences. That Lady Gregory went to such lengths over a moderately promising play by an unknown playwright was in itself evidence of her contention that 'the writer has something in him'. Her suggestions for reshaping it, encouraging its author, and even having it typed for further examination would certainly have nudged her fellow directors at the Abbey to pay serious attention to the play, even had they not been able to recognize merit in it themselves. Her report implicitly recognizes the eventual basis for their friendship: a lively interest in people and politics. It also contains the seeds of dissolution: her suggestions for improvements, changes, even the desire to help change. Lady Gregory was used to doing this kind of constructive collaboration for many new playwrights. Indeed, she was still doing it for Yeats and he for 'her. But O'Casey was not used to having anyone else meddle with his creation. When plays were returned to him, he did not, like other playwrights Lady Gregory wrote to, redraft what he had already submitted. He usually preferred to start over, with a new play, one that would be entirely his own idea. Hence his tendency to see what she considered points for modification as negative pronouncements.

What fascinated Lady Gregory in *The Crimson in the Tri-Colour* – besides O'Casey's stylistic exuberance and the skill of characterization evidenced in his handling of the Budroses – was the 'play of ideas'. Her first comment on it in her journal mentions only the political core of the play: 'the trouble sure to come between Sinn Fein and Labour'. She was as interested in the theory behind that idea as she was in dramatization of it, and she seems to have recognized that this new playwright was someone she could talk to and share her own strongly nationalist ideas with.

They met for the first time, according to her journal, on November 10, 1921, five days after she had read the play. Her account of the meeting focuses on the political aspect of the play and O'Casey's political activities as well: 'Then Casey, the author of *The Crimson in the Tri-Colour* came in, and I had a talk with him about his play, and when I said we could not in any case put it on now, as it might weaken the Sinn Fein position to show that Labour is ready to attack it, he said 'If that is so I would be the last to wish to put it on.' And he is a strong Labour man, and is collecting names to sign a message to Larkin in Sing-Sing ' (*J*: 308–09). It was evidently during this meeting that she made the oft-quoted remark that his strong point was characterization. Her comments also make it clear that she had at least some intention of producing the play, even from the beginning, an impression that is confirmed by later journal entries, in which she writes that she had wanted 'to pull that play together and put it on to give him experience, but Yeats was down on it ' (*J*: 308–08; 446).

Yeats's negative opinion of O'Casey's play prevailed, despite his admission in his opening remark that he found 'this discursive play very hard to judge for it is a type of play I do not understand'. (*L*: 102–03). He objected to the apparent absence of dramatic interest, the precipitousness of some events which were not adequately prepared for earlier in the play, and the fact that 'it is so constructed that in every scene there is something for pit & stalls to cheer or boo. In fact it is the old Irish idea of a good play . . . especially as everybody is as ill mannered as possible & all truth considered as inseparable from spite and hatred.' But he closed by saying that he would not stop Robinson from producing it, if Robinson wanted to do so. These comments prefigure his remarks about *The Silver Tassie*.

Several aspects of the handling of *The Crimson in the Tri-Colour* are significant in the way in which they prepare for future events. First impressions lingered among the directors, apparently, and resurfaced to plague O'Casey over the *Tassie*. Other aspects were similar, too. O'Casey was led to believe that the directors wanted to do his play, and then had the play rejected for reasons very similar to the ones that later caused the directors to have reservations about the *Tassie*. O'Casey was sent Yeats's verbatim comments (which appeared more negative than they really were, since Lennox Robinson edited out the crucial opening and closing sentences of Yeats's report), which led O'Casey to believe that Yeats was his chief opponent and the prime mover in the rejection of the play, when in reality the rejection mechanism had been far more subtle and complex, involving all three Abbey directors' views. When, after the *Tassie* incident, O'Casey wrote that his anger at Yeats had been brewing a long time (*L*: 249), he may have been remembering *The Crimson in the Tri-Colour*.

O'Casey's reaction to the rejection of the play is equally important for understanding his future actions. He fought back, evidently in anger, refusing to accept any validity in the criticism, answering Robinson's letter: 'I have re-read the work and find it as interesting as ever, in no way deserving of the contemptuous dismissal it has received from your reader.' (Even in its excerpted form, Yeats's criticism was clearly not a 'contemptuous dismissal'.) He went on to defend the play point by point against the reader's report, countering the objection that the play was loose and vague with the remark, 'And what could be more loose and vague than life itself?' He offered, finally, to write the play over as a comedy, and asked if Robinson thought it would be acceptable in such a form (*L*: 104–05). Not content merely to retort to Robinson, he wrote to Michael J. Dolan, of the Abbey company, enclosing Yeats's report and offering Lady Gregory's confidential one, asking for Dolan's opinion of the play's worth and asking further whether Dolan thought that the Abbey actors might perform it independently (*L*: 106).[6] Dolan replied, rejecting the play, having first solicited the opinions of two other prominent members of the company, Arthur Shields and F. J. McCormick. By this time, the Abbey was producing O'Casey's *The Shadow of a Gunman*, and it is ironic that Dolan's reason for not wanting to do the play – 'to put it on would mean undoing your good work of the Gunman' (*L*: 107) – should foreshadow precisely Lady Gregory's objection to the *Tassie* seven years later: it would hurt his reputation as a playwright. Faced with Dolan's confirming opinion and flushed with the obvious success of *The Shadow of a Gunman*, O'Casey allowed his anger over *The Crimson in the Tri-Colour* to subside, and before long he was telling Lady Gregory that he could not stand to re-read it (*J*: 512; 609) – though he did, of course, re-read it occasionally.

The Abbey's acceptance of the Gunman strengthened the growing friendship between O'Casey and Lady Gregory. He had already identified her as the most encouraging and sympathetic of the Abbey directors, and her wholehearted enjoyment of his success made him feel she was a true friend. As O'Casey described it in his Blessed Bridget O'Coole chapter, the crowds attending his play made her eyes dance and lifted years from her shoulders (*IFTW*: 165). She could share his delight at being a newly successful author: she too had begun to write comparatively late in life and had done well. She was good at sharing anyone's delight, furthermore, and self-effacing enough to revel in the success of others. Her own intuitive liking for him was magnified by the huge audiences he brought to the troubled Abbey and by her realization that he was in himself a living fulfilment of everything she had worked so hard for at the theatre. He was a man from the common people who might never have written a play had there not been an Abbey to receive it, and he had become a fine dramatist in time to rescue the theatre from financial danger.

She noted in her journal that he watched the first night's performance from the wings, that she brought him to sit with her in the stalls on the second and third nights, and that on the fourth night she sat O'Casey in one of the pair of seats reserved for Yeats and herself, sitting with the musicians in the orchestra by herself for the first act and taking Yeats's seat with O'Casey for the second. All in all, she found the play 'an immense success, beautifully acted, all the political points taken up with delight by a big audience' (*J*: 445–56). She mentions taking him around to the door before the play 'to share my joy in seeing the crowd surging in,' and then records virtually their entire conversation. While watching the crowd with him, she learned much of his life story and even probed a bit about his religious beliefs:

> Casey told me he is a labourer, and as we talked of masons said he had 'carried the hod'. He said 'I was among books as a child, but I was sixteen before I learned to read or write. My father loved books, he had a big library, I remember the look of the books high up on shelves'. I asked why his father had not taught him and he said 'He died when I was three years old, through those same books. There was a little ladder in the room to get to the shelves, and one day when he was standing on it, it broke and he fell and was killed'. I said 'I often go up the ladder in our library at home' and he begged me to be careful. He is learning what he can about Art, has bought books on Whistler and Raphael, and takes *The Studio*. All this was as we watched the crowd. I forget how I came to mention the Bible, and he asked 'Do you like it'? I said 'Yes, I read it constantly, even for the beauty of the language'. He said he admires that beauty, he was brought up as a Protestant but has lost belief in religious forms. Then, in talking of our war here, we came to Plato's *Republic*, his dream-city, whether on earth or in heaven not far from the city of God [her comment on his agnosticism]. And then we went in to the play (*J*: 446).

For so short a conversation, theirs ranged widely and deeply!

Going in to see the play, O'Casey reminded Lady Gregory that the Abbey had rejected his early effort, *The Frost in the Flower* (she recorded the title incorrectly as '*Frost and Flowers*,' an indication of how little she remembered it), but he told her that it was returned marked 'not far from being a good play'. Her journal mentions that he had sent in others, so presumably he said so, and that they discussed briefly the rejection of *The Crimson in the Tri-Colour*. She also noted in her journal – with obvious approval – that O'Casey had refused a free Abbey Theatre pass, saying, 'No one ought to come into the Abbey Theatre without paying for it.' And she quoted him further as saying, 'All the thought in Ireland for years past has come through the Abbey. You have no idea what an education it has been to the country.' Those words, she wrote, 'and the fine audience on this our last week [of the season], put me in great spirits' (*J*: 446).

So it was not merely the success of the *Gunman* that made Lady Gregory's eyes dance and took years off her shoulders; it was equally her good and easy conversation with O'Casey and his compliments about the Abbey, with their implicit tribute to her own work in the theatre. In their future conversations, they did not content themselves with exchanging pleasantries about play-wrighting, nor did O'Casey defer to her ladyship any more than in this first long conversation, which is to say not at all. He and she spoke as equals and as friends.

Elizabeth Coxhead has pointed out that O'Casey had recently lost his mother and that Lady Gregory had lost her son, and that in some ways they were fulfilling the absent party role for each other.[7] This is no doubt true, at least to some extent, but one must temper it with the realization that for both of them the losses had been moderated – even if only slightly – by the passage of several years, and it should not be allowed to undercut the fact that Sean O'Casey and Lady Gregory took to each other on their own terms. She may have reminded O'Casey of his mother – he occasionally uses phrases to describe her in his autobiography that are reminiscent of phrases he uses for his mother – and certainly he might well have thought of her simply as maternal in nature. But it is less likely that O'Casey would have reminded her of Robert Gregory. She already had a subsitute son in her grandson Richard and a further fulfilment in her two granddaughters. Indeed the good reports from Harrow about Richard's academic progress and jottings about the doings of 'the chicks,' as she called his sisters, intermingle with her journal entries about O'Casey. There were Gregorys enough to carry on the name and to keep her busy without the need of an additional son. Furthermore, her relationship with O'Casey was in some ways warmer than her relationship with her own son had been. From what can be gleaned from her journals, Lady Gregory lived in some fear of losing Robert's affection during his lifetime. Though she loved him dearly, and her letters to him are warm, he had early in young manhood expressed disapproval of her nationalist ideals – his expensive Harrow and Oxford education having converted him into an imperialist – and it was precisely for this reason, as she wrote in her diaries and in letters to her friend Wilfrid Scawen Blunt, that she had decided to work for Ireland only through the comparatively safe channels of literature and the theatre.[8] Her oft-repeated phrase, 'we are not working for Home Rule, but preparing for it', takes on a more poignant undertone when viewed in the light of her concern for what Robert would think of her. And it is worth remembering that when Robert Gregory left wife, mother, children and home to fight for England in the Great War, he was not a youth but a fully mature man of thirty-four.

Lady Gregory's affection for O'Casey, who in almost no way resembled her son, was based in O'Casey's exuberant personality, his welcoming her into conversational intimacy as though he had known her all his life, his commitment to Ireland, and his over-whelming dramatic talent. These transcended all obvious differences in class, stature, and age between them and made them friends. O'Casey claimed to marvel at the fact that they could have become friends, given all the opposites they represented, in a letter written to Elizabeth Coxhead after the appearance of Lady Gregory's biography: 'I loved her, and I think she was very fond of me – why, God only knows. Our friendship-affinity was an odd one: she from affluence, I from poverty; she an aristocrat, I a proletarian Communist. Yet, we understood each other well, talking, eating, and laughing easily together.'[9] He gave the reason in the Childer-mess chapter near the end of his autobiographies: 'Each had travelled his or her own different way, very different ways, yet, in the winter of her life, in the late summer of his, they had suddenly met, each facing towards the same direction. The pattern of life she was weaving, and the one he wove, mingled and stood out bravely in the tapestry of Irish life.' (*S&ES*, 31)

Their friendship fully flowered during the production of O'Casey's next play, *Juno and the Paycock*. Lady Gregory described opening night, March 7, 1924, as if savoring the occur-rence, chronicling impressions in the order of her noticing them: 'a long queue at the door, the theatre crowded, many turned away, so it will be run on next week. A wonderful and terrible play of futility, of irony, humour, tragedy.' She noted that she met O'Casey after the performance in the greenroom and had asked him to tea the next day, only to learn that he would be working with cement next day "and that takes such a long time to get off." He reminisced with her about his past poverty and – again – the earlier rejection of *The Crimson in the Tri-Colour*, telling her, 'I owe a great deal to you and Mr. Yeats and Mr. Robinson but to you above all. You gave me encouragement. And it was you who said to me upstairs in the office – I could show you the very spot where you stood – "Mr. O'Casey, your fort[e] is characterisation." And so I threw over my theories and worked at characters and this is the result.' (*J*: 511–12). She was obviously delighted at his success and pleased with his giving some of the credit for it to her: 'that full house, the packed pit and gallery, the fine play, the call of the mother for the putting away of hatred – "give us thine own eternal love! " – made me say to Yeats "This is one of the evenings that make me glad to have been born".' (*J*: 512).

The day after the first performance, she bought cakes and brought them for tea to the greenroom, returning then for the evening performance. Because of the full house, she allowed her own seat to be sold to the public and took O'Casey with her to sit in the musicians' chairs in the orchestra. She was very much involved in the play: 'When the mother whose son has been killed – "Leader of an ambush where my neighbor's Free State soldier son was killed" – cries out "Mother of Jesus, put away from us this murderous hatred and give us thine own eternal love" I whispered to Casey 'that is the prayer we must all use, it is the only thing that will save us, the teaching of Christ". He said "Of humanity". But what would that be without the Divine atom?' (*J*: 512–13) She took O'Casey along to Yeats's next Monday evening, and spent most of her time ignoring the talk of current literary affairs and conversing instead with O'Casey, who 'interested me most'. (*J*: 514). She recorded his opinions as if she were learning from them – as indeed she was – making notes carefully and striving for accuracy of recollection about everything he said. He was clearly an important influence and friend.

O'Casey recorded his first visit to Coole in a poetic narrative form in the Where Wild Swans Nest chapter (*IFTW*: 182–199) of his autobiographies. It is interesting to note that Lady Gregory had to race back to Coole from Dublin in time to receive him, as he told her at the Abbey on June 4 that he would like to come up, accepting her invitation, the next week. She was ill, besides, but his presence there distracted her from her own troubles and made her happy. For the whole of his visit, her journal records his words, stories, and impressions almost verbatim. He is at work on Penelope's Lovers, a play, he dislikes the current fashion of boasting about what one did during the Rising, he thinks women are

braver than men, and more besides. Lady Gregory learned much
about his life during the week. He told her the story of his mother's
death and funeral. (He seems to have begun writing his autobiography in these recollective narratives for her: the manner
in which she recorded them in her journal sounds strikingly
similar to the way in which they appear, more fully detailed, in
his books.) She learned about his eye trouble, and noted with
obvious approval that he refused an operation because there was
'a thousandth chance he might go blind and so remain ignorant'.
She delighted to hear that the first book he had ever read was
D'Aubigny's *History of the Reformation*, a book she knew as a
child at Roxborough. She chronicled his early reading, noting that
he memorized much of Shakespeare from a Globe Edition of the
works which he bought for a shilling. They discussed politics:
Jim Larkin was the topic of conversation across many days. She
invited him to lecture at the Abbey, but he declined, on the
grounds that there would be too much competition from the
cinema. And, knowing from the autobiographies how desperately
hard it had been for O'Casey to stay awake during her reading
of Thomas Hardy, it is ironic to read, 'I am reading him now *The
Dynasts*. He is tremendously struck with it.' (*J*: 546–58).

By September the Abbey was rehearsing O'Casey's one-act
play, *Nannie's Night Out*,[10] and O'Casey was frequently at the
Abbey for chats with Lady Gregory. It was during one of these
visits that she began reading to him Upton Sinclair's play, *The
Singing Jailbirds* (not at Coole, which is the impression one gets
from O'Casey's autobiographical account, where time and place
are deliberately blurred for effect). A comparison of O'Casey's
version with hers shows something about the gentleness with which
O'Casey could be forceful and even dogmatic in person. In Where
Wild Swans Nest, he said it was the only protest he ever made at
her reading: 'Oh, stop, woman, for God's sake! he had bawled,
forgetful of where he was, rising and pacing to the far end of the
room: the Labour Movement isn't a mourning march to a jail-
house! We are climbing a high hill, a desperately steep, high hill
through fire and venomous opposition. . . . Perhaps you're right,
Sean, she had said hurriedly putting the book away, something
ashamed at having so delightedly praised such an insignificant
work.' (*IFTW*: 184–85). Lady Gregory's version does not mention
that he asked her to stop. As she tells it, 'at the first scene he said
"rather melodramatic" which it is. But then he was very much
impressed, thinks it a "terrible play." He has an idea of a Labour
play himself, says it came to him when looking at my [*The Story*

Brought by] Brigit, the idea of one man giving himself for the people.' (*J*: 584) Evidently O'Casey managed to say that he thought it was a terrible play without conveying to her the least sense of irritation. The outcome of the *Tassie* incident might well have been very different, had the two of them been able to be face to face. And ironically, George Bernard Shaw was to do something very similar with the phrase 'one hell of a play' and the *Tassie*, writing it positively in a letter to Sean O'Casey and negatively in a letter to Lady Gregory and allowing each to take his meaning differently, as he knew they would.[11]

Shortly afterwards, she noted in her journal that O'Casey's eyes were very bad and that he was in pain, undergoing 'slight operations, very painful, every few days, can read very little, but can write a little and has begun a new play *The Plough and the Stars*.' (*J*: 593–94). She was prepared for anything startling the new play might offer by an incident outside the Abbey that same evening which proved how accurate O'Casey's portrayals of Dublin life in fact were: 'As I left the theatre . . . the street was rather crowded and we saw a girl being brought along by two policemen, on each side. Her hair was flying and she looked young and defiant, was singing – the very song "Nannie" sings in Casey's *Nannie's Night Out* – "Mother of mine". A tragic sight, the reality of what had been put on the stage.' (*J*: 594).

As her journals indicate, by now O'Casey was regularly visiting the Abbey in the evenings, and when he did, she and he, along with Lyle Donaghy and Jack Yeats, made frequent conversational partners. She enjoyed these talks enormously, not only because they were interesting in themselves and she was learning new things, but also because they seemed to her so much more lively and important than the gossipy conversations of her social peers. A month after the *Nannie* episode, she recorded in her journal one such obvious dichotomy: tea with Lady Ardilaun, where the talk centered around which minister had been rebuked by the king for wearing tweed to a royal garden party, and then 'back here, and Casey for the evening, talking about *The Plough and the Stars* which he is working on.' She already had some idea of its tumultuous reception forming in her mind: 'It may not be popular, giving the human side and not the heroic side, the reverse of the battle [sh]ield.'[12] But she supports his right to give 'the human side' by adding that he told her he knew of a woman whose son had been killed and who had shouted curses on Connolly. On this evening O'Casey also offered her his 'The Grand Oul' Dame Britannia' for her book of ballads, but she had already included it. She 'had read it to Yeats the other day, saying it was though fine hardly simple enough for my book, and he had said I should put it in "it had literary quality".' (*J*: 608–09). So although she was aware of O'Casey's authorship of the ballad in November 1925, she did not ascribe it to him in the book, published in 1926, presumably to preserve the folk aspect of the songs.

The radical difference she felt between her social world and her theatre circle received final treatment in her journal entry for November 30, 1924, and in it she made her preference obvious:

> Yesterday wet. Worked at *Bourgeois* [*Gentilhomme*] and wrote letters. Then to Abbey matinee, good stalls; the play went well. Lady Ardilaun had a party there and took me back to tea at 42 Stephens Green, a pleasant change, the house full of beautiful flowers. And it was like a change of plays at the Abbey, from my intercourse with what I may call progressives, Jack [Yeats] and the others [Donaghy and O'Casey] last night, and the actors in the greenroom, all living in a world that is alive, and these in a decaying one. A sort of *ancien régime* party, a lament for banished society. Mrs. Plunkett, the Bishop's wife talked of the burned houses "and if they rebuild them they will be burned again. And if they are not burned who will want to live in them with no society? And all we are paying in postage! And the posts so slow in coming . . ." (*J*: 610).

It would not be difficult to prefer the greenroom at the Abbey to 42 St. Stephens Green, and although she delighted in the flowers in the garden and in the friendship of Lady Ardilaun, who helped financially with the Abbey, Lady Gregory much preferred, as she told O'Casey herself, the company of creative people. (*J*: 615).

When O'Casey was awarded the Hawthornden Prize for *Juno and the Paycock*, Lady Gregory went along to London too. She had work to do for the Lane pictures, attempting to convince the Irish delegation to Parliament to work harder for the return of her nephew's precious collection of thirty-nine French Impressionist paintings to Dublin.[13] Her conversations with O'Casey, if anything, had increased her certainty that Dublin needed the paintings, so that men and women like him, who wanted to teach themselves about art, would have great art at hand in their own city.

Their joint visit to T. P. O'Connor, M.P. for Ireland, is one of the more hilarious episodes in the whole O'Casey autobiography, detailed in the Childermess chapter of *Sunset and Evening Star*.

It gives a good picture of their close and easy friendship at this
point of their lives, and shows the great good humor between them.
In his account, O'Casey gives the impression that both of them
were responding to the mock-regal crimson decor for the first
time, but Lady Gregory's journals show that she had been to
visit O'Connor previously about the Lane bequest. O'Connor was
sympathetic to her cause and mentioned the visit with O'Casey
in his column 'Men, Women and Memories' in the *Sunday Times*
for April 14, 1926. O'Casey's highly negative view of O'Connor,
enjoyable reading though it may be, does not really do justice to
O'Connor's efforts on behalf of Lady Gregory's crusade for the
return of the Lane pictures to Dublin.

The battle for the Lane paintings was one which drew Lady
Gregory and O'Casey close together. For her, it was not merely
a battle to regain something of her nephew's work; rather, it was a
fight for Ireland and for everything she held sacred for Ireland
in precisely that 'safe' channel of art and literature that she had
dedicated herself to working in. One cannot help but see her
stamina in the fight against England as deriving from the root of
her being. She continued to write letters, visit politicians, hound
influential persons and research legal precedents until her death,
and she continually confided in O'Casey, seeking both his help
and his advice. Significantly, during the estrangement which
followed immediately upon the *Tassie* incident, the Lane pictures
made the one topic of conversation about which she and he continued to correspond. She seems to have tried even to use O'Casey's
natural sympathy with her in this one cause to maintain what was
left of the fragile tie between them in the years which followed
the *Tassie* fight.

The production of *Juno and the Paycock* at the Abbey was
followed closely by the appearance of *The Plough and the Stars*,
the play which sent O'Casey's name around the world, as Yeats
predicted it would to the angry crowd that disrupted the second
night's performance. The play had run into trouble backstage
before its first performance, from the cast and from one of the
directors, George O'Brien,[14] but not from Yeats or from Lady
Gregory. She had liked it immediately and had organized a group
to read it to. Even the words of the prostitute's song at the end
of the second act did not give her pause, though the song itself
was later cut from the Abbey production. As O'Casey wrote to
Gabriel Fallon, 'It was rather embarrassing to me to hear her
reading the saucy song sung by Rosie & Fluther in the second act,
but she is an extraordinarily broad-minded woman, & objects only

to the line "put your leg over mine, Nora"; not because it is objectionable, but because she's afraid it may provoke a laugh from the wrong people.'[15] Her ready acceptance of the play, with its salty dialogue virtually intact, and Yeats's rallying defence of it in confrontation with angry playgoers and a hostile press, left O'Casey ill-prepared for their reception of his next play, *The Silver Tassie.*

The *Tassie* was the ultimate test of the strength of the friendship between O'Casey and Lady Gregory, and the friendship foundered. Looking back at it when the worst was over, Lady Gregory noted in her journals, 'just bad stars'. (*J*: LR 109). And truthfully, an unfortunate combination of circumstances worked almost inexorably towards disaster. Primary among them was the fact that all four directors and O'Casey himself were at great distances from one another geographically when the play arrived at the Abbey. O'Casey was in London, Yeats was in Rapallo, Lady Gregory was in Galway, Starkie was away and was too late reading the play to participate in the decision. That left Lennox Robinson in Dublin by himself, and it meant that no real discussion ever took place until it was too late: all communication took place exclusively by mail. As even the earliest Abbey play reports make clear, the prevailing style of succinct, almost epigrammatic, dissection of a play could easily be taken for callousness of tone, even when it was not intended as such. The reader had to assume the good will of the writer, and for a variety of complex reasons, O'Casey assumed the opposite.

Perhaps of equal importance was the fact that all the principals, with the possible exception of Lennox Robinson, incorrectly assumed that the others understood them well enough to interpret tones of letters positively. Both Yeats and Lady Gregory thought that O'Casey knew them sufficiently well not to misinterpret their well-meaning concern for his reputation and that this would tide him over the difficulty of accepting a negative verdict about the current state of the play. They had no reason to expect that he would react angrily to what he would see as an attack on the play as a whole. He had previously rewritten parts of plays at their request (although this had always been after the play was accepted for production), and Lady Gregory had been able to talk him out of his anger at players' balking over lines in *The Plough and the Stars* by telling him that she, Yeats, and Synge had all allowed actors to make small changes when they felt them to be important.[16] And they did not think that they were rejecting the play. In fact, they did not reject it initially; the intention was to wait till the next

season, as they were so close to the end of their spring season when the play arrived. O'Casey, of course, assumed they were rejecting it, but the fact that they were still discussing whether or not to produce it before O'Casey published their correspondence in the *Observer* indicates that there was still a likelihood of an Abbey production. Before the printing of the *Tassie* letters in the press, both Yeats and Lady Gregory wanted to do the play (Robinson did not). Afterwards, everything was different.

There were other misunderstandings as well. O'Casey apparently thought that since both Yeats and Lennox Robinson had visited him in London to ask whether he would offer his new play to the Abbey, the Abbey would take *The Silver Tassie*. His phenomenal success with his previous three plays at the theatre would have augmented that conviction. However, Yeats and Robinson were more likely not sure of O'Casey's future intentions towards the Abbey. He had left Ireland, as he explains in *Inishfallen, Fare Thee Well*, with much bitterness towards the people and press of Dublin and the actors at the Abbey.[17] There would have been legitimate doubt among the directors about his willingness to offer a play again in Ireland. (Eventually, O'Casey decided that Yeats and Robinson had asked him to send the play simply to set him up for the rejection, which he felt they had decided upon before ever seeing the play. One hopes that even in the midst of great disillusionment he would have seen that such a plan is not credible. And, of course, the evidence disproves it.)

Finally, there could not have been worse timing all around. Largely because O'Casey was preparing for imminent publication of the play, the entire procedure operated irregularly and outside channels at a much faster pace than was desirable: there was no time for second thoughts. O'Casey himself was at a crucial phase of life, having only recently married Eileen, and he was finishing the *Tassie* in the midst of making the enormous adjustments to married life at the age of 47. He was, further, confronted simultaneously with the psychological strain of his first close proximity to pregnancy (as the youngest of his mother's children he would have had not even an unconscious memory of it), and he was about to accept the responsibilities of fatherhood. Worried about Eileen and the baby, in the closing days of her pregnancy he had also to handle his mother-in-law, and the day before Yeats's letter arrived, he had to eject his mother-in-law from the house, as her comments about him and the child had made Eileen hysterical. He had been through an emotional wringer.[18]

Although the closest O'Casey ever comes to saying it is in

statements that he had 'a kid on the way,' Eileen says in *Sean* that
the letter about the *Tassie* arrived the morning after he became
a father. Not only did O'Casey rightly perceive himself as the
Abbey's most popular contemporary playwright, expecting a
congratulatory letter of confirmation, but he also was full of the
multitudinous emotions of new fatherhood, not the least of which
are the feelings of pride and wonder. Under the circumstances,
the letters Lady Gregory sent him must have seemed comically
incomprehensible and petty beyond belief. He was in no condition
to read them calmly and with detachment.

On the other hand, although the directors certainly knew
O'Casey was their most popular playwright, there is nothing in
journals or letters to indicate that they knew that O'Casey was on
the brink of fatherhood. In letters to Lady Gregory, he had
described the house, announced the coming play and its title, but
he did not mention the baby. He wrote to her for help with his
royalties[19] which he needed for the doctor's bills, but he did not
tell her why he needed money so urgently. Had Lady Gregory
any idea that a child was on the way, she would almost certainly
have rethought her strategy of sending him all the bad news at
once, and perhaps she might have fought harder for the *Tassie*
or been more sensitive to O'Casey's emotions.

As it was, the strategy to send the letters was hers alone. She
did not do what Yeats had asked – summarize and soften his
letter; she did not wait to hear from Starkie; in her haste to send
the word to O'Casey in time for him to make changes in the *Tassie*
proofs, she did not write out her own criticism in detail and
contented herself instead with the general statement that Yeats's
letter represented 'what we all think'[20] – inadvertently laying the
whole burden on Yeats, giving the erroneous impression that she
was primarily deferring to Yeats's views. But she had thought that
the *Tassie* was not good before hearing from Yeats, and although
she later said that the Abbey ought to have produced it, she never
completely changed her mind.

For a fuller undestanding of what went wrong, the precise
chronology of events is important. The *Tassie* had been long and
eagerly awaited, and anticipation had led the directors to expect
not only another good play from O'Casey, but one even better
than *The Plough and the Stars*. When O'Casey wrote to tell Lady
Gregory that he had finished the play, on March 1, 1928, he offered
his opinion – which in retrospect seems crucial – that: 'Personally,
I think it is the best work I have yet done. I have certainly put my
best into it, and have written the work solely because of love

and a deep feeling that what I have written should have been written.' (*L*: 239). The comment emphasizes the emotional stake which he had in the play. It is not the sort of statement which Lady Gregory was used to hearing from Yeats, who in the euphoria of a completed work regularly wrote to her that this last was the best he had ever done. O'Casey meant every word of his opinion of the *Tassie* far more deeply than Lady Gregory apparently realized. She replied by return post that she would be reading the play at Coole, presumably to cheer him and to remind him of their good times there together. O'Casey, in return, invited himself to Coole for his next trip to Ireland, which would, of course, be his visit to produce the play. (*L*: 237).

When the play arrived at the Abbey, apparently around March 18 (*L*: 232), Robinson wrote a congratulatory 'Three cheers!' to O'Casey, read the play and sent it with critical commentary to Lady Gregory. Lady Gregory would have taken his criticism with several grains of salt, because she would have remembered his letters to her at Coole during rehearsals for *The Plough and the Stars*, which, while complaining of the play's loose construction and long-windedness, nevertheless added the caveat that Robinson's own style was diametrically opposite to O'Casey's and noted that O'Casey's style was absolutely right for O'Casey.[21] So Lady Gregory was aware from Robinson's previous warning – if she was not able to intuit it – that there was some rivalry involved in anything Robinson might say. On March 28, she wrote down her comments, and they betray disappointment at the play she had just read:

Sean O'Casey's play came yesterday, I read it through. Well, I absolutely agree with L.R.'s criticism, the beginning so fine, the two first acts, then such a falling off, especially in the last, the 'persons' lost in rowdiness.

I must have written something like this to L.R. for he writes in return: 'I was very relieved to get your letter today and to find that you agreed with me about O'Casey's play. If you had disagreed with me I should have suspected myself of all sorts of subconscious feelings. I shall send the play at once to W.B.Y. and avoid writing to Sean till he has read it. We can't do it before the end of this season and if W.B. agrees with you and me Sean will have time to think over his last acts before July and August. It looks to me as if he had put very careful work into acts 1 and 2, and finished the other two acts haphazard because everyone

was beginning to say he would never write a play again and he
wanted to show that he could – but the play as it stands won't
increase his reputation. I see the end of his play as a single
tenement act with the maimed heroes back and everyone sorry
they've come and the girl gone off with the other fellow. This is
obvious, but the idea of O'Casey's play is always obvious; it is
treatment that makes the difference, makes the genius. (*J*: LR
104–05).[22]

After she had read the play, Lady Gregory received O'Casey's
kind letter, written March 28, about the Lane pictures. (*J*: LR 105).
Ironically, it worsened the situation, because she read in it a 'call
to courage': 'I like best his last sentence "You can always walk
with your head up. And remember you had to fight against your
birth into position and comfort as others had to fight against their
birth into hardship and poverty, and it as difficult to come out of
one as it is to come out of the other, so that power may be gained
to bring fountains and waters out of the hard rocks." ' (*J*: LR 105).
One of Lady Gregory's lifelong maxims was 'doing the hard thing
first,'[23] and O'Casey's letter would probably have abetted her
belief that although the medicine would be harsh, it would also be
best for him, hard as it would be to write such news to him. His
letter would also have reminded her that he was a fighter, the kind
who would surely bounce back from any disappointment, no
matter how serious it seemed. She wrote back on April 2, thanking
him for his encouragement about the Lane pictures, but
scrupulously avoided mentioning the *Tassie* until she should hear
from Yeats.

O'Casey wrote again, on April 20, telling her that he was correcting proofs for the *Tassie*, promising her the first copy of the
play – 'to be published in a few months time' – and inviting
himself to Coole on the next Irish trip. (*L*: 237). She received it
two days later, and it saddened and worried her, 'because he
supposes (rightly) that I have read his play sent to L.R. by now. . . .
And L.R. is abroad, and I don't know if Yeats has read it, and I
can't write until all – Starkie also – give their opinion, and don't
like to think he may print it without their criticism – and without
seeing it on the stage.' (*J*: LR 105–06). From this, it is evident that
Lady Gregory intended not rejection of the play, but rewriting.
She thought that O'Casey would be willing to rework the play and
then make further adjustments in rehearsal, as she and Yeats
regularly did, before arriving at the final text for publication. Had
she written a detailed analysis of the strengths and weaknesses of

the *Tassie*, as she had done long before for *The Crimson in the Tri-Colour*, O'Casey might have been willing to follow her suggestions. She could persuade him when others could not. But largely because she was convinced that the play as it stood was not a good one and therefore she was afraid its publication would prove an embarrassment, she did not wait to write an analysis once the word came from Yeats, and, worse, she allowed her lack of extensive commentary to imply agreement with Yeats's opinion, possibly hoping that hinting her criticism to O'Casey would be less painful to him than detailing it precisely.

Yeats's famous letter (*L*: 267–69) arrived at Coole on April 27. It made her happy, because it was so forcefully, clearly, and well written, indicating that Yeats was fully returned to health at Rapallo and that he had come back to Dublin in his full strength. Her first comment on the letter in her journal was 'Such a fine letter', but later events caused her to cross it out three times in the manuscript, and the phrase does not appear in the printed text of her journals.[24] The sentiments in the letter did not shock her, of course, because she had already arrived at similar conclusions about the play, and besides, she had heard Yeats make the criticism that O'Casey was less good writing about people and events he 'didn't know' before.[25] She decided, therefore, to ignore Yeats's advice and to send the letter directly to O'Casey as it was. Yeats, meanwhile, was gradually moving from a consideration of the play in the abstract to an evaluation of it in its context: O'Casey's situation vis-à-vis the Abbey. He wrote again to Lady Gregory, asking her, if she agreed with him that they could not take the play as written, to suggest to O'Casey that he withdraw it himself. He seems to have hoped that she would not yet have written to O'Casey and that this suggestion would replace some of the implications of his earlier letter. Before long, he and Lady Gregory would be urging Lennox Robinson to let it be staged at the Abbey.

But Lady Gregory decided to send the letters to O'Casey without editing or annotation. Looking back, she evaluated what she had come to see as a mistake in judgment, though an understandable one: 'I sent even Yeats' letter to me that he might see there was nothing kept back and my own note of criticism from my diary. He had stayed here and I looked on him and treated him as a friend I could speak or write openly to. He had accepted our criticism in other cases, had rewritten one of the scenes of the *Plough and the Stars* at Yeats' suggestion, and I did not think he would have refused to consider this.' (*J*: LR 110). So Lady Gregory sent Lennox Robinson's letter, Yeats's letters, and her own brief comment immediately to O'Casey, without waiting for Starkie to return from Spain, or without allowing everybody's initial impressions that the *Tassie* was not the equal of its predecessors to be balanced against O'Casey's worth to the theatre and the debt they owed him. She was totally unprepared for the vehemence of O'Casey's reaction.

On the day that she sent him the letters, she noted in her journal that she expected that Yeats's letter particularly 'must be a severe blow, but I believe he will feel its force, its "integrity", and be grateful in the end.' (*J*: LR 106). On May 4, she began to worry that the lack of response from O'Casey was a bad sign: 'he may be trying to find a London producer. That would be best for us but not, I think, for him. But he may shrink from a rewriting or not accept our opinion. I am sad about it all.' (*J*: LR 106).

She had unintentionally hurt O'Casey far worse than she knew, and she took the blame upon herself for it, but O'Casey was about to repay her in kind. Her opinion of her friend dropped steadily as he retaliated and counterattacked in the days and months ahead. She had not thought him capable of such anger and bitterness, and although he tried to be gentle to her and to exempt her from his criticism of the Abbey directorate, it was precisely in his attacks on Yeats, AE and others of her friends that he hurt her most.

He waited to write to her until after he had written to Robinson and to Yeats, and so she received his response to the criticism in its harshest form by hearing it from them. The letter, she wrote, 'grieved me and angered them'; she apparently found it hard to believe his logic – that the Abbey had rejected the play out of spite – and was surprised that he had refused to accept their judgment. She thought he had been 'very ungracious about Yeats's second letter, 'a kindly meant one'. (*L*: LR 107). In a portion of her journals not yet published, she adds: 'I am very sorry – for him, for I don't think his reputation will be helped, and for the Abbey, we had hoped so much of this new play. And for the breaking of a friendship that had been a pleasure and interest to me.' That night she did not sleep, and the next day she sat down on the sofa and fell asleep almost immediately for three hours, and the long nap revived her spirits. She felt, she wrote, 'much the better for it, this last week had been very tiring and I had felt as if a breakdown must come.' (*J*: Berg TS, 37: 41).

Then O'Casey's letter to her arrived (*L*: 270), and she wrote back with some relief that she was glad of its tone, for she would have been sorry had there been 'any break in a friendship I value'.

(*L*: 242–43). Then, as if that made an end of the affair, she went
on to talk of the current successful Abbey production of the *Plough*
and of a Dublin meeting about the Lane pictures. But the incident
was not yet finished; indeed, it had hardly begun, and Lady
Gregory was to feel a few more shocks before it was over. Yeats's
conciliatory letter to O'Casey, mentioning the packed houses for
the *Plough* and saying 'Had my admiration for your genius been less
my criticism had been less severe. I think that is true of Lady
Gregory and Robinson also' (*L*: 242) – was answered by a bitter
and sarcastic note. In it, O'Casey called Yeats shallow, asked him
'What have packed houses, enthusiastic (cheering, says Mr.
Robinson) audiences for *The Plough* got to do with your contention
that *The Silver Tassie* is a bad play?' and, after referring to Yeats's
'delightful sense of Irish humour,' bid him farewell. (*L*: 274) The
letter was so bad, Lady Gregory recorded, that 'George [Mrs.
Yeats] will not let him see it yet – a sorrow to me.'[26] (The doctors
were still worried about his blood pressure.) The next day, Lady
Gregory received 'a very nice letter' from O'Casey (*L*: 246),
making no mention of *The Tassie*. It prompted her to hope 'we may
come together about the Silver Tassie after all,' though she added
that when she showed the letter to Yeats, he was 'frigid'. Can this
be written by the same hand that wrote that letter to Yeats[?]'
she wondered, and hoped that it was a sign of a softening on
O'Casey's part.[27] She had sent him a copy of her *Three Last Plays*,
signed 'with affection and humility', and she hoped that he had
taken its spirit as his own. She and Yeats tried to persuade
Robinson that the play should be done anyway, to let O'Casey see
its good and bad points on the Abbey stage, but Robinson was
adamant about performing it, given the circumstances, and neither
Yeats nor she had changed their estimate of the play. As she noted
in her journal, 'reading it again it seems, after the first act, weaker
than before, and I thought this especially when looking at the
triumphant progress of the *Plough*, every character so clean-cut,
an etching of life caught up in tragedy. In the *Tassie* the characters,
equally vivid in the first act, become lay figures, lantern slides,
showing the horror of war.' (*J*: LR 108–09). She could not see that
as a virtue, whether it was deliberately done or not, and she
wished that O'Casey would remember her advice that his strong
point was characterization.

Then O'Casey published the correspondence, and there seemed
to be no going back. After that, her letters to him restricted themselves to the neutral ground of the Lane controversy, and even
there some petulance emerged, when she wrote to O'Casey that she

had been told Jim Larkin would attempt to disrupt a meeting planned to consider a gallery for the Lane pictures. O'Casey wrote back, 'Oh nonsense,' though he signed himself 'Affectionately yours.' (*L*: 255–56). Worse than that, the publication of the letters made trouble at the Abbey for Lady Gregory, because Starkie found out that she had sent their opinion to O'Casey without waiting for his advice. (He had thought the letters were not sent out before he had read the play and expressed his views to the directors.) It brought her face to face with the responsibility for the trouble that she had already acknowledged to herself, and she wrote to Starkie, apologizing for not waiting, explaining the need for haste, and taking all the blame for the *Tassie* trouble. (*J*: LR 109–110).

The following day, June 6, the *Observer* arrived with its reprint of the letters, and she noticed that O'Casey had left out her own little note that said she agreed with Lennox Robinson's criticism. She had slept little, and she gave way to uncharacteristic gloom: 'It was great ill luck, L.R. and Starkie abroad, Yeats just back and falling on it with new energy of criticism, and my excess of consideration, thinking O'Casey ought to see his opinion before the proofs were out of his hands, and believing he would make alterations. And I am sad. Just bad stars.' (*J*: LR 109).

On June 9, she wrote in her journal that she was glad O'Casey had not given her personal letters for publication in the *Irish Statesman*, as she wanted 'to keep out of the skirmish which has caused, to me, much regret and vexation of spirit'.[28] As each new letter from O'Casey appeared in the papers, her journal recorded the hope that this was the last of the incident, but her assurance dwindled steadily, and she was plainly hurt by O'Casey's letter in the *Irish Times*, June 21, saying 'I feel that the rejection of the play has done more harm to the Abbey than it has done to me, and it would be unhuman of me to say that I was sorry for that.' (*L*: 289). She noted it in her journal, adding, 'The end for the moment of a sad business.'[29]

O'Casey sent her the promised copy of *The Silver Tassie*, inscribed 'With Pride and Warm Affection', and dated at London on June 26. With it, came a letter of reconciliation which she copied into her journal. It read, in part,

'And you shouldn't let what has happened cause you grief. You had really very little to do with it all. I knew the play would be rejected long before it was sent in – in fact when it was only half finished. . . . I can guess the reason which has no association whatever with you.' (I dont know what he thinks the reason was) 'Now I am sending you a copy of the play in the old feeling of respect and affection, and I hope you will be good enough to take it from me.'

I am glad he is sending it – Juno and the The Plough looked lonely without it. (*J*: Berg TS: 38: 41).

When it arrived, on June 30, it gave her pain to look at it, but it did not cause her to retract her initial opinion. Her only comment was that she was glad he could think kindly of her part in it, 'all meant in kindness if he but knew'. And she wondered if his excusing her from blame was based on a belief that she was doting. (*J*: LR 111). Even a letter from Shaw, saying they ought to have done the play whether it was good or not, did not cause her to change her mind. Her journals continued to lament the occurrence, but she did not ever enter a wish to retract her opinions of the play. Furthermore, she made no attempt to explain herself to O'Casey, neither correcting his impression that her share in the decision was minimal, nor specifying how she felt about his campaign in the press. She may have learned to distrust communication on sensitive issues by mail – and she had certainly learned that O'Casey was sensitive to criticism of his work. She also appears to have been fairly certain that they would meet again, and that they might, if the mood and the time were right, make everything clear. It seems possible, finally, that O'Casey's virulent counterattacks on any and every negative comment that appeared in print – occasionally tearing into friends like AE as well as Yeats – made her value his friendship less than theirs and caused her to worry less about whether he knew the whole truth. She stopped losing sleep over O'Casey's feelings when he turned to the newspapers for a forum. And on August 5, after a particularly harsh attack on AE in the *Irish Statesman*, she noted 'I am sad, for it is not worthy of him as I knew him.' (*J*: Berg TS, 38: 51).

When the Abbey performed *The Plough and the Stars* again, in the last week of October, she wrote O'Casey to tell him how well it went, to talk some more about the Lane pictures, and to bring him up to date on Abbey business and her family. In response to her remark that she was managing the Abbey as Yeats was in Italy and Robinson in the States, O'Casey broke the cordial tone of his answering letter:

You will have to forgive me for ceasing to care where W.B.Y. is or what L.S.R. is doing. I can't forget their sneakiness in the

rejection of 'The Silver Tassie' [presumably a reference to his
belief that they had decided to reject it before seeing it]. What
Robinson does, or does not, doesn't matter much – he'll never
add one jot or tittle to life or literature – but Yeats's action
must be counted unto him for unrighteousness. He has over-
thrown his own original constitution of the Abbey Theatre, in
which he wrote about 'the freedom to experiment which is not
found in Theatres in England.' We must change that now to 'the
freedom to experiment which is found in the English Theatre
but is no longer to be found in the Abbey Theatre of Dublin.'
(*L*: 317–20).

Obviously that would have hurt her. They had all, she felt, criticised
the play honestly – she would have had no idea what O'Casey
meant by Yeats's and Robinson's 'sneakiness' – and of course the
Abbey was as dear to her as life itself. She apparently did not
reply – or at least she did not record replying – and no letter
survives until that of December 1, in which she asked O'Casey for
a photograph of the portrait Augustus John had done of him –
perhaps a hint that she would not be seeing him soon. (*L*:
324–25).

In January and February there was another brief spurt of
correspondence, mostly about things other than the *Tassie*. A
comment made in a letter to Gabriel Fallon around this time is
notable: 'Her [Lady Gregory's] letters are always kind and
gracious, but never an answer to a criticism about LR, or AE, or
Yeats or [Will] Shields. This may be a divine dignity, or it may be
a fluttering fear.' (*L*: 342). It was more likely a silent demurring
from his opinion and an implicit hint that criticism of others did
not belong in his letters either.

An apparent pause in their correspondence ended July 15, when
Lady Gregory again initiated their communication with a long,
conversational letter about family news and A.E. Malone's new
book, *The Irish Drama: 1869–1928*.[30] Moved by the kindness of
her tone, O'Casey responded with a gentle and gracious letter:
'Thanks for your letter, and its core of kind remembrance.' (*L*:
350). This friendly touch was undercut slightly by a fuss over
remarks attributed to Yeats by an English journalist, which Yeats
denied making, and more seriously by a disagreement with the
Abbey Theatre over the rights of the theatre to exclusive production of his plays. After letters back and forth between lawyers and
O'Casey, the problem was resolved on O'Casey's terms: Lady
Gregory was to be sole guarantor of all his future Abbey dealings.

(*L*: 351–360). So it was clear that he still trusted her and believed she had his best interests at heart. She must have felt that this re-established the bond between them, because when he wrote to her of the rehearsals of *The Silver Tassie*, she wrote back asking to see him when she went to London to see the play. His famous and ungracious reply is given in full in the *Letters* (p. 369), where David Krause adds a footnote saying that O'Casey, hearing his own words read back to him thirty-four years later, 'groaned and remarked' 'That was one letter I should never have written, especially that cruel last sentence, to my poor dear Lady Gregory! But I suppose my wounds were still raw and I wasn't strong or wise enough to forgive and forget.' To Elizabeth Coxhead, he wrote in a similar vein, 'I made a grim mistake in refusing to see her when she asked if she could come to see us in London: that mistake is a bitter memory within me too.'[31] The letter is remarkable for its combination of emotions. O'Casey was attempting to be kind, to spare her from hearing the anger he continued to feel about the rejection of the *Tassie*; but as he said to her himself, the production had brought back the incident freshly to mind, and recent state-ments attributed to Yeats, whether true or not, had increased his bitterness, and it would have been hard for him to restrain himself in her presence from saying things about her friends which would hurt her. Having said that, he immediately penned a sentence that was surely intended to hurt, the final sentence of the letter: 'So, knowing how I feel, & guessing what I would say about the many Artistic & Literary Shams squatting in their high places in Dublin, I feel it would be much better to set aside, for the present, the honour & pleasure of seeing you & talking with you.' Though he mentioned Robinson in passing, and though AE is clearly one of the 'literary shams' he intends, it is Yeats who is the primary target of O'Casey's wrath, and the letter suggests that perhaps the root of O'Casey's displeasure with Lady Gregory lay in his realiza-tion that despite her obvious affinity and even friendship for him, she had sided with Yeats and not with him when it came to a choice between them.

She replied graciously and frankly, telling him his letter had grieved her – 'perhaps I deserve that' – and asking him with some urgency to change his mind. She had, she wrote him, only a few days left in London. She could, she said, see him the next day – 'If you give me leave.' (*L*: 370). Evidently she had detected that the letter was intended to punish her, and she hoped that O'Casey would think that she had been punished enough without inflicting upon her the kind of ostracism that she had endured many years

before in Gort over the *Playboy* controversy. So she asked him
again if she could visit. She did not, however, play upon his
sympathies nor did she tell him that there was a chance she might
not live to see him again (she had undergone surgery for cancer).
She simply presented herself for acceptance or rejection, in a
rather emblematic turnabout of the *Tassie* incident, and O'Casey
rejected her. He did not answer her letter, nor did he write to her
again, no matter what she wrote to him, for the rest of 1929 and
all of 1930.

Before returning to Ireland, she wrote to O'Casey, saying in
measured and restrained tones that she was sorry not to have seen
him. She enclosed a copy of a letter she had written Yeats, after
seeing the *Tassie*, arguing that the Abbey ought to have produced
the *Tassie*. (*L*: 372). Her note to Yeats did not argue that the
Tassie was a good play, only that they should have done it – and
would have done it better. The letter is more complex than it
seems. On the one hand, it is an atonement, a retraction of the
negative statement she had once written. On the other hand, in
its dignified way, it is very hard on O'Casey. She accuses him of
injustice by not accusing him at all, by saying simply that she
'missed the pleasure of seeing you'. With some pride, she suggests
that the Abbey remains a better producer of his old and new plays
than what he has found in London. She mentioned having worked
more successfully than usual on behalf of the Lane pictures,
leaving unsaid the obvious fact that this time she had had to work
alone. And what she did not mention may have been the strongest
message in the letter: that she had forgiven O'Casey's unkindness
enough to write to Yeats on behalf of the *Tassie*, despite the fact
that O'Casey could not forgive her enough to speak to her.

As he did not reply to that letter, O'Casey also left unanswered
her congratulatory note of six months later, concerning the April
revival of *The Plough and the Stars* at the Abbey. (*L*: 401). She
wrote again in May, mostly of family and theatre business, and
O'Casey's only response was a mocking paraphrase of her words in
a letter to Gabriel Fallon. (*L*: 406–08). In October she mentioned
that she had not heard from him for a long time, and asked him if
the rumor that he would be visiting Ireland were true: 'It would
be a pleasure to me to see you again – and make acquaintance
with your wife and son – so be sure to let me know if you do
come.' (*L*: 421). She wrote to him for Christmas, beginning her
letter with the words: 'It is long since I have had news of you –
I hope all goes well with you and your wife and the son. There
was a rumor a while ago that you were coming back on a visit to

Ireland – but it died away.' (*L*: 423). This letter, aided no doubt by
the spirit of the season, brought a reply from O'Casey: 'I had
decided never to look Westward in thought again, but your kind
letters have (like a still small voice) whispered in my ears that it
would be something lower than bad manners if I continued to
ignore them.' (*L*: 427–28). In the very next paragraph, he launched
again into 'another cause for bitterness' and attacked Lennox
Robinson and Dudley Digges for a bad production of the *Tassie*
in New York. The issue was evidently never going to die between
them, and O'Casey at least would never be able to overlook it or to
overcome it.

In October, less than seven months before her death, she replied
to a letter from him, rejoicing in seeing his handwriting again.
The letter is full of Yeats, who had spent much time with her (she
was in great pain most of the time, but never mentioned it to
O'Casey). Her final words had an ominous ring: 'Perhaps one day
you will bring your wife here. I am sorry not to have met her.'
(*L*: 439–440). An uncharacteristic use of the past tense suggests
gently that her life will soon be over. She died without seeing
O'Casey again.

In his autobiographies, O'Casey seems to have tried to make it
up to her. His is the loveliest portrait of her written by a contemporary, and the one closest in spirit to the Lady Gregory of
the diaries and journals, full of laughter and enthusiasm for life,
skilled and dedicated at her work, and endlessly giving of her time
and energy. But O'Casey cannot resist noting her imperfections,
partly, one feels, to flesh out the portrait and give it more
credibility, but also apparently to blunt the edge of her critical
taste and take the polish off her expertise. The 'lisp' he assigns her
is really nothing more than the hard-edged 'd' of the Connacht-
flavored English she grew up with. It can still be heard today in
the region. But it has the effect of diminishing her stature as well
as of livening her speech. It seems to distance her from him, even
when they are closest.

Given the length of both their lives, their friendship was a
fairly brief one. It was born in the encouragement which Lady
Gregory gave to O'Casey in his early, struggling attempts to write
a play for the Abbey, and it grew steadily through his first three
Abbey successes. Without her encouragement and guidance, there
would almost certainly never have been a playwright named Sean
O'Casey, and the world would have been a poorer one. She founded
the theatre he started to write for, she kept it firmly under control
and kept it alive against great odds until he was ready for it, and

once she found him and recognized his talent, she fostered his genius and turned to him as a friend. They grew closer, becoming congenial companions in Dublin and during his visits to Coole, until O'Casey left Ireland for London, when the geographical distance between them began to become a psychological distance as well. Then *The Silver Tassie* changed everything. Although he tried to minimize her role in the affair and directed most of his residual bitterness at Yeats, O'Casey was grievously wounded by her handling of the *Tassie* and the lingering thought that even she had not liked his play. Their friendsip never really recovered from the damage.

It is tempting to speculate on alternative courses of history. Had Lady Gregory known about the impending arrival of the O'Casey baby, the *Tassie* might have been treated in context and not in the abstract – and she would have had a personal concern for O'Casey to balance the sympathy she felt for the ailing Yeats. Had she not rushed the directors' letters to him for correction in proof, had she given him a more detailed analysis of her own, had she realized that O'Casey could never really take 'no' for an answer but would acquiesce to changes in a play after he had first heard 'yes,' O'Casey might not have become so angry as to make the break with the Abbey inevitable. The Abbey might have done his play, and although the press would almost surely have been hostile, he would have revelled in the support of Lady Gregory and Yeats – and perhaps even of Lennox Robinson – and would have brought Eileen and his son to walk in the woods of Coole. Different plays might have written in the years to come, and there might have been a friendship between O'Casey and Lady Gregory to rival the closeness she had with Yeats.

As it happened, O'Casey never allowed the reconciliation that might have made at least some happy ending possible. After the *Tassie*, one senses instead an uneasy distancing on both sides, a growing formality of speech, a trying to recapture an intimacy of tone that had been lost forever. It needed a confrontation of the problem, a face-to-face meeting, a clearing of the air, a forgiveness, to bring their promising friendship to maturity. Though Lady Gregory tried many times to bring that about, O'Casey never let her do so and never offered reconciliation himself. If to forgive is indeed divine, then O'Casey was all too human.

Although they occasioned some of each other's happiest moments and contributed significantly to strategic phases of each other's careers – she at the commencement of his and he at the culmination of hers – in the final analysis, the 'friendship-affinity'

of Sean O'Casey and Lady Gregory makes only a brief chapter in
two very full lives.

Notes

1 Sean O'Casey, *Inishfallen Fare Thee Well* (New York: Macmillan, 1949), pp. 164–65. Hereafter abbreviated in the text as *IFTW*. Similarly, *Sunset and Evening Star* (New York: Macmillan, 1955) is abbreviated as *S&ES*.

2 Volume I (New York: Macmillan, 1975). Hereinafter abbreviated as *L*.

3 [Isabella Augusta Persse, Lady Gregory.] *Lady Gregory's Journals*, ed. Daniel J. Murphy (Gerrards Cross: Colin Smythe, 1978), hereinafter given in the text as *J*. Quotations from Lady Gregory's Journals which are dated prior to February 24, 1925, are taken from this text. Quotations from after this date are from either of two sources: the excerpted edition of *Lady Gregory's Journals*, ed. Lennox Robinson (New York: Macmillan, 1947), abbreviated in the text as *J: LR*; or from unpublished sections of Lady Gregory's typescript in the Berg Collection, given as *J: Berg TS*. These are published by kind permission of The Henry W. & Albert A. Berg Collection of the New York Public Library, Astor. Lenox & Tilden Foundations.

4 Elizabeth Coxhead, *Lady Gregory: A Literary Portrait*, second edition (London: Secker and Warburg, 1966).

5 *The Harvest Festival* and *The Frost in the Flower*.

6 Abbey actors occasionally rented the theatre for their own productions.

7 Coxhead, p. 184.

8 Isabella August Persse, Lady Gregory, unpublished diaries, Berg Collection, New York Public Library, January 1, 1899 ff.

9 Coxhead, p. 192.

10 Produced at the Abbey Theatre on September 29, 1924.

11 To O'Casey, Shaw wrote, 'What a hell of a play! I wonder how it will hit the public.' To Lady Gregory, he wrote, 'It is literally a hell of a play, but it will clearly force its way on to the stage and Yeats should have submitted to it as a calamity imposed on him by the Act of God, if he could not welcome it as another *Juno*.' (L: 284–86).

12 The published version (*J*: 608) gives this as 'the reverse of the battle-field', but the Berg typescript clearly shows 'battleshield,' a reading which makes more sense.

13 Lady Gregory's nephew, Sir Hugh Lane, had bequeathed a collection of thirty-nine French impressionist paintings to England, because of frustrations encountered in trying to get the Dublin Corporation to build a gallery to house them. He drowned in the sinking of the *Lusitania* in 1915, and after his death an unwitnessed codicil was found to be in his desk, changing the bequest and returning the pictures to Dublin. England, while granting that his wish was to restore the pictures to Dublin, nonetheless chose to enforce the letter of the law and to refuse to return them. For further details, see Lady Gregory's

   Hugh Lane's Life and Achievement (Gerrards Cross: Colin Smythe, 1973).

14 O'Brien, after writing an approving letter to Lady Gregory about the play, began to have doubts about the propriety of parts of it and to hint strongly in a letter to Yeats that the Abbey might lose its government subsidy if *The Plough and the Stars* were performed as was. (Letter from George O'Brien to Lady Gregory, August 8, 1925, Berg Collection; *J: LR:* 87–99; *L:* 144–47.) The Abbey company was angry with O'Casey for his pointed criticism of its recent production of Shaw's *Man and Superman. (L:* 138–140).

15 The fact that Lady Gregory gave this as her reason for objecting to the prostitute's song is not in itself sufficient evidence that she was broad-minded, but it does indicate how tactful she could be in making her objections known and reinforces the idea that she might have treated the *Tassie* with more diplomatic skill if she had been near O'Casey or in his presence, rather than across the Irish Sea.

16 *J: LR* 94. Lady Gregory's treatment in her journals of *The Plough and the Stars* echoes most of what is already known about the audience reactions, actors' squabbles, and success. She was not in Dublin for the opening, and heard about it by letter from Lennox Robinson. (Berg Collection, February 9, 1926).

17 *IFTW:* 370–396. Like other writers before him, O'Casey felt the pressure to amend his work to conform to social standards, or to actors' and producers' preferences stifling, and so he left Dublin permanently for the comparatively greater freedom of London, though he continued to wage war in the Irish newspapers against his critics.

18 Eileen O'Casey, *Sean,* ed. with an introduction by J. C. Trewin (London: Macmillan, 1971), pp. 81–82.

19 *L:* 227. This was a recurring problem at the Abbey, and Lady Gregory replied that her own had been kept overdue as well. (L: 228).

20 *L:* 239. Lady Gregory enclosed her own note to Robinson, copied from her journals, agreeing with Robinson's critique, but this was so brief as to sound like nothing more than an echo of Robinson, and would probably have reinforced O'Casey's perception that she had no real objections of her own.

21 Letter from Lennox Robinson to Lady Gregory, February 9, 1926. Berg Collection.

22 Robinson's 'unconscious feelings' would have stemmed from the trouble he had had with O'Casey and with the actors during the production of *The Plough and the Stars,* as well as from any sense of rivalry.

23 Unpublished diaries, back cover. Berg Collection.

24 Unpublished journals, holograph copy, April 27, 1928. Berg Collection.

25 *L:* 146–47: 'What is wrong is that O'Casey is there writing about people whom he does not know, people he has only read about.'

26 *J:* Berg TS, 37:44. 'A very bad letter from S O'C to W.B.Y. this morning.'

27 *J:* Berg TS, 37:46. Actually, she received two letters, the first about the Lane pictures and the second thanking her for sending O'Casey her *Three Last Plays. (L:* 245–246).

28 *J:* Berg TS, 38.15–16. She added that she spent so restless a night

that she upset her candlestick and broke its glass, 'which strews the floor'.

29 It was not.

30 *L:* 49–50. The letter ends as follows: 'I hope your boy continues to grow in health & strength. And I do hope you are well & strong [she was in failing strength herself] – and I do honestly hope for the success of the Tassie – please believe this – & believe me affectionately your friend [.]'

31 Coxhead, p. 192.

THE DRUIDIC AFFINITIES OF O'CASEY AND YEATS

DAVID KRAUSE

> The arts are at their best when they are busy with battles that can never be won.
>
> W. B. Yeats

> God be my judge that I hate fighting. If I be damned for anything, I shall be damned for keeping the two-edged sword of thought tight in its scabbard when it should be searching the bowels of knaves and fools.
>
> Sean O'Casey

1. Tribal Dance and Drums

Yeats and O'Casey were usually at the top of their artistic form when, in their separate ways, they won or lost the battles that couldn't be won. The heroic Yeats won most of his battles as a lyric poet; the mock-heroic O'Casey won most of his battles as a tragicomic dramatist; but both men, in the best meaning of artistic defeat in the cause of a visionary theatre, have up to the present time lost the battles of their later experimental plays. The symbolic verse plays and comic fantasies that Yeats and O'Casey wrote for an impossible theatre of the future are seldom if ever produced in the commercial theatre, or even at their own Abbey Theatre, and only isolated art theatres or small university groups are willing to take the risk of performing these innovative and controversial works.

A typical Irish controversy arose in 1938 when Yeats's *Purgatory* was first produced at the Abbey Theatre, and one of the vocal critics who objected to the anti-Christian meaning and merit of the play, the Rev. Terence Connolly, S.J., turned out to be the same American priest who three years earlier had attacked O'Casey's *Within the Gates* as a blasphemous and obscene work and succeeded in having the play banned in Boston. The aged Yeats, only a year away from his death, was too weary and suspicious of what he called the impermanence of controversy to defend his play, as he explained in a letter to Edith Shackleton Heald on 15 August 1938: 'The trouble is outside. The press or the clerics get to work – the tribal dance and the drums. This time the trouble is theological. As always I have to remain silent and see my work travestied because I will not use up my fragile energies on impermanent writing.' Perhaps the much honoured Yeats could now afford to remain artistically aloof about a cranky Jesuit critic who, as a mere nuisance and having no influence in Dublin, couldn't interfere with the production of the play or damage Yeats's reputation. Lacking the stature and confidence of a Nobel Prize poet, O'Casey, who always wrote the kind of play that was destined to cause trouble outside, felt he had to join 'the tribal dance and the drums' in his own defence, as he had explained in his characteristic 'two-edged sword of thought' reply in a September 1931 letter to Charlotte F. Shaw, who had urged him 'not to be too belligerent'. His public anger was inseparable from his aesthetic passion; his magnificent belligerence was an essential and permanent aspect of his art. And we should remember that the seemingly detached Yeats could also be magnificently belligerent and rise to 'an old man's frenzy' in his *Last Poems* (1939), for as he says in 'The Spur':

> You think it horrible that lust and rage
> Should dance attention upon my old age;
> They were not such a plague when I was young;
> What else have I to spur me into song?

In 1938 when the Abbey Theatre rejected *The Silver Tassie*, Yeats had spurred himself to heat up the controversy with his belligerent letter of rejection to O'Casey. On that occasion, and even more openly and vigorously when he had defiantly defended *The Playboy* and *The Plough* against rioters in the theatre, a younger Yeats had histrionically contributed his share to the tribal dance and drums. In his rejection letter of 20 April 1928, however, he was urging the chastened O'Casey to avoid war and politics, and opinions about both subjects in his plays, warning him to suppress all references to historical events in the theatre. But Yeats himself had often broken this quaint principle and beaten a political drum in his early nationalistic plays, as well as in his later comments on 'The Troubles' in his poetry. In 'Easter 1916,' for example, Yeats did not hesitate to take a political stand, though he cautiously avoided the kind of savage irony with which O'Casey looked at the sacrificial rhetoric and patriotic death in

The Plough and the Stars, Juno and the Paycock and *The Shadow of a Gunman*. In the historical context of the poem, Yeats's refrain line, 'A terrible beauty is born' – which O'Casey later mocked in his autobiography as 'A terrible beauty is borneo' – placed more emphasis on the beauty than the terror in an obvious concession to patriotic sentiment; and sometimes the theme of the poem is blurred when Yeats tries to have it both ways by dividing his loyalties between the green glory of the martyrs and the stony hearts of the people. The last section begins:

> Too long a sacrifice
> Can make a stone of the heart.
> O when may it suffice?
> That is Heaven's part, our part
> To murmur name upon name,
> As a mother names her child
> When sleep at last has come
> On limbs that had run wild.

These elegaic lines have a direct parallel in Mrs. Tancred's tragic lament for her dead Republican son in *Juno*, a lament later repeated by Juno Boyle with even sharper emphasis when her son is killed by the Republicans, except that O'Casey adds a heartbreakingly ironic dimension to Yeats's stoical acceptance of despair by allowing Mrs. Tancred to echo the hearts of stone but also imply that Heaven was not doing its part to save a mother's child:

> Mother o' God, Mother o' God, have pity on the pair of us! . . . O Blessed Virgin, where were you when me darlin' son was riddled with bullets, when me darlin' son was riddled with bullets! . . . Sacred Heart of the Crucified Jesus, take away our hearts o' stone . . . an' give us hearts o' flesh! . . . Take away this murdherin' hate . . . an' give us Thine own eternal love!

May Craig, the distinguished Abbey Theatre actress who first created the role of Mrs. Tancred, established the tradition of reading this speech with a quiet and reverent intensity which always made a powerful impact. But this is not necessarily the only way to deliver the speech. It should be pointed out, for example, that on one fairly recent occasion, which was recorded in the *Irish Times* on 26 July 1975 by Kane Archer in his review of Maureen Toal's one-woman show, 'Tributes,' that speech was interpreted in a different and darker tone: 'As Mrs. Tancred, her cry to the Mother of God is not a plaint but an outright angry accusation of betrayal.' This wild accusation of a heavenly betrayal is probably more appropriate to the theme of O'Casey's anti-heroic play, and there is little of this tribal savagery in Yeats's poem. Briefly, in his comment on one of the 1916 martyrs, John MacBride, the husband of Maud Gonne, as 'A drunken, vainglorious lout', Yeats darkens the irony, though he then goes on to soften it by conceding that even MacBride was 'transformed utterly' by the terrible beauty. There is also a scornful reference to the 'shrill' political voice of Countess Markiewicz, who spent her days 'in ignorant good-will', with which judgment O'Casey would readily have agreed, since he was forced to make a belligerent protest against her strident patriotism when he resigned from the Irish Citizen Army in 1914 because he felt she was undermining the labour movement in Dublin.

In the concluding lines of his poem, however, Yeats abandons all irony and, contrary to O'Casey's irreverent treatment of patriotic sacrifice, exalts the beauty in the terror with an unqualified glorification of the martyred heroes who died for excessive love of Cathleen Ni Houlihan:

> And what if excess of love
> Bewildered them till they died?
> I write it out in a verse –
> MacDonagh and McBride
> And Connolly and Pearse
> Now and in time to be,
> Wherever green is worn,
> Are changed, changed utterly:
> A terrible beauty is born.

The suffering mothers and the hearts of stone are forgotten now. Bearing in mind Yeats's advice to O'Casey in his letter rejecting *The Silver Tassie*, one is tempted to suggest that perhaps the fire of lyric poetry should have burned away Yeats's display of these sentimental patriotic opinions. The sceptical O'Casey would never experience the guilt Yeats felt at the end of his life when, in 'The Man and the Echo,' the poetic Yeats sat in judgment on the political Yeats and wondered if his early nationalistic play, *Cathleen Ni Houlihan* – in which his noble title-heroine had chanted her dirge for the dead heroes, 'They shall be remembered forever' – had been a spur to the martyrdom of the Rising:

>   Did that play of mine send out
>   Certain men the English shot?

In contrast to this political question, Yeats took a more objective
and less exalted view of Ireland's suffering in 'Meditations in
Time of Civil War,' a more complex and powerful poem than
the facile and sentimental 'Easter 1916,' when he wrote:

>   We had fed the heart on fantasies,
>   The heart's grown brutal from the fare;
>   More substance in our enmities
>   Than in our love. . . .

It is more likely that these poignant lines will be remembered
forever, and Yeats wrote them in 1923, a year after the Civil War
and the same year that O'Casey's first play, *The Shadow of a
Gunman*, was produced at the Abbey Theatre. In this play most
of the comically discredited characters have fed so long on
fantasies of heroism that their hardened hearts have made it
impossible for them to see or love one another as human beings.
Seumas Shields, the sardonic jester who reflects O'Casey's mock-
heroic meditations on the Civil War, often stresses and expands
Yeats's theme of brutality and enmity, as he does in this scene
with Donal Davoren, the shadow of a poet who tries unsuccessfully
to remain aesthetically aloof from the tribal dance of death:

Seumas. I wish to God it was all over. The country is gone mad.
Instead of counting their beads now they're countin' bullets;
their Hail Marys and paternosters are burstin' bombs – burstin'
bombs, an' the rattle of machine-guns; petrol is their holy
water; their De Profundis is 'The Soldiers' Song,' an' their
creed is, I believe in the gun almighty, maker of heaven an'
earth – an' it's all for 'the glory o' God an' the honour o'
Ireland'.
Davoren. I remember the time when you yourself believed in
nothing but the gun.
Seumas. Ay, when there wasn't a gun in the country; I've a
different opinion now when there's nothin' but guns in the
country – An' you daren't open your mouth, for Kathleen ni
Houlihan is very different now to the woman who used to
play the harp an' sing 'Weep on, weep on, your hour is past,'
for she's a ragin' divil now, an' if you only look crooked at
her you're sure of a punch in th' eye. . . . I'm a Nationalist right

enough; I believe in the freedom of Ireland, an' that England
has no right to be here, but I draw the line when I hear the
gunmen blowin' about dyin' for the people, when it's the people
that are dyin' for the gunmen! With all due respect to the
gunmen, I don't want them to die for me.

Perhaps these dramatic lines should be remembered forever, for
they bring O'Casey and Yeats together in their now common
attitude toward Ireland's brutalized and stony heart. O'Casey
went on to intensify his loyalties for the helpless people over the
ruthless gunmen in *Juno*, when Johnny Boyle, already crippled in
the fighting, insists he would do it all again for Ireland because
'a principle's a principle', and his mother replies: 'Ah, you lost
your best principle, me boy, when you lost your arm; them's the
only sort o' principles that's any good to a workin' man.' And in
The Plough it is the prostitute, Rosie Redmond, who profanes the
sacred principles of the patriots as they march to the meeting to
hear the blood-sacrifice words of Pearse in preparation for the
Rising: 'They're all in a holy mood. Th' solemn-lookin' dials on
th' whole o' them, an' they marchin' to th' meetin'. You'd think
they were th' glorious company of th' saints, an' th' noble army
of martyrs thrampin' through th' shtreets of paradise. They're all
thinkin' of higher things than a girl's garthers.'
It was inevitable that such devastating irony and mockery
would soon lead to trouble outside, and Yeats himself became one
of O'Casey's chief defenders when the belligerent controversy
broke out. It was incredible that only two years later Yeats should
have scolded O'Casey for daring to write a controversial pacifist
play about the first World War. It was inconceivable that Yeats,
a continually controversial figure in Ireland, could have forgotten
that all significant Irish literature – many of his own poems and
plays, the plays of Synge and O'Casey, the fiction of Joyce – had
in a variety of nobly irreverent ways outraged the rabblement
and arrived to the usual accompaniment of a tribal dance and
drums.

2. Intimate Enemies

O'Casey should have been ripe for revenge after Yeats rejected
The Silver Tassie. His first three plays had rescued the declining
Abbey Theatre from artistic and financial disaster, and his new
symbolic play had been written in precisely that experimental
spirit which Yeats had called for in 1904 at the founding of his
Irish Theatre dedicated to 'that freedom to experiment which is

not found in theatres in England, and without which no new movement in art or literature can succeed.' But Yeats and Lennox Robinson, and a reluctant Lady Gregory, said no – the final decision rested with Yeats, probably the worst blunder in the history of the Abbey Theatre – and the bewildered and angry O'Casey, his career as a dramatist disrupted and endangered, was cut off from his theatre and his country. Nevertheless, in the years following the rejection, O'Casey, a man who seldom forgave an injustice, defended and celebrated the genius of Yeats, though he was understandably slow to forget Yeats's role in the rejection. And this refusal to seek revenge against his intimate enemy tells us something about the personal genius of O'Casey.

In accord with his romantic mythology, one might have expected he would see himself as a proletarian Oisin girding himself for battle against an aristocratic dragon. Instead of such an allegorical struggle, however, the two men promptly became engaged in a tribal battle of words. In their letters to each other over the rejection, recorded in *The Letters of Sean O'Casey*, Vol. I (1975), a correspondence which the wounded O'Casey released to the press contrary to Yeats's wishes, they hurled their opposing theories of drama at each other. Yeats, who had apparently reserved for himself the freedom to experiment with new dramatic techniques, seemed to believe that his own verse plays for dancers, based upon Ezra Pound and Ernest Fenollosa's version of the ritualistic Japanese Noh Theatre, were now the only viable form of drama. He objected to O'Casey's use of an historical event like the first World War as a theme for *The Silver Tassie* because, according to Yeats's newly discovered dictum, 'the whole history of the world must be reduced to wallpaper in front of which the characters must pose and speak'. It was a similarly arbitrary attitude which prompted Yeats to reject Wilfred Owen's war poems when he was editing the *Oxford Book of Modern Verse* in 1936, because he felt that poetry about war could only deal with 'passive suffering', a phrase he borrowed from Matthew Arnold, who had used it in his reflected distress over the act of suicide, not war, in his powerfully painful poem 'Empedocles on Etna'. Furthermore, since O'Casey, unlike Owen, had not served in the Great War, Yeats went on lecturing at O'Casey, he could only write out of his 'opinions' instead of direct experience, and dramatic action was 'a fire that must burn up the author's opinions'.

Apparently it did not occur to Yeats that there was no such thing as a Procrustean rule about the subject matter of a play, or any work of literature, and that O'Casey's historical world was just as valid as Yeats's wallpaper world. Whatever one thinks about the merits of such totally different works as *At the Hawk's Well* and *The Silver Tassie*, for example, they must both be accepted as legitimate and unique experiments in modern drama. Nor should the objection that O'Casey had not taken part in the War be any more relevant than an objection that Yeats had not set foot in the mythic realm of Celtic Ireland or the stylized world of medieval Japan. O'Casey was fully aware of the contradictions in Yeats's argument, and he shot back his reply at point-blank range: 'Do you really mean that no one should or could write about or speak about a war because one has not stood on the battlefield? Were you really serious when you dictated that – really serious, now? Was Shakespeare at Actium or Philippi? Was G. B. Shaw in the boats with the French, or in the forts with the British when St. Joan and Dunois made the attack that relieved Orleans?' Then, with an ironic blast aimed at Yeats himself and his 'The Wandering of Oisin,' he added: 'And someone, I think, wrote a poem about Tir na nOg who never took a header into the Land of Youth.'

Since Yeats had only the highest praise for O'Casey's first three plays, plays that had all dealt with the history of the Irish War of Independence and Civil War, 1916 to 1922 – a series of events that Yeats had used in his poems – and those early plays had clearly reflected the dramatist's 'opinions' about the conflict, O'Casey was understandably puzzled by the logic as well as the aesthetics of Yeats's objections to the new play: 'I have pondered in my heart your expression that "the history of the world must be reduced to wallpaper", and I find in it only the pretentious bigness of a pretentious phrase. I thank you out of mere politeness, but I must refuse even to try to do it. That is exactly, in my opinion (there goes a cursed opinion again), what most of the Abbey dramatists are trying to do – building up, building up little worlds of wallpaper, and hiding striding life behind it all.' There was only one way to accomplish Yeats's impossible aim, O'Casey concluded: 'It is all very well and very easy to say that "the dramatic action must burn up the author's opinions." The best way, the only way, to do that is to burn up the author himself.' Behind O'Casey's sacrificial jest lies the conviction that the objective or impersonal theory of art as a private communion of aesthetic value, in the work of a Yeats or Eliot, should be countered by an equally valid subjective or personal theory of art as a public commitment of social or humanistic value, in the work of a Dickens or an O'Casey. Unfortunately, the champions of these two approaches to art are often intolerant of each other's position, but there must always be room for both points of view, the wallpaper and the historical worlds of art.

Yeats refused to allow O'Casey's play to appear in the Abbey Theatre, and he was only prepared to make one concession to O'Casey's injured pride, a minimal concession that turned out to be a tactical blunder. In an awkward attempt to suppress the controversy, he let it be known, indirectly in a letter to Lady Gregory, that O'Casey might save face by telling the press he had decided to withdraw his play for revisions, and thus there would be no embarrassing publicity about the Abbey's rejection of the play. Whereupon O'Casey let it be known, indirectly in a letter to Lennox Robinson, how he felt about Yeat's concession: 'If W. B. Yeats had known me as faintly as he thinks he knows me well, he wouldn't have wasted his time – and mine – making such a suggestion. I am too big for this sort of mean and petty shuffling, this lousy perversion of the truth. There is going to be no damned secrecy with me surrounding the Abbey's rejection of the play. Does he think that I would practise in my life the prevarication and wretchedness that I laugh at in my plays?'

Yeats had misjudged O'Casey as well as *The Silver Tassie*, and O'Casey had reason to be roaring mad. Nevertheless, consistent with his fierce sense of honesty, O'Casey resorted to anger not vindictiveness, even though the rejection had hurt his career as well as his pride. In the fifth volume of his autobiography, *Rose and Crown*, he described his reaction in the following manner: 'Yeats's denunciation of *The Silver Tassie* had done Sean's name a lot of violence. The Nobel Prize winner, the Leader of English literature, was a judge against whom there was no appeal for the time being. Sean's flying start had been rudely curtailed of its fair proportions, and he would have to start over again, and fight the battle anew.' Although neither he nor Yeats appreciated it at the time, he was ironically fighting the artistic battle that can never be won, the quest for absolute integrity of vision in art, the ultimate battle with one's craft, against all private weakness and public pressure, as Yeats himself had declared on a different occasion. Significantly, then, instead of seeking revenge against Yeats and hardening his heart on that enmity, O'Casey resumed his personal battle by doing the one thing he felt he knew best: he started to write another innovative and controversial play about the symbolic fate of modern man, *Within the Gates*. At the same time, in the early 1930's, a group of backbiting writers in

Dublin tried to recruit O'Casey to their case of undermining the
reputation and influence of Yeats, but O'Casey unhesitatingly
gave them the back of his hand. He was, as he had said, too
big for that sort of prevarication and wretchedness, especially in
relation to Yeats.

The first sign of a reconciliation between them came in 1935
when, after seven years of stony silence, they met on two
occasions. They met in the Spring in London, after O'Casey had
returned from his first and only trip to New York where he had
helped supervise the American premiere of *Within the Gates*;
and they met again at the end of the Summer in Dublin, where
O'Casey had gone with his wife to spend a brief holiday on his
last visit to Ireland. On the first occasion O'Casey had made the
initial gesture by writing in February to inquire about Yeats's
failing health; and on the second occasion in September it was
Yeats who made the first move by inviting O'Casey to his Dublin
home, Riversdale, in Rathfarnham. After so much controversy
and so much silence, it was remarkable that there was no bitterness
between them. 'At last,' O'Casey wrote in *Rose and Crown*,
'Yeats had stretched out a hand of friendship; and the heart within
Sean rejoiced greatly.' And in a March letter to Olivia Shakespear,
Yeats reacted with similar pleasure and relief: 'O'Casey has
written me a friendly letter about my illness, and this – the first
sign of amity since our quarrel – has given me great pleasure.
He has attacked propaganda plays in the *New Statesman* and
that may have made him friendly to me.'

Yeats's remark that O'Casey may have become friendly again
after he had attacked propaganda plays is related to an ironic
set of circumstances that grew out of another typical O'Casey
controversy. Early in 1935 after he had returned from America,
he had been trying to earn some extra money by writing reviews,
and when his negative review of the published text of Ronald
Gow's *Love on the Dole* appeared in February in the *New
Statesman and Nation*, at a time when the play was still enjoying
a long run in the West End, Ethel Mannin, a friend of Yeats's,
was one of several correspondents who wrote letters of protest
to the magazine in defence of what they believed to be a proletarian play of great merit. O'Casey had attacked the play on
artistic as well as political grounds, first stating that the plot
was too transparent and the predictable characters were all still-
born, and then objecting to what he called the glib pandering to
the proletariat by an intellectual playwright whose sympathies
were stronger than his talent. He insisted that condescending

propaganda for the masses was not likely to produce good drama.
It was in this context that he concluded that the artist 'is above the
kings and princes of this world, and he is above the Labour Leaders
and Proletariat, too.' He was specifically thinking of those labour
leaders and proletarians in England who had automatically
praised the play. A day after he read Miss Mannin's abusive letter
in which she indignantly defended all proletarian propaganda and
sneered at insensitive artists like O'Casey who should 'get a kick
in the pants from the proletariat' – an ironic accusation to hurl at
a genuinely proletarian artist – a day later the frustrated and
isolated O'Casey instinctively turned to a kindred artistic spirit
and wrote a warm and friendly letter to the ailing Yeats. The
irony continues when we remember that Yeats had rejected *The
Silver Tassie* because he felt O'Casey was indulging in anti-war
propaganda, and now O'Casey was sharing with him a common
ground of artistic integrity. Although O'Casey had always been
militant about his working-class loyalties, he never believed that
a mere sign of sympathy for the workers in a work of art was
sufficient reason to praise it. The proletarian as well as the
aristocrat refused to place politics above art. The intimate enemies
were not completely united, though they shared some common
ground, but they were at last drawing closer together.

3. The Bee and the Wasp

If Ethel Mannin had inadvertently brought the two men
together, their reconciliation didn't mean that O'Casey had
decided to forsake the legitimate theme of social commitment in
art. He had only objected to blatant propaganda and condescending art. He remained convinced that all art contains a personal
point of view, some form of functional opinion or propaganda
that is organic to the work and not something that is merely
imposed upon the creative process. In an article on 'The Theatre
and the Politician' that he wrote in 1945, in which he also talked
about religion and drama, he stated that 'Every town that has a
church should have a theatre', and he made the following comments on politics and drama: 'Then there is the question of what
is called propaganda in a play. There are very few plays in which
the artist doesn't give an opinion about life as he sees it; or gives
forth a sigh for what he would like it to be; or laughs at its follies,
applauds its courage, or lashes out at its hypocrisies. There is, of
course, at times, the play that is nothing but a wearisome string
of political party platitudes, containing no element, in character
or lyricism, of a play at all. The writers of this sort of thing have

in them no spark of the love of humanity, but are merely hangers-out of opinions, voiced by puppets dressed up for the occasion in the garments of men and women.' He might have been thinking about a play like *Love on the Dole* here.

Yeats might have agreed with O'Casey's conclusion about the hangers-out of opinions, though he probably would have added that all opinions hang out in a work of art and must therefore be burned away by the fire of creation. It should be remembered that Yeats had stated his absolute opposition to all literature that reflects a writer's opinion or point of view in his 'General introduction For My Work' in 1937: 'I knew, though but now and then as young men know things, that I must turn from that modern literature Jonathan Swift compared to the web a spider draws out of its bowels; I hated and still hate with an ever growing hatred the literature of the point of view.'

Yeats was alluding to Swift's *Battle of the Books* and its famous 'sweetness and light' episode, the burlesque Aesopian fable about the controversy between the allegorical bee and spider. Representing the classical writers, the bee created honey and wax which provided man with sweetness and light, or beauty and wisdom, while the spider was a venomous modern creature who created its seamy writing out of its own entrails and ignored the tradition of the ancients. But perhaps Yeats's love of tradition and obsessive hatred of ideas in modern literature was not entirely Swiftian, since no writer ever dedicated himself more savagely to the expression of his own point of view than the satiric Swift, who, in spite of his comic allegory, could write with the brilliant venom of a spider as well as the fine enlightenment of a bee. And the same judgment might be made of the sharply satiric O'Casey, who could be even more Swiftian than Yeats in this dual sense. There is more of the savage indignation of Swift in *The Silver Tassie* than in *At the Hawk's Well*, for example, and this is in no way meant as a denigration of Yeats's beautifully esoteric and romantic play; nor is it an attempt to deny that the lyrical Yeats could often rise to a Swiftian rage in his poetry, which reflected a very fixed point of view, particularly, for example, when he had cause to comment on the modern age in 'The Statues' as 'this filthy modern tide', or referred to the modern democratic masses in 'Under Ben Bulben' as 'Base-born products of base beds.' Perhaps Yeats didn't so much hate opinions as much as he hated opinions that differed radically from his own opinions.

To continue the Swiftian allegory in O'Casey, it was he who had assumed the persona of an avenging wasp in the same year that Yeats was identifying himself with the bee, when in *The Flying Wasp* he counter-attacked the English critics who had rejected the innovative and symbolic plays of O'Neill and O'Casey in preference to the stereotyped drawing-room drama of Coward and Lonsdale. His chief opponent then was James Agate, the reigning monarch of the London drama critics, who had dismissed *Within the Gates* in 1934 as 'pretentious rubbish', and on another occasion complained: 'There is a nest of wasps that must be smoked out because it is doing the theatre infinite harm.' The waspish O'Casey should be forgiven for replying to his genteel adversaries with more light than sweetness in his laughing criticism of the critics, for he administered his satiric sting with a relentlessness that owed a strong debt to the spirit of Swift. Twenty years later when replying to his less than genteel Irish critics in *The Green Crow*, he continued in the mock-allegorical mode of Aesop and Swift by assuming the persona of a sly and belligerent crow who refused to be silenced when he was maligned or mistreated. And he was extremely honest and accurate when he characterized himself in the following manner: 'Some Latin writer once said, "If a crow could feed in quiet, it would have more meat." A thing this Green Crow could never do: it had always, and has still, to speak and speak while it seeks and finds its food, and so has had less meat than it might have had if only it had kept its big beak shut.'

Paradoxically, O'Casey seemed to thrive on controversy as well as suffer from it, for it apparently contained that spur of indignation over injustice that quickened his pride and released his creative energy so that he could go on fighting the battles that Yeats said couldn't be won. Yeats may have been less sanguine about controversy, yet he himself was often in the centre of it, usually as a result of his obsessive hatreds, or his vigilant efforts to defend his principles of poetry, to protect the Abbey Theatre and its playwrights from angry mobs, to protest against oppressive censorship laws in Ireland, to fight for his unpopular theatre of verse and dance plays. He maintained that he tried to keep controversy out of his poetry, and he was largely successful in this effort, though his uncompromising hatreds and reactionary sentiments shine out powerfully and controversially in some of his best poems. He hated the literature of ideas, represented most dramatically by Bernard Shaw, who Yeats saw in a dream as a perpetual motion sewing machine, and he was probably over-reacting to Shaw's vitalist eloquence because it was diametrically opposed to his own mystical eloquence. In 1917 in his 'Anima Hominis' Yeats had written his famous dictum: 'We make out of the quarrel with others, rhetoric, but of the quarrel with ourselves, poetry.' But like attractive aphorisms this one must be qualified lest it be taken as an absolute rule for the purity of poetry, as often happens when it is invoked by Yeatsian disciples, for it should be apparent that there is poetry in rhetoric and rhetoric in poetry; there are images in ideas and ideas in images. This fusion of contraries must be apparent in the works of Dante and Milton, Shakespeare and Goethe, Calderon and Keats, Blake and Pushkin, Swift and Shaw, Whitman and Eliot, Melville and Yeats, Synge and Joyce, Dickens and O'Casey, and many more writers who explored the infinite possibilities of poetic vision. They all quarrelled with others as well as themselves.

To complete the Swiftian analogy, Yeats was in a sad and allegorical mood when he was passing through London on his way to his retreat in Rapallo in October 1928, six months after *The Silver Tassie* controversy, and not long after he had delivered his eloquent speeches against government censorship of literature in the Irish Senate and resigned from politics, having served as a Senator for six years. In an interview in *The Observer*, reprinted in the *Irish Independent* on the 22nd of October, titled ' "As a Bee – Not as a Wasp," Senator Yeats in His Old Age,' he made the following statement: 'We have created a native literature – a vigorous intellectual life in Dublin, but the blundering of a censorship may drive much Irish intellect into exile once more, and turn what remains into a bitter polemical energy. We have created something at once daring and beautiful and gracious, and I may see my life's work and that of my friends, Synge, "AE," and Lady Gregory, sinking down into a mire of clericalism and anti-clericalism. I am glad to be out of politics. I'd like to spend my old age as a bee and not as a wasp.'

The disillusioned Yeats was still thinking of Swift, one of his favourite 18th century heroes, and he obviously had in mind the benign bee with its sweetness and light, in contrast to the entrail-spinning spider, now associated with the angry wasp. Although O'Casey had not yet identified himself with the avenging wasp, Yeats must have felt that the controversial dramatist was the antithesis of the bee. Furthermore, there are some implicit contradictions in his somewhat sentimental statement. The native literature and vigorous intellectual life which he and Lady Gregory and Synge had created in Dublin was a daring achievement, but it was seldom so remotely beautiful or gracious that it was free from bitterly rhetorical confrontations with the clerical and political enemies of the arts in Ireland. In fact, it was largely as a result of Yeats's genius for polemical energy and fearless courage under fire that the literary and dramatic renaissance in Ireland had been able to survive. In the non-professional sense, he was always a shrewd and formidable politician in his literary endeavours; in his strategic friendships with influential female friends and patrons; and in his founding of significant literary and dramatic societies. In his autobiography O'Casey had appropriately called Yeats 'the great organizer'. Therefore, while he was now looking forward to the serene and sweet life of a bee in his old age, it must be recognized that he had already served with great honour as a battle-scarred wasp in the cause of a free and distinguished literary movement. He was right to issue his warning about the dangers of government censorship of literature, yet he must have known that clericalism and anti-clericalism were hardly new forces in a country where the historically reactionary Catholic hierarchy had consistently opposed the fight for political freedom as well as the freedom of the literary movement, and had indeed exerted its considerable influence to persuade the government to impose the censorship bill. And as a final irony, it should be noted that there was little of the bee's sweetness or light in Yeats's arbitrary censorship of O'Casey's play.

Joyce also played with insect and animal fables in *Finnegans Wake*, and they have some relevance to the quarrel between the bee and the wasp. The Ondt and the Gracehoper represents his version of La Fontaine's fable of the Ant and the Grasshopper, in which Joyce's Shem, the artistic son of Earwicker, is the fun-loving Gracehoper whose carpe diem philosophy is preferred to the smug asceticism of his twin brother Shaun, the philistine, who is the prudent Ondt. In the Mookse and the Gripes, which is based on Aesop's fable about the Fox and the Grapes, Shaun becomes the magisterial Mookse associated with the infallible Pope, while Shem represents the independent Gripes, or the rebellious artist who refuses to submit to the authority of the Pope. There are palpable affinities here for O'Casey's rebellious wasp and crow, who are closer in spirit and action to Joyce's liberating Gracehoper and Gripes than they are to the repressive Ondt and Mookse, or to Yeats's remote and temporizing bee. Nevertheless, it should also be remembered that the persona of a raging and foolish old man which emerges in Yeats's *Last Poems* tends to place him closer to the comically creative and

angry crow of O'Casey's later years. In this context Yeats and
O'Casey share an affinity with Joyce's creative and eccentric
Shem, who is a wildly clownish as well as rebelliously artistic
figure, an attractive 'shemozzle' – a comic fool in Yiddish. In
many paradoxical ways, then, the bee and the wasp were drawing
closer together.

4. Druidic Affinities

Without trying to convert each other, the bee and the wasp had
decided to sit down together in a friendly manner in 1935. When
they first met in the Spring in London, Yeats made a peace
offering by suggesting that the Abbey Theatre should produce
Within the Gates, a play that Yeats curiously enough said was
far superior to *The Silver Tassie*, but O'Casey replied with typical
candour that they should do *The Silver Tassie* – a play that might
be easier for an Irish company to produce than the other work
which had so many Cockney and British characters to portray –
though he made a special point of leaving the final decision with
Yeats. He chose *The Silver Tassie*. It was too late for redemption,
but O'Casey must have felt relieved. On 12 August 1935 the
Abbey finally performed the Irish première of the play, but for a
limited run of one week, since prior to and during the performances a typical Dublin storm of abuse, the old tribal dance and
drums of controversy, as usual provoked by religious and nationalist pressure groups, was turned loose against Yeats for his
capitulation and against O'Casey for his 'blasphemous' play. A
month before the play was produced, an article from Dublin
appeared in the *New York Times*, 'And Back Home', by Hugh
Smith, datelined July 1st, printed on the 14th, apparently inspired
by the always active anti-Yeats faction, implying that a new board
of directors had overruled the poet with a 'bold and courageous'
policy of better things to come at the Abbey now that the theatre
had at least done belated justice to O'Casey. Refusing to take
advantage of this attempt to embarrass Yeats, however, O'Casey
quickly swung into action as soon as he had received a copy of
the paper and wrote a corrective letter on July 26th printed on
August 11th, defending Yeats and giving him full credit for the
decision to produce the play, stating publicly: 'Mr. Yeats will
never be anything less than a great poet and a great man.'

The two men were brought closer together by common enemies,
the Irish rabblement and the second-rate Irish backbiters who
envied both of them. To this day some of those disgruntled
writers and their Joxers in Dublin continue to sneer at the names

of Yeats and O'Casey, and they have on some occasions sought
jaundiced comfort in Patrick Kavanagh's cruel and unjust line
about Yeats as 'A cautious man whom no sin depraves.' When
O'Casey recorded his impressions of Yeats in *Rose and Crown*,
he was too forthright to go to the other extreme and draw a completely flattering portrait; he stressed his admiration of the poet's
genius and courage but had reservations about the way the man's
aristocratic bias added a quality of arrogance and remoteness
to his life and work. 'There was no braver man among the men
of Eireann than W. B. Yeats,' he wrote. 'In every fray of
politics, in every fight for freedom in literature and art, in every
effort to tempt Dublin's city into the lure of finer things, the
voice of Yeats belled out a battle-cry.' Nevertheless, no doubt
with the limitations of his own proletarian bias, O'Casey also
felt that Yeats was equally capable of retiring into that 'wallpaper
world' which he had tried to impose upon O'Casey: 'The poet
had played with his toys too long. Aristocratic toys, self-fashioned;
a few coloured with a wild philosophy, all tinged with beauty,
some even with a gracious grandeur; but he had played with them
all too long.' Then in an amusing aside, he speculated: 'Born
into the proletariat, Yeats would have made a magnificent docker.'
Fortunately, O'Casey realized, the world that lost a magnificent
docker gained a magnificent poet.

Yeats died on 28 January 1939, and at the end of the year, for
the December issue of a Russian magazine, *International Literature*, O'Casey wrote an article called 'Literature in Ireland', in
which he presented an introduction to Irish culture, politics and
literature. He stated that Joyce was the greatest novelist and Yeats
the greatest poet in the English language, but again he qualified
his judgment of Yeats. Next to Joyce, he said, 'The greatest
of these big figures was, undoubtedly, Yeats, the strange, dreamy,
faraway poet, who could, all in a moment, be so practical in the
affairs of the theatre. He is the great poet of the period, and so
far, possibly (to me, certainly), the greatest poet writing in the
English language.' After so much praise, however, he added that
for all his greatness Yeats sometimes 'fled too far away from the
common people, turning the poet into a cold aristocrat who
turned his head up to the heavens, looking at no-one below the
altitude of a star; failing to see that many, especially among the
workers, were themselves, in their own way, seeking a vision, more
roughly, perhaps, but no less deep than his own.'

It took a few more years, and in 1946 O'Casey finally overcame
his proletarian bias when he wrote a moving essay on Yeats

called 'Ireland's Silvery Shadow,' in which he composed a lyrical tribute of unparalled devotion to the memory of his once intimate enemy, now possibly his most kindred spirit. The angry wasp proved that he could write like a mellow bee. This little-known piece, originally commissioned by the B.B.C. Spanish Service and broadcast in a Spanish translation, has been resurrected and printed in English for the first time in Ronald Ayling's excellent edition of *Blasts and Benedictions* in 1967, three years after O'Casey's death. On this special occasion O'Casey had at last made his peace with the formidable wraith of Yeats. Now he celebrated Yeats's 'strange and magnificent genius' by comparing him to Parnell, and placing him among Lady Gregory's 'Gods and Fighting-men': no Irishman 'bore a tougher shield, a brighter sword, or a loftier crest, than W. B. Yeats, the poet' – and this was the highest praise which until now O'Casey had only bestowed upon Dublin's mighty Jim Larkin, the promethean labour leader. But even in the full flush of this myth-making mood, O'Casey, with the natural instinct of a dramatist, characteristically brought the god-like Yeats down to earth by giving him his fair share of human frailties: '. . . arrogant at times, not always wise; but vigorous, poetic, and of unbreakable integrity.' O'Casey might have been describing himself in these balanced phrases. In retrospect, therefore, when circumstances demanded a Swiftian metamorphosis, the bee could sting like a wasp and the wasp could sing like a bee.

Finally he addressed himself directly to the charge which he along with many others had levelled at Yeats, that he often assumed the attitude of a detached dreamer. He recalled one of Yeats's early poems, 'Fergus and the Druid,' in which King Fergus, tired and disenchanted with the life of action, somewhat like the aged Yeats who longed for the serene life of the bee, makes a bargain with a druid to exchange his kingdom for a miraculous bag of dreams. The king is now transformed into a poet, but in taking upon himself the druid's poetic insight he also becomes grey-haired and hollow-cheeked. Fergus willingly accepts the bargain, saying to the druid:

> A wild and foolish labourer is a king
> To do and do and do, and never dream.

O'Casey had used a pre-1925 edition of Yeats's poem which contains this early version of the poem. In later editions, however, Yeats revised and improved the lines to read:

> A king is but a foolish labourer
> Who wastes his blood to be another's dream.

Although O'Casey had a copy of the revised version, he apparently
felt that the earlier lines were more symbolically relevant to his
concern about the alternatives of *doing* and *dreaming*, the constant choice of action vs. art in Yeats's life and work, and also
in his own. Yeats often tried to reconcile the life of action and the
life of art, mythically in his series of Cuchulain plays, especially
in the personal allegory reflected so poignantly in *At the Hawk's
Well*, and more directly in his poem 'The Choice':

> The intellect of man is forced to choose
> Perfection of the life, or of the work,
> And if it take the second must refuse
> A heavenly mansion, raging in the dark.

The world-weary Fergus chose to rage in the dark by abandoning his kingdom for the druidic gift of dreams, the life of
imagination, the Yeatsian private mask or liberating anti-self. In
his final judgment, however, O'Casey saw Yeats as an even greater
Fergus, a poet of action who had perfected his life as well as his
art: 'Yeats, dreaming his life away, did and did as heartily as any
king. . . . This strange man, seeking the excitement of supernatural
knowledge, and, in his visionary life, casting but a careless thought
or two on the practical things which concern the movements of
a man's mortal existence; this man probing himself into the
mystery of the why and wherefore of what man called life; loving
the dream far more than the thing to do, or the thing done; yet
spent far more of his life in doing things than in dreaming about
them.' For evidence O'Casey then drew up an impressive
catalogue of 'the amazing number of active things that this man
crowded into his dreaming life': his founding of the Abbey
Theatre with Lady Gregory; his writing of plays and his untiring
work on them and the plays of others in rehearsal; his theatrical
innovations in the development of a new style of acting and
original scenic design; his constant search for and encouragement
of new playwrights; his courageous defence of his theatre and its
playwrights from continuous attacks by the Irish puritans and
patriots; his editing of a magazine in which he formulated and
publicized the principles of his theatre; his unceasing fight for
Ireland's ownership of the Hugh Lane Pictures; his notable
participation in political issues as a member of the Irish Senate;

and many more constructive deeds in the practical world. 'So you see,' O'Casey concluded, 'Yeats was a doer, and a hearty one as well as a dreamer.'

At this point in his essay, after so much praise of the life of militant action, O'Casey was prompted to consider his own creative impulse in relation to his active deeds. Touched by the druidic affinities himself, he revealed his innermost feelings by presenting his own version of Fergus's choice, his defence of the life of art, the *dreaming* as superior to the *doing*: 'To do and never to dream is worse than to dream but never to do; for to dream and never to do is to at least live in a rich state, even though it be an unnatural condition to striving humanity; but to do, and never to dream, is to humiliate that humanity into insignificance, and to dishonour the colour and form in that arrangement of things by God which man calls life.'

This revelation by O'Casey the artist should not come as too great a surprise, for there can be no doubt that while he was a lifelong socialist committed to political change and the improvement of living conditions for all people everywhere, and often fought for that belief, he also lived and wrote in a rich state of powerful dreams. In his early plays he had exposed and laughed at cowardly dreamers like Donal Davoren and 'Captain' Boyle because they humiliated humanity by following the wrong selfish dreams, pipedreams as O'Neill called them. In *The Silver Tassie* and *Within the Gates* he had attacked those illusions which prevented people from seeing that perhaps more than anything else, war and poverty 'dishonour the colour and form in that arrangement of things by God which man calls life.'

Furthermore, it might be said that O'Casey expanded his own bargain with the druid when he turned to a comic affirmation of dreams in his later plays: in the carnival of fantastic dreams presided over by Philib O'Dempsey and the Irish rustics in *Purple Dust* (1940); in the mystical transformation of Dublin in the dream sequence on the banks of the Liffey inspired by Ayamonn Breydon and the Celtic heroes in *Red Roses For Me* (1942); in the liberating dances of the good women led by Robin Adair and the miraculous Cock in the Aesopian and Swiftian *Cock-a-Doodle Dandy* (1949); in the prophetic masquerade of the festive tostaleers looking for God in the street in *The Drums of Father Ned* (1958); and, finally, in the heroic and comic six-volume autobiography, that great dream-book which has druidic affinities with the great dream-books of Joyce. For all the characters in those plays, and for O'Casey himself, who emerges from his epic dreams with a mighty 'Hurrah!', it must be said that, in the spirit of Yeats's druidic epigraph from an Old Play, 'In dreams begins responsibility.' Dreamers all, and many of them visionary clowns who weave laughter into the fabric of the dream, they are responsible to themselves, to mankind, and to God's arrangement of things.

Late in August 1931, only a few days before O'Casey expressed his eloquent rage in his letter to Charlotte Shaw about wielding his two-edged sword of thought, Yeats finished a poem about intemperate speech in which he summed up this final affinity between these two angry and visionary Irish titans:

> Out of Ireland have we come.
> Great hatred, little room
> Maimed us at the start.
> I carry from my mother's womb
> A fanatic heart.

SEAN O'CASEY
ART AND POLITICS

ROBERT G. LOWERY

The artist must take sides. He must elect to fight for freedom or slavery. I have made my choice.

Paul Robeson

Every art is rooted in the life of the people – what they see, do, how they hear, all they touch and taste; how they live, love, and go to the grave.

Sean O'Casey

What do you think an artist is? An imbecile who has only his eyes if he is a painter, or his ears if a musician, or a lyre at every level of the heart throbs if he is a poet . . . ? On the contrary, he is at the same time a political being, constantly on the alert to the heart-rendering, burning, or happy events in the world, molding himself in their likeness.

Pablo Picasso

Much of what has passed for criticism of Sean O'Casey's politics has tended to qualify his sympathies for Communism. This is due in part to a general anti-Communism among Western critics, a distrust of all ideologies, and a feeling that ideologies have a detrimental effect on artists and writers. What one critic wrote about Brecht has been said a hundred different ways about a hundred different writers who professed Communism:

The lost paradise – the romantic fairy tale garden of Baal – must be replaced by a new modern and more palpable paradise. This is why Brecht, like so many others who at one time were infatuated with an unrestrained freedom, found himself in the ranks of the totalitarians.[1]

Many western critics have for a long time indulged in this what-if,

121

isn't-it-a-pity kind of criticism, and several who followed the career of O'Casey have expressed the same sentiments.

O'Casey's sympathy with Communism has been seen as something foreign to his nature, alien to his development, harmful to his art, and as an aberration of 'real' Communism to which his endearing qualities were a natural antithesis. It was dark, conspiratorial totalitarianism on one hand and O'Casey's passionate egalitarianism on the other, both joined together in an inexplicable sense of illusionary imbalance. Brooks Atkinson could write, with complete sincerity, that 'O'Casey's Communism is *really* a dream of a better life for mankind' (emphasis added)[2] for this was the image of goodness that the dramatist imparted: a humanist who saw the future and asked why not.

While bourgeois critics lamented the politics of the later O'Casey, Leftist critics have lamented the early O'Casey. He has been found guilty of political degeneracy because of his criticisms of James Connolly; guilty of male chauvanism because of his antagonism toward Countess Constance Markiewicz and for the way in which women were dramatized in his plays; and guilty of slandering the working class in his three major plays. These critics have counterposed O'Casey against a gamut of experts ranging from Lenin to Mike Gold and the conclusion is always the same: at best, the dramatist's early works were naive; at worst, they were counter or anti-revolutionary and harmful to the labour movement.

It should not be surprising that the political criticisms of O'Casey meet and overlap. For instance, Gabriel Fallon and Saros Cowasjee from the Right agree with C. Desmond Greaves and Carl and Ann Reeve[3] that O'Casey did not embrace Communism until around 1940. Cowasjee, Greaves and the Reeves are convinced that *The Plough and the Stars* contains cowards while Fallon, Greaves and Cowasjee believe that O'Casey was not a socialist in the 1920s. There are a gaggle of other critics who fall into one or the other category but who find agreement at points of political controversy.

It is the thesis of this essay that Sean O'Casey's politics can be seen as a continuation and integration of Maxist theory. 'His' Communism was not a distortion or an aberration of traditional Marxist values nor was it antithetical to the aims and goals of Marxist parties around the world. It was in fact a contribution to Marxist values. His style, considered by some to be heretical to Socialist Realism, was in accord with the experimentation promoted by the leading Marxist literary theoreticians, including

Anatoly Lunacharsky and even Karl Marx himself. His politics have been misinterpreted by most critics – both Left and Right – and not always for literary purposes. What is needed is an understanding of his politics, and especially of 'his' Communism, the philosophy by which he was most singularly identified. Within that context we need to understand his relationship to the socialist theories of art and politics which dominated his era, his acceptance or rejection of them and why, and his contribution to them. Although his political and artistic writings have been examined in the light of Irish history, they have not been accorded the same examination from the perspective of socialist history. If, as I believe, O'Casey's contributions were socialist critiques, then they must be measured against a socialist standard.

When O'Casey called for Countess Markiewicz's resignation from the Irish Citizen Army Council in 1914 and publicly rebuked James Connolly five years later, he unwittingly entered into a political controversy which has yet to be satisfactorly resolved: the socialist's response to nationalism. Although these two events may seem minor in the life of one of the world's foremost dramatists, they have become, along with the shewing-up of nationalism in his drama, the primary political events by which O'Casey is known to Irish nationalists and socialists. To both these groups O'Casey was an enigma. Although the nationalists opposed socialism and welcomed a negation of Connolly's revolutionary views, O'Casey was too much a Communist for them; although the Irish socialists disdained bourgeois nationalism, which O'Casey attacked, the dramatist had also attacked the founder of Irish socialism.

The facts may be briefly stated. O'Casey as secretary of the ICA proposed the expulsion of Countess Markiewicz because she was affiliated with the Irish Volunteers, a bourgeois nationalist army, which at that time had just come under the control of John Redmond's Irish Parliamentary Party. His motion was narrowly defeated and he resigned. In 1919, using records and papers from the ICA, O'Casey wrote a short history, *The Story of the Irish Citizen Army*. In it, O'Casey wrote that Connolly, far from being a socialist martyr in the 1916 Rising, had in fact renounced internationalism for the cause of Ireland. Later, in *Drums under the Windows* (1944), the dramatist amplified the charges against both people. He continued to believe it until the day he died.

In a capitalist society, the choice between nationalism and socialism for socialists is easy to make. In almost every normal situation the choice will be for socialism. Nationalism, the socialist believes, is and has been a sham with which to fool the working class. It sets nation against nation for the interests of a handful of capitalists who rule. The working-class's interests should be and are with the working classes of other countries rather than with the capitalist class of his own, for the problems of the proletariat of any country are similar to those in other countries: wages, jobs, food, rent, and peace. Moreover, the socialist believes that true democracy can only be so when the interests of the majority of people are the ruling ideas of any country and ultimately the world. Capitalism and democracy are incompatible because the power of the ruling class is vested in the hands of the minority – the capitalists – rather than with the majority – the working class. There are fundamentals and most socialists agree on them.

Problems arise, however, when situations develop which are not endemic to the theories of socialism. For instance, socialists must undoubtedly oppose the ruling class. Yet this by itself does not say whether or not socialists should stand for election to parliaments in capitalist-ruled countries. If so, should socialists form their own parties or should they 'bore from within' bourgeois parties? Socialists should assist the working class, but they should from their own trade unions, should they join and influence existing ones, or both? Socialists should oppose wars, but *all* wars? Clearly not, or perhaps it's not so clear. Socialists should support the rights of minorities, but should they support nationalist movements among minorities? Are minorities more than or part of an oppressed class? What if the 'minority' are women, not such a minority at all? There's hardly a socialist party in the world which hasn't had to deal with these problems, and some are still dealing with them.

Many of these and other problems have been attacked and seemingly resolved by socialists. Of these, Lenin, more than any other socialist, wrote on a wide range of subjects and his writings have been accepted in one form or another as wisdom. But Lenin wrote with two factors in mind: Marxist ideology and the situation at hand. While the former supposedly cuts across national and cultural difficulties, it itself has often evolved from specific national and cultural difficulties; it is, therefore, not as workable in one situation as it is in another. Local conditions, with historical and ideological considerations, have almost always determined the course of action for most socialists.

Such was the case with Ireland. The original Marxist standard on Ireland came, appropriately enough, from Karl Marx who, with Friedrich Engels, was deeply interested in and extraordinarily knowledgeable about Ireland's history, culture and politics. Ireland, they believed, was probably the most important country in the world *vis* international socialism. While industrial England was the key to world revolution because of its power and far-flung empire, Ireland was the key to the British workers' class-consciousness. England's working class, Marx wrote, would never accomplish anything, much less establish socialism, until they had forced the ruling class to divest themselves of Ireland. At the same time, a free Ireland, however gained, would free the British working class from their chauvanistic attitudes toward the other colonies and would precipitate England's downfall. Therefore, concluded Marx, Ireland, because of its special relationship to England, had an obligation to be more nationalistic than internationalistic.[4]

James Connolly developed his own theory which, though not incompatible with Marx, was more attuned to local conditions. In essence, it was a two-stage programme for freedom. The Irish people, Connolly believed, must have national independence before they could achieve socialism. The centuries-old national question was an albatross which had to be discarded before the working class could evolve to a state of class consciousness necessary to establish socialism. From a tactical standpoint, Connolly believed it made better sense to present socialism with an Irish face to Irish workers and to demonstrate that Irish socialists were as deeply believing in national independence as the most fervent nationalist. The roots of Irish socialism, therefore, were in the long struggle for freedom by the Irish people.[5]

But Connolly was a rare bird, and his theories were not shared by the majority of his comrades in the world socialist movement – the majority of whom, it should be pointed out, were from independent countries. It is easy to forget that the years of the Second International (1880–1914) fostered the unerring belief that nationalism in every form was anathema to socialism. As with most absolutes this one went to ludicrous lengths. For instance, Harry Hyndman, leader of the British socialists, argued against recognition of Connolly's Irish Socialist Republican Party (ISRP) at the International Socialist Congress in Paris in 1900, believing that his, Hyndman's, party represented all the workers in the British Isles. Connolly, Hyndman stated, was only encouraging nationalism by insisting upon separate recognition. The British and other socialist parties had their own colonial policy and worked on the theory that socialism would come to

Ireland and the other colonies when socialism came to the mother countries.[6]

The socialist policy of those years was given great impetus by the writings of Rosa Luxemburg, an outstanding socialist from Poland. In 1908–09 she wrote a series of articles which in effect argued against the independence of her own country, at that time erased from the map of Europe. Luxemburg formulated the theory that while Poland had a moral right to national freedom from the Russians, Germans and Austrians, independence was illusionary because it would only reinstitute the powers of the Polish nobles and bourgeoisie, who were not much better than foreign oppressors. Self-determination, she said, was only meaningful if it was not in the abstract, as for instance with the concept of nationhood. Self-determination for the bourgeoisie was not the same thing as self-determination for the working class. Far better, she believed, to agitate for socialism among the working class and bypass the stage of so-called independence. In the end, only an international socialist revolution would solve the problems of national domination of one country by another and Poland should join with the already-independent nations to bring about that revolution.[7]

In 1913, at the behest of Lenin, Stalin was directed to answer Luxemburg. The result was the poorly-written *Marxism and the National Question*. Stalin found that, 'In its essence, the national struggle is always a bourgeois struggle, one that is chiefly favourable to and suitable for the bourgeoisie.'[8] Though Lenin praised Stalin's pamphlet, he couldn't have been satisfied with it since he wrote his own rebuttal to Luxemburg one year later: *On the Right of Nations to Self-Determination*. It was a difficult position for Lenin to be in. He, like Luxemburg, opposed splitting up the world into new, small and non-viable states. Both believed in the Marxist principle of the economic advantage of larger units and federations. And, of course, he too believed in an international socialist revolution which took precedent over all nationalist claims. Despite the fact than Lenin's rebuttal was overruled by a majority of the Communist Party of the Soviet Union in 1919 (and the slogan of the right of self-determination removed from its platform), his arguments are quite persuasive and they remain the basic Marxist position on the national question.

Almost ten years previously, Lenin, in response to the Armenian Social Democrats' demand for self-determination for Armenia, wrote: 'We on our part concern ourselves with the self-determination of the *proletariat* in each nationality rather than with the self-determination of peoples or nations.'[9] In 1914, though, Lenin approached the question in terms of the duties of socialists from oppressor countries toward the nationalist movements in oppressed countries, with particular reference to Asia and Africa. To Lenin, self-determination of nations means 'Political self-determination, state independence, and the formulation of a national state.' Toward that end: 'The bourgeois nationalism of *any* oppressed nation has a general democratic content that is directed *against* oppression, and it is this content that we *unconditionally* support.'[10] In her articles, Luxemburg had called Polish independence 'utopian' and had asked rhetorically, why not raise the demand for the independence of Ireland? Lenin responded to this only by repeating Marx's position on the question, saying that his writing 'has lost none of its immense *practical* importance'.[11] He added one unexplored and illuminating note, though: 'In England the bourgeois revolution had been consummated long ago. But it had not yet been consummated in Ireland [in Marx's time]; *it is being consummated only now*, after a lapse of half a century by the reforms of the English liberals' (emphasis added).[12]

Lenin's comment about the reforms taking place in Ireland is valuable because it sheds light on the validity of Connolly's theory. Marxists have believed that certain stages of history are not only inevitable but necessary. The jump from feudalism to socialism cannot take place without an intermediate bourgeois revolution, for it is this stage which transforms and revolutionizes the means of production so necessary for socialism. The capitalists develop capital – factories and equipment – to such a high degree that its ownership becomes societal, necessitating socialism. The attractiveness of Connolly's two-stage theory is obvious: it seems to correspond to Marx. Connolly was saying that Ireland could not develop a socialist political movement without first achieving bourgeois reforms. In most colonized countries of Asia and Africa where conditions approached serfdom, Connolly's theory would have had more merit. But the political reforms in Ireland, despite it being a colonized nation, were, in Lenin's eyes, being consummated in 1914, not by Ireland itself but 'by the reforms of the English liberals'. It would seem to indicate less of a need, from Lenin's view, for Ireland to go through a bourgeois revolution than it would have been where such reforms were lacking.

It is clear that O'Casey's arguments closely paralleled both Luxemburg and Lenin. Implicit in their position was the theory that the political freedom and economic development was sufficient to allow for socialist education and organization: prime requisites for developing a revolutionary socialist movement. Equally important: O'Casey and Luxemburg believed that their respective countries had a strong base of industrialization and an active, urban, revolutionary working class. In Ireland, the latter was most dramatically demonstrated during the 1913 Lockout when the city of Dublin was virtually paralyzed for several months. That the Lockout was won by the employers does not invalidate the workers' actions: their sustained militancy showed them to be not merely a class *of* itself but one *for* itself – one of Marx's maxims for revolutionists. The Lockout and the many strikes before it had not negated the national questions: far from it. But the workers' militancy had given the question more of a social content than was present in the Land League struggles of the late 19th century: enough, in O'Casey's opinion, to change the emphasis of the struggle. The economic development was manifested by a large Irish bourgeoisie – large for a country of Ireland's size – which, though dependent upon England's co-operation (as capitalism is always dependent upon free trade), was distinctly Irish-oriented. The William Martin Murphys were ruling Ireland more for themselves than for England. In O'Casey's view, therefore, Ireland was a developed country, both politically and economically, and was not too primitive to proceed to socialism. Primitiveness was more a mark of the Russian economy of 1917.

Objectively, O'Casey's attack on Countess Markiewicz was a classic case of local conditions imposed on ideology and flavoured with personality clashes. Though the Irish Volunteers and the ICA were founded almost simultaneously in late 1913, they served different causes. The Volunteers arose in response to Lord Edward Carson's Ulster Volunteers and the threat of partition while the ICA was formed to protect the workers during the Lockout. The two armies' class composition, while similar among the rank and file, was radically different at the leadership level. One was dominated by bourgeois politicians, such as John Redmond, Home Rulers, and petty capitalists; the other was led by trade unionists and revolutionaries, such as James Larkin and Connolly. The 'democratic content' which Lenin urged socialists to support would have been hard to find among the leadership of the Volunteers during the Lockout, for many of them opposed the strike and condemned Larkin, Connolly and the ICA. Despite class antagonisms, though, efforts were made to unite the two, if only provisionally. Mutual gatherings and debates were suggested, a sharing of meeting halls was proposed, and joint marches to Wolfe Tone's grave at Bodenstown were formulated. All these united front efforts emanated from the ICA, probably at the instigation of Larkin who realized the danger of workers being fooled by nationalist propaganda. The results were that at nearly every turn the ICA was rebuffed. Eoin MacNeill, chief of the Volunteers, steadfastly refused to allow the Volunteers to meet with the ICA. O'Casey, as secretary, was involved in every facet of these efforts: drafting requests and proposals and being the first to hear of the denial.[13]

Countess Markiewicz was on the staff of the Volunteers during this time and could have played a role in influencing them to accept or reject the ICA's offers. Although O'Casey and Larkin had been hostile to her since the Lockout, they submerged their antagonisms in the interest of unity. Certainly they made no move to oust her though Larkin wasn't above embarrassing her as when he exercised a pocket-veto of a union proclamation honouring her. (It was finally given to her by Connolly after Larkin had left for the U.S. and after O'Casey had left the ICA.)[14]

The hostility of the Volunteers' leadership toward the ICA combined with two other events to force a confrontation between O'Casey and Markiewicz. First, the Volunteers acceded to the demand of the Irish Parliamentary Party for the inclusion of a large number of nominees upon their Provisional Committee. O'Casey and Larkin immediately increased their attacks upon the Volunteers through the *Irish Worker*. Neither Markiewicz nor Connolly agreed with or took part in the attacks and O'Casey suggests that, by their isolation, they grew closer together.[15] Second, Larkin had announced his intention of leaving for the United States for a lecture and fund-raising tour and that he was leaving P. T. Daly in charge of the union. After much discussion and behind-the-scenes squabbling, Larkin was overruled and Connolly was chosen by the future Free State union leadership to be Larkin's successor.[16] It is not hard to imagine Larkin's and O'Casey's chagrin at this turn of events. It is also not difficult to understand the attack (led by O'Casey but undoubtedly approved by Larkin) on Markiewicz. She was vulnerable in both cases: she was close to the Volunteers, objectively the class enemy, and she was close to Connolly.[17]

What then of Connolly? After the Rising, the world socialist community was aghast. Connolly was a well-known and valuable socialist, and the majority opinion was that he had sacrificed himself without reason. While in prison awaiting execution, Connolly had allegedly remarked to his daughter: 'The socialists will never understand why I am here. They will all forget that

I am an Irishman.'[18] He was only partially right. The socialists
of Europe and America, both Right and Left, knew what he did
and they attributed it to the fact that he was indeed acting like
an Irishman. William Bohn spoke for many when he wrote:

> James Connolly stands as a warning and as a guide. Under
> different circumstances he might have played a part in the world
> movement like that of Keir Hardie or Bebel. As things are,
> he goes down fighting in a heroically foolhardy skirmish.[19]

James Larkin was 'stunned' and Victor Berger was amazed that
Connolly would die in such a way. Hyndman, typically imperialistic
and by now more a British nationalist than a socialist, called those
in the Rising 'reckless fanatics' who took 'hopeless risks at a most
serious crisis in *our* foreign and domestic affairs' (emphasis
added).[20] The *Socialist Review*, organ of the Independent Labour
Party, wrote: 'In no degree do we approve the Sinn Fein Rebellion. We do not approve of armed rebellion at all, any more than
any other form of militarism and war.'[21] The Glasgow socialist
Forward, which had published many of Connolly's articles, commented: 'One must be either a nationalist or an internationalist.'[22]
Two Bolsheviks, Karl Radek and Leon Trotsky, disdained the
Rising. Radek called it a 'putsch' and Trotsky wrote that the
reason for its failure was that the Irish working class 'attracted
to itself the young intelligentsia and some nationalist enthusiasts,
who in turn have ensured the preponderance, in the working class
movement, of the Green Flag over the Red.'[23] In Ireland, James
Stephens, while not a socialist but who was a witness to the
rebellion, wrote essentially the same thing:

> The organised labour discontent in Ireland, in Dublin, was not
> considerable enough to impose its aims or its colours on the
> Volunteers, and it is the labour ideal which merges and dis-
> appears in the national one. The reputation of all the leaders
> of the insurrection, not excepting Connolly, is that they were
> intensely patriotic Irishmen, and also, that they were not
> particularly interested in the problems of labour.[24]

Once again, though, Lenin saw things differently and
approached the Rising from another perspective. He avoided
moralizing over whether or not Connolly should have taken part
in the Rising. That wasn't the important point. To Lenin, the
Rising was part of the crisis of European imperialism. Along with
this insurrection, there had been a mutiny among Indian troops

in the British Army in Singapore and attempts at rebellion in French Annam and in the German Cameroons. National revolt had broken out in the colonies and in Europe, and this went far to sharpen the revolutionary crisis in Europe. As for Ireland, in no way could that be called a putsch:

> For to imagine that social revolution is *conceivable* without revolts by small nations in the colonies and in Europe, without the revolutionary outbursts of a section of the petty bourgeoisie *with all its prejudices*, without a movement of politically non-consciousness and semi-proletarian masses against landlord, church, monarchal, national and other oppression – to imagine that means *repudiating social revolution*. Very likely one army will line up in one place and say, 'We are for socialism,' while another will do so in another place and say, 'We are for imperialism,' and that will be the social revolution! Only from such a ridiculously pedantic angle could one label the Irish rebellion a 'putsch'.

> Whoever expects a 'pure' social revolution will *never* live to see it. Such a person pays lip service to revolution without understanding what revolution really is. (Lenin's emphasis throughout.)[25]

Lenin concluded by invoking the same geographical standard formulated by Marx and echoed by himself two years previously: 'A blow delivered against British imperialist bourgeois rule by a rebellion in Ireland is of a hundred times greater political significance than a blow of equal weight in Asia or in Africa.'[26]

However concise and illuminating Lenin's arguments are, they leave many unanswered questions. Is it significant that Lenin does not mention Connolly? Three years earlier he had paid tribute to Larkin's role in the Lockout[27] (and was thus aware of the personalities), but his analysis of the Rising has nothing to say about Connolly. If he specifically endorsed Connolly's role, would this have been taken as a blanket approval for socialists around the world to go to the barricades for every nationalist insurrection against imperialism? Would this have not been suicidal for the socialist movement, a movement whose members were already deserting in droves for the cause of nationalism and patriotism? It is doubtful, then, that Lenin's defence of the rebellion was a statement of general policy. More likely, it was a specific defence of a specific action. Evidence for this is found

in the fact that Lenin consistently tied the Irish insurrection
directly to the European crisis. Moreover, the Bolshevik leaders
had long believed that for a Russian revolution to succeed it must
be accompanied by revolutions in the West. World War I had
precipitated a crisis which, Lenin hoped, would hasten those
revolutions. Ireland, again because of its geographical importance,
could have been the starting point. Objectively, Ireland was
important to the international socialist revolution, and a rebellion,
any rebellion against imperialism, with or without labour's or
Connolly's participation, would have been approved of by Lenin.
Lenin was far too objective and scientific in his approach to
revolution to let something like the class content of the insurrection sway him. His concern was always the objective results
of the event.

Lenin's writings on the Rising, which weren't translated into
English until 1929,[28] have often been used against O'Casey.[29]
According to this reasoning, Lenin's approval of the Rising
constitutes an approval of Connolly which signifies an approval
of Connolly's tactics, i.e., of joining forces with the nationalists
in a united front. Since O'Casey criticized this tactic, this is
tantamount to criticizing Lenin. As I've tried to show, this
reasoning is fallacious. Connolly's united front was hardly original,
having been attempted by Larkin and O'Casey. There is even
some question whether or not Connolly's united front attempts
were as successful or as well thought out as his supporters
maintain. O'Casey and others have written of the 'revolutionary
change' that occurred in Connolly's behaviour during the months
of 1915.[30] The Irish Communist Party have said that with the
outbreak of the war, Connolly quit working for the formation
of a strong political party.[31] This was certainly a major change
in emphasis from his earlier actions. All his energies went into the
ICA. His alliance with the Irish Volunteers was directed to pushing
them into revolution, but his writings reveal that he was
exasperated by their indecision.[32] The Volunteers, led by Eoin
MacNeill, had not set a date for a rebellion and were probably
more concerned with the threat from Carson's Ulster Volunteers
and the possibility of partition. Elements within the Volunteers
were sympathetic to Connolly's plans and would have followed
him into rebellion, but Connolly's impatience wore so thin that
he threatened to take his small army out alone, even if no one
supported him. One can only speculate what Lenin's reaction
would have been had this transpired: the cream of the Irish
working class going out alone, in Connolly's words, 'to be

slaughtered'.[33] In the end, of course, it was not Connolly who set the date for the Rising; it was the IRB who, in January 1916, co-opted or kidnapped Connolly for fear his actions would precipitate a premature British reaction. The IRB had already set a date, Easter Sunday, and would surely have risen, with or without Connolly, just as Connolly would have risen, with or without the IRB or the Volunteers. This fortuitous timing and the link between Connolly and the IRB, then, can hardly be seen as a grand scheme for a united front.

Brooks Atkinson thought it was significant that O'Casey never joined the Communist Party. Perhaps it was, for O'Casey made a point in his autobiography of mentioning that he was 'a voluntary and settled exile from every creed, from every party'.[34] Of course, Marx, when he too was once in limbo, wrote that he belonged to no organized party except that one which 'naturally grows, everywhere, from the soil of modern life'.[35] Metaphors aside, though, Atkinson's comment raises several questions. What were O'Casey's experiences with all radical parties during the 1920s and 1930s? What was his relationship to the Communist Party and how was he perceived by them? How did his commitment to Communism affect his writing?

There were good reasons for O'Casey to distrust political parties. He had belonged to several and his 'bent for criticism' often got him in trouble. He left or was expelled from the Irish Republican Brotherhood because he criticized their refusal to establish links with the labour movement. He left the Gaelic League after criticizing their reluctance to recruit working-class Protestants. His Citizen Army sojourn ended abruptly when his efforts to expel Countess Markiewicz failed. Here, he had the temerity to criticize Larkin and lost a valuable ally for a while. O'Casey joined the Socialist Party of Ireland, the forerunner of the Irish Communist Party, around 1917, probably out of sympathy with the Russian Revolution, but he did not stay for long.[36] No reasons were given for his departure but it was probably due to several. First, the SPI was dominated by William O'Brien and Cathal O'Shannon, two of Larkin's rivals. Second, O'Casey's dramatic efforts were beginning to occupy more of his time. And, third, he had met and fallen in love with Maura Keating and that occupied much of his time.

O'Casey resumed his political activities in earnest in November 1921 as secretary of the James Larkin Correspondence Committee, which was set up to agitate for Larkin's release from Sing Sing

prison in the United States. Although he seems to have played
a role in the closing of Dublin's docks for one day to protest
Larkin's imprisonment, his primary job was as secretary, sending
out thousands of letters and appeals. When Larkin returned to
Dublin, he made a bid to recapture the labour movement, but
O'Casey seems to have played little part in it. Even Larkin's
election to the Comintern in Moscow in 1924 and the triumphant
torch-light parade on his return to Dublin doesn't seem to have
involved O'Casey. Of course there is little doubt that Larkin
wanted O'Casey, not only because of his long years of loyalty
but also because of O'Casey's skill as secretary. Yet O'Casey
abstained, probably because he realized that he was a political
liability and would only hurt Larkin's chances.[37] O'Casey was
still known as the man who criticized the Easter Rising.

The Easter Rising, O'Casey wrote, produced 'a curtain of dark
separation'[38] between him and other socialists, and this can be
seen as one of the primary reasons for his curtailed political
activity during the 1920s. It was an extraordinary thing for
O'Casey to write what he did in the *Story of the Irish Citizen
Army*. In 1918, the martyrdom of the leaders of the Rising was
sweeping the country like a mania. Its publication came on the
heels of the 1918 General Election when the Irish Parliamentary
Party was swept out of existence and Sinn Fein was riding a tidal
wave of support. It was also a courageous thing for O'Casey to
write what he did and for Darrell Figgis to publish it. It was, it
seems safe to assume, read widely within the Republican and
labour movements, and it surely stamped O'Casey as someone
to be avoided.

For O'Casey's part, the feeling was mutual. There is no
evidence that he sought to return to the labour movement. He had
no desire to re-enter the trade unions, for they had embraced
Connolly and the Rising as political symbols. Moreover, those in
control of labour, O'Shannon and O'Brien, were his and Larkin's
past enemies, and all the old animosities came to the surface
when they launched a bitter campaign to prevent Larkin from
taking over the labour movement.[39] Aside from this, O'Casey
believed that labour was selling out its demands of the Free State
government for the sake of 'unity,' and he had heard that story
in the years before the Rising. When labour raised no protest
against the appointment of Countess Markiewicz as Minister of
Labour to the First Dail, O'Casey must have reasoned that there
was little to be saved in the labour movement.[40]

The fledgling Communist Party of Ireland (CPI), which would

have been O'Casey's only other choice (if only because they expelled O'Shannon and O'Brien) was also found wanting. They too adopted Connolly as their spiritual founder and appointed Connolly's son, Roddy, as first secretary. In addition, Larkin, upon his return, refused to have anything to do with the CPI because it had little following among the working class. Larkin's decision was sound for the Party soon disbanded and many of its members joined him.[41] It is doubtful, then, that O'Casey would have felt comfortable in the Communist Party.

From their friendship, O'Casey must have known that Larkin was privately critical of Connolly's role in the Rising.[42] Yet Larkin could not say so publicly for fear of losing what support he had and giving his enemies new ammunition. In effect he too had to embrace Connolly and the Rising. So O'Casey's decision not to rejoin Larkin was wise. It was one thing to oppose the bourgeois trade union leaders: even Larkin did this. But it was entirely different to have gone on record as opposing Connolly, the martyr, and, more important, the Easter Rising. With *The Plough and the Stars*, of course, the separation between O'Casey and practically all Irish socialists became irrevocable, and even Larkin couldn't have helped him. No party would have wanted him.

There is reason to suspect that O'Casey's inability to function within the Irish political structure contributed to his decision to leave Dublin. It could not have been an easy decision to make. He had, after all, been intensely involved as either a participant or observer in the making of modern Ireland. He had witnessed or helped make momentous events in his country's political and cultural history. He had rescued the Abbey Theatre from certain bankruptcy and he was clearly the toast of Dublin's artistic circles. But his success as a dramatist was blunted by hard realities. O'Casey was far too cagey to be fooled by his stature as one of Ireland's premier playwrights. While the success of his three major Dublin plays insured him some income it by no means set him up for life. Theatre history is full of examples of dramatists who wrote a few good plays and then faded away into obscurity, grubbing for the odd dollar and trying once more for the magic moment. O'Casey knew that he had to continue to write plays in order to live and it was evident that he had pushed his luck to the limit. He had ridiculed and condemned the Easter Rising, the War of Independence, the Civil War, and the labour movement, and it was only a matter of time before fate caught up with him. He was putting his views on stage for all to see and, in time, his drama was sure to be censored (as had been tried with the *Plough*).

Soon, his views would be stifled and his living would be curtailed. Yeats and Lady Gregory, who had done the most to encourage him, were ageing and the directorship of the Abbey was passing into other hands: to people from whom O'Casey might not gain a sympathetic hearing. Unless his success continued he knew that he would have to find another way of earning a living. From his days as an agitator during the 1913 Lockout, O'Casey knew that Dublin offered no security to a man who was politically blackballed. Those who controlled the civil service and other employment were unlikely to take a chance on him in view of his work record, his past associations, and his open hostility to what was fast becoming a Catholic state. Those he had actively opposed and castigated were now in power: the capitalists, the nationalists, and the church. Since there was not much call for a half-blind fifty-year-old labourer and since returning to the dole was unthinkable, the choice seemed to have been made for him. It didn't take a weatherman to know which way the wind was blowing.

Most literary studies of O'Casey begin their analyses of his sympathies with Communism with the play, *The Star Turns Red*. It is a logical starting point if one's aim is to outline chronologically the *use* of Communism in his plays.[43] It does, however, lead to the erroneous conclusion that since this play is the first work in which he wrote about Communism, then the date of the play (1940) is the date of his 'conversion'. Using that logic, one might as well conclude that 1928 was the date O'Casey first became interested in World War I and that 1940 was the time of his interest in the 1913 Lockout.

The conversion theory is fallacious for two reasons. First, it ignores O'Casey's common sense. To suggest that a man of sixty years of age, especially one with O'Casey's intelligence – and scepticism – would suddenly convert to Communism at the time of the attacks on the validity of the Moscow trials, at the time of the Nazi-Soviet pact, and at the time when the British *Daily Worker* was being suppressed is nonsense. Those were not what anyone would call inspirational times. Second, the conversion theory does not satisfactorily address itself to O'Casey's political beliefs before the 'conversion'. Mike Gold, the American Communist writer, referred to O'Casey in 1937 as a 'muddled liberal'.[44] The dramatist was busy writing *The Star Turns Red* and defending Spanish democracy with his pen at the time, and he never replied to Gold. C. Desmond Greaves refers to O'Casey's 1930 period as being one of an 'artistic elite'. Stephen Spender, who was in the Communist Party all of one week (out of which came two books: a record), called the *Star* 'Christian socialism'. If we put this all together we find that O'Casey went from the extreme nationalism of the Gaelic League and IRB to the revolutionary socialism of the Transport Workers' Union, ICA, and SPI to a combination 'muddled liberal'/'artistic elite' in the 1930s, and finally to Communism/'Christian Socialism' in 1940. A muddled path, indeed, if it were true.

It is important to realize that the late 1920s and 1930s were disjointed years for O'Casey, years not conducive to political activism. They were years of retrenchment, re-evaluation, and consolidation of the gains he had made as a dramatist. He was now exclusively a playwright, earning his living in no other way and having no other source or potential source of income. Even when times were good, they were not prosperous. When times were bad, they were very bad, a pattern of life that was to plague O'Casey for the rest of his years.

Although he left Ireland in March 1926 feeling bitter, things looked promising. The move to London signalled a fresh start and wider vistas. He was a celebrated dramatist coming to accept a prestigious literary award (which he received with a few words of Gaelic) and a full season of his plays had opened at the Fortune Theatre.[45] He was at work on a new play ('the best play I've written') and was already thinking of an autobiography. Within a short time he met Eileen Carey and a year after their marriage their first son was born.

Artistically, London had much to offer. O'Casey looked forward to new audiences, new directors and new actors and actresses. No longer would he be limited by the small confines of the Dublin stage, for, although London did not have a national theatre like the Abbey, it had ten times the number of theatres and this dramatically increased his chances of getting his plays staged. Further, London, as always, abounded with artists and intellectuals and writers and poets, including his soon-to-be close friends, Augustus John and George Bernard Shaw. There is probably little truth to the charge that O'Casey's head was 'turned' by this new environment but it is certain that he enjoyed the new associations and found them stimulating. Moreover, the church in England, at least the Roman Catholic Church, was less prominent and this, O'Casey believed, was a gain for artistic freedom, especially his artistic freedom. No longer would he have to contend with actors who consulted priests before appearing in his plays and no longer would he tolerate the mutilation of his scripts for the sake of zealous clerics.

Politically, England differed from Ireland. O'Casey arrived only a short time before the outbreak of the General Strike which he half-hoped would cripple Great Britain.[47] The English workers were different from the Irish though, and 10 Downing Street stood for a long time afterwards. There were, however, other features to Britain's political life. In contrast to Ireland, England was sophisticated. There was more variety of thought and greater variety of discussion about world issues, especially about the new Soviet state which assumed prominence with the appearance of the 'Zinoviev Letter'.[48] Moreover, England had a strong Labour Party and a Labour government in which O'Casey apparently placed some faith.[49] Too, the age-old Irish question, while always an issue to old-line imperialists, was of secondary importance in British politics, and this in itself was a relief to O'Casey. He no longer had to worry about offending the sensibilities of a nationalist population, then celebrating the tenth anniversary of the Easter Rising, and he didn't have to contend with the familiar faces and old enemies who were always quick to remind him that they knew him 'when'. With a new environment the old arguments became superfluous and faded into obscurity.

All these hopes were shattered when Yeats and Company rejected *The Silver Tassie*. It is difficult now to appreciate the harm the rejection did to O'Casey, since he continued to write and to write well, but there is little question that he felt it did him severe damage.[50] It was important that the first play he wrote after leaving Dublin be a success, not only from a financial standpoint but from an artistic one. Success in both areas would have insured his independence and this was vital to his psychological well-being. From an artistic point of view, the rejection was damaging because *Tassie* was O'Casey's first serious venture outside the realist mode that dominated his Dublin plays. The rejection raised questions about O'Casey's competency with expressionism and led people to begin wondering if his leaving Dublin was wise. Moreover, the rejection, accompanied by the publicity generated by O'Casey's publication of his correspondence with the Abbey, would make it more difficult for his next play to be accepted, not only because theatre boards would be reluctant to correspond with him if they feared their words would end up on the front page of *The Observer*, but because O'Casey gave no indication that he was returning to his more successful (and profitable) Dublin style. Financially, the rejection was a blow because the dramatist was raising a family. Had he been alone with no one dependent on him, he wouldn't have felt as great a responsibility or pressure to earn a comfortable living. He himself had and could live on considerably less than it took to support a wife and child. Once again, though, he must have relived in his mind the haunting Dublin days of poverty and insecurity.

Although deeply wounded by the rejection it is to O'Casey's credit that he did not rush into print with a play reminiscent of his Dublin works; yet, it must have done something to his self-confidence. Approximately five years elapsed between the completion of *Tassie* and the beginning of this next play, *Within the Gates*, the longest time span between any of his works.

Despite problems, O'Casey continued to develop politically by incessant reading.[51] The capitalist nations were in the midst of a deep economic depression while the Soviet Union was announcing the success of their first Five-Year Plan. Unemployed actors and writers lined the streets in the West while from Moscow came news that theatres were packed. In the 1931 British elections (to which O'Casey devotes a chapter in *Rose and Crown*) the Labour Party was removed from office in favour of the Conservatives who promised a stronger capitalist system. With this election, British intellectuals moved to Communism.[52]

O'Casey's experiments with expressionism in *Tassie*, with poetic symbolism in *Gates*, and with the stream-of-consciousness in *I Knock at the Door* would seem to run counter to the dominant mode of revolutionary drama and writing of the turbulent 1930s (hence Greaves's charge of 'artistic elitism'). Although parts of *Tassie* and *Gates* had scenes with techniques popular with the agit-prop and socialist realist dramas of those years (such as the Mass chant and choral arrangements), O'Casey had been moving increasingly away from the realism of his Dublin period: a realism so strong that he was labelled a 'photographic artist'. Beginning in the early 30s his essays denounced realism as an outmoded and worn-out style of writing, a conviction he held the rest of his life. In 1934, the year socialist realism was institutionalized, he wrote:

> Realism, the portrayal of real life on the stage, has failed, for the simple reason that real life cannot be shown on the stage; realism has always failed to be real. Nothing can be more artificial than the play that claims to be true to life. In setting out to gain everything it has lost all. Realism died years ago and the sooner we bury the body the better.[53]

In 1960, he complained that 'present-day drama is beset by the worship of realism,'[54] which O'Casey believed was never enough to capture the magic of life. Taken alone, these statements suggest that O'Casey and socialist realism were never together long enough to part company.

In a characteristically frank letter in 1955, O'Casey stated categorically that he did not believe in socialist realism. He also confessed that he did not know what socialist realism was.[55] O'Casey's confusion was not singular. Many writers of the 1930s who were sympathetic to Communism felt an ambiguity toward this new doctrine. On one hand they deeply believed in the Soviet revolution and its goal of socialism. On the other hand they believed in their own artistic talents. To begin writing in a new form would bring problems that negated much of their power and artistry.

This ambiguity was compounded by an uncertainty of definition, for the definition of socialist realism varied from writer to writer, country to country, and even from year to year. It was a poor ideology insofar as being imposed or universally accepted. As formulated by Maxim Gorky at the 1934 Soviet Writers Congress, socialist realism was literature which was realistic in content, socialist in politics and affirmative in tone.[56] This, however, was subject to interpretation of the nature of realism, the nature of socialism, and the nature of affirmation. As an example, the French Communist Party did not accept Brecht until the late 1950s, long after the dramatist found acceptance in other socialist countries and Communist parties. On the other hand, the British Party seemed to have no criteria for judging socialist realism and accepted humanists of all stripes. The French/Brecht/British dichotomy was by no means peculiar. Picasso, O'Casey, and many other writers and artists traversed the same path of acceptance in one country and non-acceptance in others. Some Communists liked them; some didn't.

Even the best known theorists, Brecht and Georg Lukacs, could not agree on a definition. Both laboured for years and came to diametrically opposite conclusions as to what constituted socialist realism. At the same time, the apodictic Zhdanov in the Soviet Union seemed to have no theory at all and appeared to be arbitrary and capricious. Writers who were praised in the 1930s during the United and Popular Front periods found their same works condemned during the Cold War period of the 1940s. The confusion O'Casey felt, then, was appropriate.

Most theorists believed that socialist realism was an application of Marxism.[57] Though neither Marx nor Engels wrote a study of literature both were well-read and balanced in their approach to the arts. Marx was very familiar with literature; his favourite authors were Shakespeare, Balzac and Heine. Indeed, Shakespeare appears to have been as important an influence on Marx as he was on O'Casey. Marx was so fascinated by the dramatist that he once embarked on a study of the playwright's originality. Moreover, Shakespeare was a valuable aid to Marx's efforts to learn the English language. He knew the dramatist's works by heart in German and it was a logical step to tackle them in English. To both Marx and Engels art was viewed axiologically rather than ontologically. Art had no history of its own other than the particular milieu out of which it grew. Personally, they both preferred realistic works, such as those by Balzac who, though a staunch Catholic and rank royalist reactionary, was in Marx's eyes a superb writer and a chronicler of the follies, decadence and weaknesses of the bourgeois class. But both Marx and Engels also detested propaganda novels which Engels termed 'tendentious'. It was not enough or even important to have the 'correct' opinions. Indeed, 'the more the author's views are concealed the better the work of art'.[58] (One thinks of Yeats's advice to O'Casey that the author's opinions should be burned up in the action of the play.) To Engels, whatever social significance a work had should flow from the development of the narrative rather than be imposed by the author.

The stature of Marx and Engels as revolutionaries and their choice of realism naturally put them on the side of the 'art is a weapon' school of the 1930s. There is some question whether they would have concurred with this, though they did give every indication of not believing in the concept of art for art's sake. To both, art was a tool for learning about and understanding the past and for imparting the knowledge of today. To many critics, though, the main problem of the 1930s and beyond was not with the concept of art as a weapon as it was with the belief that every literary weapon was art. The early stages of socialist realism seemed to revolve around the deduction that since both socialist realism and art were weapons, then socialist realism was art. It was a golden age for tendentious writers.

In the Soviet Union, the campaign for realistic art was enlisted in the service of eliminating illiteracy. In this regard, the makers of the first socialist state faced enormous odds. An entire generation had suffered through world war, revolution, and a devastating civil war. This condition was added to the already dismal state of the Russian working class and peasantry whose education ranked

low on the Czar's priorities. The problem was compounded by
the diversity of languages in the Soviet state – 180 by one count –
many of which were not written languages. Realism was considered the most appropriate tool for education, and literature
took the form of folk pageants and socialist novels whose primary
task was to educate, encourage and inspire. Undeniably, this
democratization of culture had an effect on the quality of literature and drama. Equally undeniable, art became more utilitarian
and served a greater purpose to a larger number of people than
it ever had in the past.

But there was another side to socialist realism. It should not
be supposed that all theorists laboured to justify folk pageants
and socialist novels, important though they may be for education.
In the Soviet Union, for instance, Anatoly Lunarcharsky differed
with Zhdanov's version of socialist realism. Lukacs and Brecht,
while disagreeing with each other, agreed on their dislike of
Zhdanov. From some writers, such as C. Day Lewis, came the
theory that any great work of art, socialist realist or not, was a
plus for Communism, a view O'Casey partially shared.[59] O'Casey's
friend, Hugh MacDiarmid, placed his faith in a relatively obscure
party resolution from a 1925 Central Committee meeting:

> The Party must combat attempts at pure hot-house 'proletarian'
> literature. . . . Marxist criticism must decisively expel from its
> midst any pretentious, semi-literate and smug communist
> conceit. . . . While gaining a deep and unerring knowledge of
> the socioclass content of the literary streams, the Party can in no
> way bind itself in adherence to any one direction in the sphere
> of artistic form. . . . The Party must completely eradicate
> attempts at crude and incompetent administrative meddling in
> literary affairs.[60]

O'Casey always believed that Communists were selling themselves short by applauding simple and didactic forms of realism.
Life, he felt, was complex and, like art, could not be reduced to
a formula. Though he denounced realism, he never denied that his
own works were realistic, but he always insisted they had other
ingredients, such as fantasy and stylized imagination, which
heightened the realism. Indeed, it is clear that the dramatist did
not denounce *all* forms of realism; just those which did not allow
for a more truthful, imaginative, and deeper expression of life,
as he saw it. In the 1934 essay, he wrote: 'the veneration of
realism, or, as Archer calls it, pure imitation, must cease, and

imagination must be crowned queen of the drama again.'[61] And in 1950, he reiterated this belief: 'A lot think that anything fiery, fierce or commonplace is realism, but realism is but a form of writing in which imagination has no place. It is the setting down of things and characters as they are, without change, selection, modification, or arrangement.'[62] To O'Casey, fantasy and imagination must be part of any living play for both were part of the living world.

In this regard, O'Casey was in accord with the more sophisticated theorists of socialist realism. Lunarcharsky, for instance, wrote:

The revolution is bold. It loves brightness of colours . . . revolution gladly accepts those extensions of realism that are indeed in its sphere. It can accept fantastic hyperbole, caricature, all sorts of deformations. . . . If effective presentation demands depicting a certain social feature in a distorted or caricatured fashion to reveal what is hidden behind an appealing or nondescript exterior, then this device is, of course, profoundly realistic.[63]

Later, he wrote: 'Writers and, in particular, playwrights belonging to the movement, to the school, to the era of socialist realism, can create their works in highly diverse styles.' Moreover, fantasy, the grotesque, and caricature are fully appropriate for realism if 'their role is to deepen reality, to illuminate its artistic interpretation'.[64]

Lukacs took the same approach, writing, 'Marxist aesthetics is clearly opposed to any trend which limits itself to the photographic reproduction of the immediately perceived surface of the outer world.'[65] It takes no stretch of the imagination to link Lukacs's comments to O'Casey's works:

even the most extravagant play of the poetic imagination [*Within the Gates*], even the fartherest reaching fantasy [*Cock-a-Doodle Dandy*] in the representation of phenomena, is completely compatible with the Marxist concept of realism. It is no accident that some fantastic tales of Balzac or E. T. A. Hoffman count among the works which Marx rated very high.[66]

Lukacs concluded that 'the fantastic tales of Balzac and Hoffman constitute high points of realist literature since in them, precisely with the help of imaginative representation . . . essential forces are portrayed'.

Today, it is this view which prevails among socialist realist critics. A Soviet critic recently concluded:

> It is irrelevant to set down which structure, which form [literature] uses. It is possible to give a true view of the world through the use of inner monologue or literary montage, but it is also possible to distort it, and the same applies to the Aristotelian dramatic rule versus the non-Aristotelian. What matters is that a work of art, to quote Brecht, 'while laying bare the social causal nexus, should give an insight into the social machinery'.[67]

The question of form in O'Casey's plays, therefore, is of no consequence insofar as socialist realism is concerned. The expressionism of *The Silver Tassie,* the poetic symbolism of *Within the Gates,* and the fantasy of *Cock-a-Doodle Dandy* are all compatible with Marxist aesthetics. Indeed, from the perspective of theorists like Lukacs and others, what has been of utmost importance in socialist realism has not been technique but 'the expression of a personal world view' and 'a creative attitude toward life'.[68] This world view is not Oswald Spangler's 'Man is a beast of prey, I shall say it again and again.' Rather it is Gorky's 'Man is more miraculous than the miracles he accomplishes.' It is the world of the old versus that of the new. Valderman von Knoeriger wrote: 'The basic area of contradiction, which cannot be resolved and which divides both worlds, is the essence of man, his internal essence. It is the battlefield on which the future of mankind must be determined.'[69] The Soviet critic, Anatole Ovcharenko, commented: 'We are saying that because the artists of the new world have an unshakeable faith in man, in his final triumph, they can depict the world more profoundly, more fearlessly.'[70]

This 'unshakeable faith in man' is the socialism in socialist realism. By definition it is affirmative. It implies a progressive view of history, an understanding of the multi-layered political and economic forces in capitalist society, and belief in the ability of mankind to shape, control, or determine its own destiny. In short, it is the artist's view of life that carries the most weight with socialist critics. Lukacs wrote: 'Marxist aesthetics requires only that the essence conceived by the writer should not be represented abstractly, but as the essence of the phenomena in which surging life is organically hidden and out of which it grows.'[71] Another critic said:

The socialist realist cannot be only concerned with an interpretation of reality. For him reality has many layers; it is
constantly evolving. For his point of view, which corresponds
to the dialectic of life, not everything has the same value, the
same specific weight. In real life, the new and the old, what
is becoming and what is decaying, coexist, often within the same
social phenomenon.[72]

O'Casey instinctively understood all these concepts and said
much the same thing (though a little more poetically):

I have always aimed . . . at bringing emotion and imagination
on to the stage, in the shapes of song, dance, dialogue, and
scene; each mingling with the other, as life does, for life is
never rigid. . . . nothing changes so often, so inevitably in city
and country, in field, factory, workshop, and home.[73]

For Lukacs's 'organically hidden surging life,' O'Casey could
write as far back as 1934: 'There is a deeper life than the life
we see and hear with the open ear and the open eye, and this is
the life important and the life everlasting.'[74] Finally, of all
O'Casey's criticisms of literature, none is so pervasive as his
objections to those works 'in which man is arrayed against forces
stronger than himself, completely beyond his control, and the
characters . . . invariably set down on the animal plane.' This
theme was the basis for his criticisms of the 'great galaxy of
darkened stars dulling the human sky': Kafka, Ionesco, Greene,
Eliot, Genet, Orwell, and, to a lesser degree, Beckett ('though
Samuel Beckett wears his rue with a difference. He is a poet,
and there is sly humour as well as music in his writing').[75] O'Casey's
'unshakeable faith in man' also formed the basis for those writers
he championed: Shakespeare, Burns, Shelley, Whitman, Gorky,
Shaw, and Yeats. For, like himself, these exceptional souls
championed his creed:

Man is the only form on earth that can see its form and love its
grandeur; he has enriched the world, for without him it would
have no meaning and look dead; it would be deah. He has
ennobled the star we stand on; exceptional souls give things
exceptional beauty.[76]

If the form and content of O'Casey's plays were not antagonistic
to Marxist aesthetics, what about other factors? Critics have

maintained that the case for O'Casey's Marxism is weakened
by important distinctions, all of which are termed 'unorthodox'.
The critics include the use of religious symbols and language in
his works; his independence which was so strong as to negate
any observance of Communist orthodoxy; and his romanticism
which was not in accord with the 'steel-like' discipline of Communists.

The charge that O'Casey professed an unorthodox brand of
Communism is tricky. I have tried to show in this essay that
orthodoxy and unorthodoxy in the Communist movement were
relative terms. Communists rarely used them, for obvious reasons.
One can easily grant that all great writers and artists who at some
time in their career professed sympathy for Communism, were
unorthodox. By definition they were so. Greatness in any artistic
sphere is the product of an unorthodox mind. Just as they were
able to perceive and recreate the world in their own distinctive
way, so too did they perceive Communism in a special manner.
But this is not extraordinary. The tailor, the baker, the farmer,
and the electrician who believe in Communism all bring their
own perspective to politics, a perspective more often than not
determined by how they earn their living and by the problems
incurred at the workplace. Their perception is also unique and
distinctive. While the artist and the worker may differ on a vision
of reality because of their differing experiences, both have in
common a shared vision of what the world can be. Further, no
purpose is served by setting up dual standards for artists and
workers. Competency in an artistic area does not negate competency in the political arena. It is, after all, one of the principles
of democracy that an educated people, who are usually competent
in their occupations, will be able to render fair political judgements. The critics' problem has been in accepting that Communism is a fair political judgement.

Organized religion was frequently the *bête noire* in O'Casey's
plays, yet he never tired of using religious allegory and biblical
rhetoric for illustrative purposes. Some critics have seen this as
a primary reason why O'Casey cannot be considered an 'orthodox'
Communist. Saros Cowasjee, for instance, wrote in two places
of O'Casey's play, *The Star Turns Red*: 'The Communists feel
that O'Casey is unnecessarily recreating a God that they have
killed' and 'Some Communists may not approve of O'Casey's
enthusiasm for God and religion.'[77] Disregarding the fact that
Cownsjee doesn't quote a single Communist authority for his
statements, his confusion is apparent. For to come to Communism

by way of Christianity or to infuse Christian symbols may seem strange in view of Marx's often misquoted statement: 'religion is the opinion of the people' (found first, incidentally, in Charles Kingsley).

Yet it is not so strange. The symbolism of Christ as 'the first Communist' or counterposed against capitalism, and of Christianity as the basis for Communism is pervasive throughout socialist and non-socialist literature. Its imagery is frequently found in twentieth-century Communist writings and the whole idea was the basis for the Christian Socialism of the nineteenth century. One of the most famous works in which the Christ symbol is used is Alexander Blok's poem, *The Twelve*, where Christ is portrayed leading the revolutionary proletariat, the modern twelve apostles. In Henri Barbusse's poem, *Jesus*, Christ is a Communist and an atheist whom the capitalists nail to the cross. In the first Soviet play, *Mystery-Bouffe* by Mayakovsky, produced on November 7, 1918 in celebration of the first anniversary of the October Revolution, Christ is the symbol of the Man of the Future. Replete with a Sermon on the Mount, this Christ of Communism tells his listeners that there is no heaven, that the only real heaven is the one built by human hands on earth. Other examples include Art Young, a leading Communist artist for the *Daily Worker*, who drew the highly-popular 'Wanted' poster of Christ, satirizing the capitalists' fear of those like Jesus who preached dangerous social ideas. Day Lewis was moved to write a 'Marxist morality play,' *Noah and the Waters*, using the biblical story to present a conflict between Noah – the life of capitalistic exploitation – and the new life of the Flood (as O'Casey may have used the Flood at the end of *Purple Dust*). The list could go on and on, for many Communists have not hesitated to use the Christ symbol as a symbol of Communism or as a protest against capitalism. How effective it has been artistically is another question, but the symbol is in no way anathema to Communist writing.

Like Marx and other Communist writers, O'Casey used the language and cadences of religious expression as a weapon and as a tool for satiric and dramatic purposes. Compare, for instance, the language he used in one passage in *Inishfallen, Fare Thee Well* with two Communist works: Mike Gold's classic *Jews Without Money* and Wangenheim's *Chorus of Work*:

(O'Casey) Morning star, hope of the people, shine on us! Star of power, may thy rays soon destroy the things that err, things

that are foolish, and the power of man to use his brother for
profit so as to lay up treasure for himself where moth and rust
doth corrupt, and where thieves break through and steal. Red
Mirror of Wisdom, turning the labour in factory, field, and
workshop into the dignity of a fine song; Red Health of the
sick, Red Refuge of the afflicted, shine on us all. . . . The sign of
Labour's shield, the symbol of the people's banner; Red Star,
shine on us all!

(Gold) O workers' Revolution, you brought home to me, a
lonely suicidal boy. You are the true Messiah. You will destroy
the East Side when you come, and build there a garden for
the human spirit. O Revolution, that forced me to think, to
struggle, and to live. O great beginning!

(Wagenheim) Our Communism
Which art in deed
Hallowed be your name
Your kingdom come on earth
Not in heaven . . .
For thine is the kingdom
The power and the humanity
May this be granted
By the Comintern
And the KPD.

None of these passages will live forever. Nor should they. But
for O'Casey at least, this method of writing had a utilitarian
purpose. In a letter to Timofei Rokotov, he wrote of those in
religious organizations he wished to reach. It is a good thing, he
said, 'to try to confound them with the words that come out of
their mouths. . . . Were Red Jim [in *The Star Turns Red*] to speak
as a Marxist, the audience here or in America . . . would take no
notice; only those converted, those already Marxists would
listen.'[78]

There is no doubt, of course, that religion was an important
influence in O'Casey's life, however much he may have used it
as a weapon or literary device. But this fact alone puts him in the
company of many other Communists and in no way does it
single him out as exceptional. André Gide wrote: 'What leads
me to Communism is not Marx but the Gospels.'[79] Day-Lewis
saw his Communism having a 'religious quality'.[80] Rockwell Kent
reflected that in his youth he was an ardent reader of the New

Testament. One can only guess the number of non-writing
socialists and Communists who started with a belief in Judaism
or Christianity, who saw in Christ a powerful revolutionary figure,
and who found themselves immersed in the ideals of the early
apostles. Indeed, to some, there was a quality about Christianity
that led them to Communism, as illustrated by a conversation
between the Dean of Canterbury and Paul Robeson in which
the Dean said:

> There is nothing more fundamental about Christianity than the
> one brotherhood of man. Grant that, and the demand for
> justice, freedom, and abundance of creative life for each
> individual together with an ever-widening fellowship, follows
> as day follows night. Grant that, and an economic order, which
> not only frustrates science but produces and tolerates wealth
> beside poverty, creates and perpetuates class distinctions, and
> fails to provide opportunity for all in the matter of work,
> leisure, education, or security, stands condemned.[81]

The religious influence on individual Communist writers must,
however, be kept in perspective. There is no general rule that
applies to all. Sometimes Communism successfully picked up
where religion left off, exchanging one set of values for another.
Other times, and less successfully, Communism was just an
extension of religion, as in the case of Gide and Day-Lewis,
incorporating one set of values with the other. Often, as expected,
the two values clashed, especially if each was carried to its
logical conclusion and promoted the examination of man's
relationship to the world around him. To Marxists, man's
existence was social and with his fellow man, while religion was
essentially individualistic and egoistic, separating man from his
communal existence. Christianity was a religion, a relationship
between God and man in which man acknowledged the supremacy
of God. Christianity saw itself as an answer to man's fate on
earth but only in the light of God. Marxism denied all transcend-
ence and metaphysical questions. One believed that all was
knowable; the other believed that the essential spirit escaped
human knowledge. To Marxists, only that which denied mystery
made science possible, for to admit that reality was unknowable
was a view which limited man's potential and capacity to control
and conquer it. Given the choice between a religious and a
scientific view of reality, Marxism chose science. And to O'Casey,
science was everything:

What is beyond us outside the world of what we see, hear, smell, taste, and touch, we don't know. Not one of the philosophies that have tried to hem us in or bring us out has told us, or can tell us anything outside of ourselves and the world. Science has told us a lot, will tell us more, and we must wait for science to tell us all.[82]

But to Gide, Day-Lewis and others who tried to religionize Marxism, it was a God that failed. O'Casey's strength was that he never worshipped at the altar.

Robert F. Aickman posed a dichotomy once by writing: 'Mr. O'Casey is a Communist. A romantic Communist, of course.'[83] In this way he both described and negated the dramatist's political views in a mere ten words. To describe O'Casey thusly quite naturally led people to believe that O'Casey was a hopeless utopian, lost in a world of his own. On one hand was O'Casey, the passionate romantic; on the other were a band of steely-eyed Bolsheviks led by the bloodless theories of the equally steely-eyed Marx and Lenin. Once again though, the critics misread both the theoretical and practical content of Marxism.

Marxism has always had within it two currents of revolutionary activism, the theoretical and the romantic, described by Ernst Bloch as sobriety and enthusiasm and alluded to by many Marxists. Bloch wrote: 'Nothing is more distant from true Marxist sobriety than common sense, which is not so healthy and not so human, but is more likely to be replete with petit bourgeois prejudices. On the other hand, nothing is closer to genuine sobriety than the quality of *bon sens*, as found in Marxist enthusiasm.'[84] These warm and cool currents of Marxist thought have been and are present in nearly all Communists, from the rank-and-file to the leadership, but they vary in degree of dominance. Whether one is a sober or an enthusiastic Marxist depends, to a large extent, on the personality of the believer. A relative few have a predilection for intellectualism and cool realism. But the vast majority of Communists have not mastered the theoretical intricacies of Marx and Lenin (few have) and they are distinguished by their passionate and romantic enthusiasm, corresponding to the dynamic *élan* of society. This is not to imply that one facet is superior to the other; only that from a Marxist view one is not contradictory to the other. Indeed, Marxists such as Bloch see as the strength of Marxism its ability to harmonize the two. 'Marxism,' he wrote overcomes the rigid antithesis of sobriety versus enthusiasm by bringing them both to a new state, and enabling both to work together for precise anticipation and concrete utopia. It is not the function of sobriety merely to remove fantasy, and it is not the function of enthusiasm, precisely as imagination in action, to operate exclusively with absolutes, as though revolutionary romanticism coincided with quixotism.[85]

It takes a stretch of the imagination to accuse O'Casey of not having a realistic view of life and of being overly romantic. He spent the first forty years of his life in decidedly unromantic poverty and financial insecurity, existing on meagre wages, the dole, and whatever else was available. He spent years as a labourer on the unromantic scrap-heap of capitalism, learning the value of his and others' labour. He devoted a considerable number of years to political movements, learning and teaching the tactics of trade unions and revolutionary parties. He was, by all accounts, a voracious reader on a wide variety of subjects, ranging through drama, history, literature, nature, politics, and economics. What has been termed O'Casey's romanticism is nothing more than the dramatist's view of reality and his conviction that, despite its woes, life has a richness and a fullness that is not adequately recognized. To him and to most other Communists, the *élan* of society was quite real. It was the dynamism in every home, factory, field, and workshop. It was in the lives of the lowly as well as in that of the mighty. It was song and sorrow, love and beauty, comedy and tragedy. It was far in advance of the understanding of even the most revolutionary parties, and yet it was the oldest subject for artist and writer who tried for centuries to capture it on canvas and paper. Lenin recognized the same force, writing:

History generally, and the history of revolutions in particular, is always richer in content, more varied, more many-sided, more 'subtle' than the best parties and the most class-conscious vanguards of the most advanced classes imagine. This is understandable, because the best vanguards express the class consciousness, the will, the passion, the fantasy of tens of thousands, while the revolution is made . . . by the class-consciousness, the will, the passion, and the imagination of tens of millions.[86]

The 'imagination of tens of millions' that Lenin wrote of was of seminal importance to O'Casey. In his essay, 'Art is the Song of Life,' he wrote:

> imagination is all: it is the focus of all achievements by man,
> it sparked off the American Revolution, it began the discovery
> of Evolution in the mind of Darwin, it flamed forth from the
> mind of Lenin, inspired Shakespeare's plays and all his songs;
> and is the burning core of form and eloquence which is present
> in a fine play, novel, painting, or musical creation.[87]

All these moments of greatness were to O'Casey the foundation of Communism, the historical heritage to which Communism must pay tribute. They were the blocks on which society was built, on which it thrived, and which gave it life. It was a dream handed down from generation to generation and passed on from father to son and from mother to daughter. It was no contradiction to Marxism nor was it overly romantic for O'Casey to believe that

> Communism isn't an invention of Marx; it is a social growth,
> developing through the ages, since man banded together to
> fight fear of the unknown, and destroy the danger from
> mammoth and tiger of the sabre-tooth. All things in science and
> art are in its ownership, since man painted the images of what
> he saw on the wall of his cave, and since man put on the
> wooden share of his plough the more piercing power of iron or
> of bronze.[88]

It was no contradiction because Marx said the same thing himself in 1843.

> It will be shown . . . that the world has long possessed in
> dream form something of which it need only become conscious
> in order to possess it in actuality. It will then be evident that
> it is a question not of a great and theoretical gap between past
> and future, but rather of realizing the ideas of the past.[89]

Saros Cowasjee wrote that 'O'Casey differs from the average Communist.'[90] Indeed he did differ. O'Casey differed fundamentally from the average Communist in that he never joined the Communist Party. I have shown earlier that O'Casey had good reason to distrust his role in political parties. Though he was well aware of the need for a revolutionary party to act as a vanguard in the struggles (as the Irish Citizen Army had done), he believed that he best served the cause in a supportive role. Some critics have read into this a hesitancy on O'Casey's part, and perhaps there was. But many writers whose Communist credentials are above question never joined a Communist Party, Mayakovsky being the most conspicuous.

To O'Casey, the Communist Party was a party representing the goals of the working class rather than the theatre. They were justifiably more attuned to the struggles of the daily worker than to the complexities of the drama, and, for that reason, he wrote: 'Most Communists are better with politics than with the things of the theatre.'[91] And so they were, for although Communists have always taken a leading role in the entertainment industry, their contribution rests more on their valuable work of unionizing the actors, stagehands, etc. and reducing the power of the movie moguls than on any long-lasting artistic achievement.

O'Casey probably would have had a difficult time in the Communist Party, and he and they had sense enough to recognize it. He had had too much experience in the past with political criticism of his plays, including criticism from his own comrades. He would have been asking for trouble by joining the Party, for there were many areas of probable contention. For instance, he was a dramatist, first and foremost. Although he always drew his strength from the working class, he realised his dreams from his skills as a playwright. He was, he said, both drama maker and revolutionist, 'one looking at life in the terms of individuals, the other [as] part of the collective urge and forward thrust of man.'[92] He had a great sense of history and of man's date with destiny. He was confident that the innate goodness of people would dominate the future and that Time would put everything into perspective. He had no desire to be remembered as a great Communist, only as a drama maker. He wrote that, from the perspective of Time, 'the dramatist is neither Tory nor Communist, but only a playwright, setting down his characters as he knew them, giving, if he can, an added depth, height, and lilt to the words he makes them speak.'[93] Moreover, O'Casey believed in a separation of drama and politics, though not in the conventional sense. Critics have not understood that a delicate balance of the two always existed in O'Casey's life and in his plays, a balance he set up and one which he maintained, though not always successfully, for though his drama and politics were separate they were also united. For example, O'Casey would hardly agree with Clifford Odets' dictum, 'art must shoot bullets' (*must*?), yet he would be the first to maintain that art could be a deadly sword

in the hands of a skilled craftsman. O'Casey was willing to use any
political tool to further his drama, yet he always denied that his
plays contained any political propaganda. He would never have
called himself a Communist writer, yet he always insisted that he
was both a Communist and a dramatist.[94] Finally, O'Casey's
subject matter was always Ireland and that was an area in which
British Communists were not particularly strong. There were,
then, areas which he was not willing to submit to judgement by
committee, Communist or not.

For their part, the Communist Party of Great Britain seemed
content with O'Casey's relationship to them. Like many other
writers, he was able to serve in an adjunct position to the Party
(though his ten-year stint on the editorial board of the *Daily
Worker* demonstrates that he was closer to the Party than most
writers were). He was always willing to lend his pen and his name
to the cause and to help in any way he could. He had his own
correspondence going with *International Literature* and with
others in the Soviet Union, and his writings brought considerable
credit and status to the British Party. From their perspective, it
wasn't really important whether or not O'Casey believed that
socialist realism was the wave of the future or that art was a
weapon. His plays *qua* plays were so proletarian that they served
as a weapon against injustice, bigotry, nationalism, and sectari-
anism, the general platform of all Communist parties.

This is not to say that Communist parties accepted O'Casey as
one of their own uncritically. On the contrary. For instance, they
rarely gave good reviews to his Dublin plays, preferring to
emphasize O'Casey's anti-imperialism rather than his lampooning
of Irish nationalism and sectarian socialism. With a few exceptions, they didn't understand *Within the Gates*, thanks to Mike
Gold, and *The Silver Tassie* was beyond the comprehension of
the British party critic in 1929. In general, it was only those plays
written after *Gates* which were well-received, most notably *Red
Roses for Me*. At the same time, nobody has championed
O'Casey's autobiographies more than the Communist parties of
Great Britain and the United States. One critic called the books
'the odyssey of man in the twentieth century' and 'one of the
greatest monuments in literature to the loveliness of life and
the greatness of man.'[95]

In some ways, O'Casey's decision to remain outside the Party
was similar to Yeats's decision to abstain from politics and devote
his efforts to poetry. The world lost nothing and gained everything
from Yeats's decision, and there is little question that the world

would have gained little from O'Casey as Communist Party Member. The difference, of course, is that Yeats had no class perspective to keep him honest, and he spent his later years flirting with fascism. O'Casey, on the other hand, had no other class perspective than that of the working class and, of course, the theatre.

This latter perspective accounts for O'Casey's friendships with and devotion to many people who were not notably working class-oriented or sympathetic to the Communist Party. His friendships with such people as George Jean Nathan and Brooks Atkinson raised eyebrows among some of O'Casey's left-wing supporters. What they forgot, though, was that, before everything, the drama, and not revolution, was O'Casey's occupation. Writing plays was his job, his craft, and his sole means of support. He took as much pride in it as the cabinet maker or the farmer took in a finely-crafted product or a well-tilled field. The good cabinet maker and the good farmer were interested in the workmanship of their fellow craftsmen, regardless of politics, and so was the good dramatist. The Nathans and the Atkinsons took a deep interest in the products of O'Casey the dramatist, and he reciprocated. Although they cared little for his politics and he cared less for theirs, he called them 'Communists', the highest compliment he could pay.[96]

I have tried to show O'Casey's relationship to the socialist theories of his era, the reasons for his acceptance or rejection of them, and his contribution to them. He was, as always, his own man and, though he kept abreast of all the important issues of his day, he was able to see it at its broadest and deepest. He was independent and he developed his theories from a combination of sobriety and enthusiasm, reflection and romanticism, and study and experience. In ancient times, he would have been a Christian; in 1789 he would have been a Republican; from 1913 he was a Communist. As a Communist he came out of the best tradition of Marxism: from those whom Marx said would 'disdain to conceal their views' and from those who believed as O'Casey did, that 'It is labour alone that keeps the world going, and it is labour alone, labour done with hand and brain that alone can make life . . . a vigorous and joyful experience.'[97] At the same time, he instinctively reflected the values and concerns of the majority of twentieth-century Communists: land, peace, bread, and a rose for the table. Like most Communists he was alienated from a capitalist world that tolerated poverty and worshipped wealth, and he turned to a society which he believed did neither: the Soviet Union. In doing so, he placed his class interests above everything, including his drama, for he was under no illusions about the long and tortuous path the U.S.S.R. had to travel. He was wise enough to know that he could never write socialist drama, for such drama is at least a reflection of socialist conditions; he was still in 'the belly of the tiger,' and his plays were always of life around him, of England and Ireland, and of life in the factory, field, home, and workshop. He was idealistic, romantic, and utopian, but he was also materialistic, a realist, and often dogmatic: just like the rest of us.

Notes

1   Jurgen Ruhle, *Literature and Revolution* (N.Y.: Praeger, 1969), p. 215.
2   Brooks Atkinson, 'Critic at Large,' *New York Times*, 13 September 1960.
3   Gabriel Fallon, *Sean O'Casey, The Man I Knew* (Boston: Little, Brown and Co. 1965). Saros Cowasjee, *Sean O'Casey, The Man Behind the Plays* (Edinburgh and London: Oliver & Boyd, 1963). Carl and Ann Reeve, *James Connolly and the United States* (New Jersey: Humanities Press, nc., 1978). C. Desmond Greaves, *Sean O'Casey, Politics and Art* (London: Lawrence & Wishart, 1979). Greaves charges that O'Casey couldn't have been a Communist in the 1920s because *inter alia* it doesn't show up in the dramatist's letters. What he doesn't say is that of the approximately 110 letters in the 1920–1927 period, 32 are to Gabriel Fallon, 26 are to Lady Gregory (and four from her to O'Casey), ten are to Lennox Robinson (one from), and seven are to Sara Allgood. There are three each to Eileen O'Casey, James Stephens (one from), Macmillan publishers, and the *Irish Statesman*. Further, there are two to Michael Dolan (one from), two from Yeats, and one each to or from the Abbey Theatre, Austin Stack, the Society of Authors, the *Leader*, and the *New York Times*. In other words, of about 110 letters, 103 are to or from people not noted for their socialist views. One might conclude that O'Casey only wrote to non-socialists. A more logical conclusion is that these were the only letters which could be recovered by David Krause (*The Letters of Sean O'Casey*, I, New York: Macmillan, 1975).

    Greaves conveniently overlooks the symbolism of such play titles as 'The Crimson in the Tricolour' and 'The Red Lily'. He ignores the meaning of the Christmas card O'Casey designed for the Larkin Release Committee: clearly pictured are a rifle, a hammer and a sickle or scythe (p. 99). He ignores O'Casey's comments about the Russian newspapers he was reading in 1925 (p. 137); his remarks about a Communist organizer in the same year (p. 123); his letter in 1928 in which he wrote of 'my fierce, jagged Communistic outlook' (p. 313); and his comments to the *Catholic Herald* in March 1930: 'in Social and Economic opinion I am a Communist' (pp. 394-95). Most of all, though, Greaves ignores the fallibility of collections of letters. For instance, for the 1914–1918 period, there are no letters about World War I. Should we assume, with Yeats, 'you were not interested in the Great War'?
4   Karl Marx and Frederick Engels, *Ireland and the Irish Question* (New York: International Publishers, 1972), especially page 332, Engels to Karl Kautsky.
5   James Connolly, *Erin's Hope – Its Ends and Means* (Dublin: New Books, 1968), pp. 21-23.

6   For an account of the debates surrounding the colonial question in socialist congresses, see Julius Braunthal, *History of the International*, v. 1 (New York: Praeger, 1967), pp. 305-19. See also Ramsay MacDonald, *Labour and the Empire* (London, 1907) and Partha Sarathi Gupta, *Imperialism and the British Labour Movement* (New York: Holmes and Meire, 1975).

7   For a discussion of Luxemburg's theories, see Horace Davis, *Toward a Marxist Theory of Nationalism* (New York: Monthly Review Press, 1978).

8   Quoted in Davis, *Toward a Marxist Theory of Nationalism*, p. 75. Davis points out that this may have been the first and last time that anti-Semitism was considered to be nationalism.

9   Quoted in Davis, *Toward a Marxist Theory of Nationalism*, p. 66.

10 Lenin, *On the Right of Nations to Self-Determination* (Moscow: Progress Publishers, 1973), 5th printing, p. 24.

11 *Ibid*, p. 52.

12 *Ibid*, p. 51. See also Lenin's 'The British Liberals and Ireland,' *Lenin on Ireland*, (Dublin: New Books, 1970), pp. 12-15.

13 O'Casey details the correspondence and contact with the Volunteers in his *Story of the Irish Citizen Army*, chapter IV.

14 Frank Robbins, *Under the Starry Plough* (Dublin: Academy Press, 1977), p. 20.

15 Sean O'Casey, *Drums under the Windows* (New York: The Macmillan Company, 1946), pp. 340-42 and 400-401.

16 Robbins, *Under the Starry Plough*, pp. 25-27. For a more scholarly account, see Emmet Larkin, *James Larkin* (London. Routledge & Kegan Paul, 1965, rpt. 1977), pp. 319-32.

17 As an example of the socialist spirit in the Irish Citizen Army, one historian wrote: 'Liberty Hall became definitely the centre of the spirit which was to be known as Bolshevist.' (W. Allison Phillips, *The Revolution in Ireland*, London, 1926, p. 26). Phillips was writing of the atmosphere that prevailed under Larkin and before O'Casey resigned. Though Connolly always remained a socialist, the close co-operation with the Volunteers hardly engendered Bolshevism or anything like it. In *Letters*, I, O'Casey distinguishes between his and Larkin's policy and that of Connolly and Markiewicz: 'I was all for a Union of Labour and the Republican movement – not "Nationalism" ' (p. 649).

18 C. Desmond Greaves, *The Life and Times of James Connolly* (London: Lawrence & Wishart, 1961), p. 338.

19 *International Socialist Review*, August 1916, p. 41.

20 *Justice*, 4 May 1916, quoted in Chushichi Tsuzuki, *H. M. Hyndman and British Socialism* (Oxford: Oxford University Press, 1961), p. 258.

21 *Socialist Review* (London), September 1916, p. 205.

22 Quoted in P. Berresford Ellis, *A History of the Irish Working Class* (New York: Braziller, 1973), p. 232.

23 *Ibid*, pp. 233-34.

24 James Stephens, *The Insurrection in Dublin* (New York: The Macmillan Company, 1917), pp. 128-29.

25 *Lenin on Ireland*, pp. 32-33.

26 *Ibid*, p. 34.

27 'Class War in Dublin' and 'A Week after the Dublin Atrocities' in *Lenin on Ireland.* pp. 7–12.

28 *The Labour Monthly*, April 1929, pp. 215–219, contains the first English publication of Lenin's 'The Irish Rebellion of 1916'. Accompanying the article is an editorial comment: 'specially translated for the *Labour Monthly*'. It first appeared in the United States in *The Communist*, January 1932.

29 Both Greaves and Reeve quote Lenin and O'Casey on the Easter Rising, as does Ellis.

30 O'Casey, *Story of the Irish Citizen Army*, pp. 51, 52. Greaves, *James Connolly*, writes that, by 1914, Connolly was 'prepared to accept aid and co-operation of any section going his way' (p. 283).

31 *Outline History of the Communist Party of Ireland* (Dublin: New Books, n.d.), p. 5: 'The Socialist Party of Ireland in this period [1914–15] did not function regularly and Connolly was involved with it only for occasional lectures. The building of a political party, with the aim of achieving socialism in Ireland, appeared no longer to hold the attention of Connolly.'

32 James Connolly, *Labour and Easter Week*, Desmond Ryan, ed. (Dublin: Sign of the Three Candles, 1966), pp. 101–19, 129–30, 155–58.

33 Quoted by William O'Brien in Connolly, *Labour and Easter Week*, p. 21. O'Brien alleges that Markiewicz was equally in favour of the Citizen Army going out alone, pp. 9–10.

34 Sean O'Casey, *Inishfallen, Fare Thee Well* (New York. The Macmillan Company, 1949), p. 370.

35 Quoted in S. S. Prawer, *Karl Marx and World Literature* (Oxford: Oxford University Press, 1976), p. 200.

36 O'Casey, *Inishfallen Fare Thee Well*, p. 8. There are several places where O'Casey gives hints that he supported the October Revolution from its beginning. In a letter to Timofei Rokotov, he wrote: 'I am, indeed, an old lover of the USSR, for I raised my voice at the Dublin meetings, held to protest the interference [the intervention by twelve capitalist nations] waged by the powers in order to down the struggling revolution.' (*Letters*, I, p. 780.)

37 See Ronald Ayling, 'Sean O'Casey and Jim Larkin after 1923,' *Sean O'Casey Review*, Spring 1977, pp. 99–104.

38 O'Casey, *Inishfallen, Fare Thee Well*, p. 392.

39 In William O'Brien's papers at the National Library of Ireland, there is a large section which contains leaflets, letters, and other material relating to this period. Larkin was accused *inter alia* of being an Orangeman and of selling out the leaders of the 1916 Rebellion.

40 In *Juno and the Paycock*, O'Casey's description of Jerry Devine reveals his disgust with the labour movement. 'He is a type, becoming very common now in the Labour Movement, of a mind knowing enough to make the mass of his associates, who know less, a power, and too little to broaden that power for the benefit of all.'

41 *Outline History of the Communist Party of Ireland*, p. 8.

42 Emmet Larkin's *James Larkin* quotes a letter Larkin sent to Connolly with instructions in late 1915 or early 1916 telling him 'not to move' (p. 190).

43 Nearly all studies use the chronology, including Greaves, Cowasjee,

Reeves, and Fallon. Cowasjee, for instance, writes: 'It is not until we
come to *The Star Turns Red* that we find O'Casey concerned with
communism.' (p. 167).

44 Mike Gold, 'Sean O'Casey and a Film,' *Daily Worker* (New York),
15 February 1937. In 'Two Letters of Sean O'Casey,' *Socialist Register
1965* (New York: Monthly Review Press, 1965), pp. 237–40, O'Casey
wrote: 'Mike Gold, a prominent Left-winger in the USA, after *Within
the Gates* appeared in New York, wrote a seething column of abuse;
the other day, 20 years later, he wrote another one, bubbling with
praise. What do I care whether he praises or blames? He doesn't know
a damn thing about literature or art.'

45 *Irish Times*, 24 March 1926. Quoted in *Letters*, I, pp. 183–85.

46 In an interview with G. W. Bishop in *The Observer* (6 October 1929),
O'Casey makes what is probably the first public mention of his intention to write an autobiography.

47 'Having fought so much for workers in Ireland, he was keenly excited,
expected to find a riot outside his windows, or, at the very least,
some form of shouting protest. But when he rose early to see what
had happened it was all quite orderly; . . . Sean, bitterly disappointed,
felt let down.' Eileen O'Casey, *Sean* (London: The Macmillan Company, 1971), pp. 50–51.

48 The 'Zinoviev Letter' was a communique purportedly from Zinoviev,
secretary of the Comintern to the British Communist Party, containing
instructions for the organization of Communist cells in the Army
and Navy. It was published in the *Daily Mail* four days before the
General Election of 1924 in an effort to create a 'Red Scare'. Henry
Pelling, *The British Communist Party* (New York: The Macmillan
Company, 1958), pp. 30–31.

49 O'Casey's interest in the Labour Party was brief and stemmed from
his admiration for Keir Hardie, who spoke in Dublin during the 1913
Lockout. O'Casey also had a short-lived friendship with Ramsay
MacDonald. By 1936, though, the dramatist was referring to the Labour
Party as 'mealy-mouthed'. (*Letters*, I, p. 632.)

50 O'Casey often mentioned the harm he felt was done to him by the
rejection of *Tassie*. In *Rose and Crown*, for instance, he refers to it
an inordinate number of times.

51 Among the items dealing with socialism and the USSR in which O'Casey
expressed more than passing interest in the early 1930s was the
chapter on Soviet drama in Hallie Flanagan's *Shifting Scenes of the
Modern European Theatre* (1928); William Chamberlain's *The Russian
Revolution*, which was to remain O'Casey's basic source for the
event; several of Shaw's books and articles, Russian films, the *Irish
Worker* (reconstituted under Larkin), and the *Daily Worker* (London).
He also had frequent correspondence and visits with Jack Carney,
Larkin's lieutenant and a visitor to the Soviet Union. O'Casey may have
had contact with Sean Shelley, an old comrade from the Citizen
Army days, whose son attended school in Moscow.

52 A. T. Tolley, *The Poetry of the Thirties*, (New York: St. Martin's
Press, 1975), p. 30: 'The collapse of the Labour government in 1931,
and the separation of its leaders from their party, seems to have been
a decisive event in the spread of Communism among British intel-

lectuals.' Pelling, *The British Communist Party*, pp. 73 *ff.*, sees the rise of Hitler as the main reason for the spread of Communism in Great Britain.

53   Sean O'Casey, 'From Within the Gates,' *Blasts and Benedictions*, Ronald Ayling, ed. (New York and London: St. Martin's Press and Macmillan), p. 116.

54   Sean O'Casey, 'Art is the Song of Life,' *ibid*, p. 78.

55   'Two Letters of Sean O'Casey,' *The Socialist Register*, 1965, pp. 237–40.

56   One writer summarized Gorky's version of Socialist Realism with the following: '(1) It is programmatic literature, it affirms something; (2) collectivism is the main factor in shaping man; (3) optimism, "the greatest happiness of life on earth"; (4) education is the central aim of this literature.' George Bisztray, *Marxist Models of Literary Criticism* (New York. Columbia University Press, 1978). There have been many books published on Socialist Realism, but one of the most concise is C. Vaughan James' *Soviet Socialist Realism, Origins and Theory* (New York: St. Martin's Press, 1973).

57   James, *Soviet Socialist Realism*, pp. 1–14.

58   Engels' letter to Harkness in Karl Marx and Frederick Engels, *Literature and Art*, (New York: International Publishers, 1947), pp. 41–43. Several writers have commented on Marx's admiration of Shakespeare. In Julius Smulkstys' *Karl Marx* (Twayne Publishers, 1974), he writes: 'Eventually, he could freely quote and identify even the minor characters from any tragedy or comedy. Once, in order to improve his English, Marx compiled all of Shakespeare's original expressions. This, in part, explains the abundance of references to his plays in *Capital* and several essays. Although there are few recorded comments by Marx on the English author, his critique of Ferdinand Lassalle's drama . . . leaves little doubt that he regarded Shakespeare as a model playwright' (p. 92). Smulkstys also quotes a letter from Marx to Engels in which Marx wrote: 'In the first act of the *Merry Wives* alone, there is more life and reality than in all of German literature.' Paul Lefargue, Marx's son-in-law, commented: 'There was a veritable Shakespeare cult in the Marx family and the three daughters knew much of Shakespeare by heart.' The best study of the influence of Shakespeare and literature on Marx is S.S. Prawer's *Karl Marx and World Literature*. Prawer wrote: 'The Shakespeare cult rife in the Marx household was noted by many observers – it brought about regular meetings of a Shakespeare-reading club called "The Dogberry Club" in Marx's house, which Marx is known to have attended and enjoyed, as well as contacts with . . . the English Shakespeare Society.' (p. 395).

59   Day-Lewis said, 'A good poem enters deep into the stronghold of our emotions: if it is written by a good revolutionary, it is bound to have a revolutionary effect on our emotions, and therefore to be essentially – though not formally – propaganda.' Quoted in Charles I. Glicksberg, *The Literature of Commitment* (Lewis-burg: Bucknell University Press, 1976), p. 259.

60   James, *Soviet Socialist Realism*, pp. 116–119. MacDiarmid refers to the document in his autobiography, *Lucky Poet* (London: Methuen and Co., 1943, p. 152), in the chapter, 'The Kind of Poetry I Want':

'A Communist Poetry that bases itself/On the resolution of the C.C. of the R.C.P./In Spring 1925 'The Party must vigorously oppose/ . . .'

61 O'Casey, 'From Within the Gates,' p. 117.
62 Sean O'Casey, 'What Thou Seest, Write in a Book,' *Blasts and Benedictions*, p. 153.
63 Quoted in A. Ovcharenko, *Socialist Realism and the Modern Literary Process* (Moscow: Progress Publishers, 1978).
64 *Ibid*. One of the most interesting statements on the use of fantasy *vis* realism comes, not from a writer, but from a scientist, Albert Einstein, who reportedly said: 'When I examine myself and my methods of thought, I come to the conclusion that the gift of fantasy has meant more to me than my talent for absorbing positive knowledge.' (William Stockton, 'Celebrating Einstein,' *The New York Times Magazine*, 18 February 1979, p. 50).
65 Georg Lukacs, 'Appearance and Essence,' in *Preserve and Create, Essays in Marxist Literary Criticism*, Gaylord C. LeRoy and Ursula Bertz, eds. (New York: Humanities Press, 1973), p. 17.
66 *Ibid*, pp. 19–21.
67 Erwin Pracht, 'Socialist Realism,' in *Preserve and Create*, p. 237.
68 Bisztray, *Marxist Models of Literary Realism*.
69 Valdermar Von Knoeringer, *Die Neue Gesellschaft*, III, 1961, p. 170.
70 Ovcharenko, *Socialist Realism and the Modern Literary Process*, pp. 122–23.
71 Lukacs, 'Appearance and Essence,' p. 20.
72 Pracht, 'Socialist Realism,' p. 237.
73 O'Casey, 'An Irishman's Plays, *Blasts and Benedictions*, p. 83.
74 O'Casey, 'From Within the Gates,' pp. 113–14.
75 Sean O'Casey, *Under a Colored Cap* (New York: St. Martin's Press, 1964), p. 135.
76 *Ibid*, p. 140.
77 Cowasjee, *Sean O'Casey, The Man Behind the Plays*, pp. 170, 175.
78 O'Casey, *The Letters of Sean O'Casey*, I, pp. 794–95. Elsewhere, O'Casey wrote in 1936 of quoting Pope Leo XIII 'rather as a weapon than in any reverent faith' (*Ibid*, p. 644). Prawer (*Karl Marx and World Literature*) writes of Marx using 'the cadences and the vocabulary of the Bible and religious tradition to attack religion' (p. 64), as, for instance, in this passage from *The German Ideology:* 'Put off thy shoes, O German patriot, for the place whereon thou standest is holy ground' (quoted on p. 157). Marx ends his critique of the Gotha Programme with a quote from Ezekiel 3:19: 'I have spoken out and delivered my soul' (quoted on p. 358). As an indication that things really haven't changed much, Edward Albee, in an interview with *The Village Times* on Long Island, said: 'I'm pretty fond of Jesus Christ; he was a very good man; the first Marxist' (31 August 1978, p. 23).
79 Andre Gidé, *Journals*, v. 2, p. 276.
80 Quoted in Tolly, *The Poetry of the Thirties*, p. 32.
81 Shirley Graham, *Paul Robeson, Citizen of the World* (New York: Simon Schuster Inc., 1946), p. 223. Brecht, when asked which book had exerted the greatest influence on him, answered in 1928: 'You will laugh – the Bible.' Klaus Volker, *Brecht, A Biography*, trans. by John

Nowell (New York: The Seabury Press, 1978), p. 6.

82 Sean O'Casey, *Sunset and Evening Star* (New York: The Macmillan Co., 1954), p. 32. In *Under a Colored Cap*, O'Casey wrote, 'the true generals now are the scientists in the laboratory' (p. 262).

83 R. F. Aickman, *The Nineteenth Century and After*, CXXXIX, April 1946.

84 Ernst Bloch, *On Karl Marx*, trans. by John Maxwell (New York: Herder and Herder, 1971), p. 34. In *Literature and Revolution*, Ruhle wrote: 'In Bloch's philosophy, there are warm and cold currents of Marxism. The first is the impulse to freedom, thinking in terms of a process, the revolutionary impulse of the dialectic; the other is realistic analysis, thinking in terms of tangible systems, the sobering insight into the possible and the useful. The one embodies Marxism's dream of the future, its goal of human salvation, the deeply humane impulse; the other the adaptation to the demands of the present, political strategy and tactics – i.e. power politics' (p. 288).

85 *Ibid*, pp. 34–35.

86 Quoted in Bloch, *On Karl Marx*, p. 35.

87 O'Casey, 'Art is the Song of Life,' *Blasts and Benedictions*, p. 78.

88 Sean O'Casey, *Rose and Crown* (New York: The Macmillan Co., 1952), p. 150.

89 Quoted in Bloch, *On Karl Marx*, pp. 27–28.

90 Cowasjee, *Sean O'Casey, The Man Behind the Plays*, p. 168.

91 O'Casey, *The Letters of Sean O'Casey*, I, p. 815.

92 O'Casey, *Under a Colored Cap*, p. 261.

93 *Ibid*, p. 262.

94 The contradiction here is that, by his own definition, O'Casey was indeed a Communist writer. From a non-ideological view, which he frequently expressed, a Communist was someone who did his best at whatever he worked at and all he could for the poor. This was not an uncommon view, as evidenced by two unrelated stories. According to Gjon Mili (*Life*, 2 October 1964), O'Casey told a troubled young doctor who was seeking advice: 'Be you the best practising doctor that ever lived – not only for those who can afford you, but also for the poor, for those who cannot afford you – and you'll be the best practising Communist that ever lived.' Compare this with a statement of a Communist interviewed by Vivian Gornick: 'If I was a doctor, it was my duty as a Party member to be the best doctor I could be. That was my obligation, that was my Communist morality.' Vivian Gornick, *The Romance of American Communism* (New York: Basic Books, 1977), p. 193.

95 Daniel Mason, 'Sean O'Casey Leaves a Legacy of Brave Joy,' *The Worker* (New York), 27 September 1964, p. 3. A similar view of O'Casey's autobiographies was expressed by the Soviet writer, A. Elistratova, who called them 'one of the finest productions of democratic literature in the capitalist world' (*Soviet Literature*, Moscow, November 1952). See also Milton Howard's article, 'Orwell or O'Casey,' *Masses and Mainstream*, January 1955 and Willie Gallogher's 'A Great Irishman,' *Labour Monthly*, April 1949. For enthusiastic reviews of *Red Roses for Me*, see 'O'Casey's "Red Roses for Me"; A Song of Human Brotherhood,' *Daily Worker*, 3 January 1956 and 'Red Roses

and Brotherhood,' *ibid*, 26 January 1956. Over the years, the Communist press has also focused attention on O'Casey in non-literary matters simply because O'Casey addressed himself to such matters. See, for intance, 'Sean O'Casey's Message to the Teacher's Union,' *Daily Worker*, 27 March 1956; 'Lenin,' *International Literature*, February 1960; 'O Woman, Weep No More,' *Worker*, 30 May 1948; 'The Song of the Soviets,' *New World Review*, November 1952; 'Keep the Flags of Friendship Flying,' *ibid*., November 1955.

96 O'Casey, *The Letters of Sean O'Casey*, I, p.

97 *Ibid*, p. 774.

EARLIEST YOUTH: PRISTINE CATHOLICISM AND GREEN PATRIOTISM IN O'CASEY'S IRISH BOOKS

WILLIAM J. MAROLDO

Pictures in the Hallway[1] is the second of O'Casey's four Irish Books; it is, in fact, their fulcrum or pivot.[2] It opens in October, 1891, with the announcement of the death of Charles Stewart Parnell, Ireland's 'uncrowned king'. And it closes sometime in 1900, that is, during Johnny-Sean-Jack Casside's twentieth year.[3] His earliest youth – *Óigeantacht,* thus bracketed, ends; so does the nineteenth century. As autobiography, this book deals with O'Casey's inaugural efforts to wrest a livelihood from the 'masters of Dublin,' amid conditions of dire poverty and personal trial; his extensive self-education, which takes him far beyond 'formal courses' denied him, even at TCD or Joyce's University College; his growing awareness of literature and art; his early interest in the theatre, which includes his participation (with brother Archie) in amateur theatricals his youthful 'pristine Catholicism', which is a likely derivative of his Protestant devotion; and his emergent Republicanism. In short, *Pictures in the Hallway* brings into focus O'Casey's first real interests in God, nation, and fellow-man: persistent aspects of his 'trinitarian' personality,[4] eventually to converge, at the end of the Irish Books, in his decision to leave Ireland and to devote his best efforts to being an artist within the larger context of the international struggle against poverty and class privilege.

The major theme detected in *I Knock at the Door*[5] is now manifest in Johnny-Sean Casside's frequent protestations of individuality and integrity, which set him apart, generally, from fellow-Dubliners whom he contacts at different junctures in his development. Furthermore, Johnny-Sean Casside's yet persistent sense of alienation is often diffused in his whole-hearted espousal of causes and the concomitant respect he wins from busy friends and associates. *I Knock at the Door* is introspective, or subjective or solipsistic, like childhood and boyhood everywhere – Johnny's book, while *Pictures in the Hallway* stresses involvement and commitment, prerogatives of earliest youth. There are lyrical interludes, to be sure, but this book is given over principally to Johnny-Sean Casside's nascent character and his worldly perspectives in the context of external events and tentative answers to questions affecting his progress in the life of Dublin and the world beyond. Moreover, Johnny-Sean Casside now addresses himself to human values and subsistent reality; he begins his search for lasting significance behind what is merely apparent in his own experience. Slowly, he approaches his place in life in terms of growing physical and spiritual consciousness; he is the moving centre of an expanding coordinate system in which perception, imagination, and hope for the future play their parts. Thus reduced, *Pictures in the Hallway*, though it is autobiography proper, shows forth many of the qualities normally ascribed to the apprenticeship novel, or *Bildungsroman*.[6] Increasing emphasis in this direction serves to differentiate further *Pictures in the Hallway* and the two subsequent Irish Books from *I Knock at the Door*.

The methods and techniques of exposition employed in *Pictures in the Hallway* are consonant with practices introduced in the previous book. Selected in response to the demands of autobiography, as literary genre and aesthetic mode (and O'Casey's *implied* autobiographical intention), they are sustained through O'Casey's use of a mask or persona (admittedly transparent) and third-person narration. However, in *Pictures in the Hallway*, he seems to rely more heavily than previously on complicated patterns of literary and historical allusion in his delineation of themes. Maintaining aesthetic distance from his material, O'Casey often eschews direct statement or expression of emotion. He strives to evoke specific emotional response in his reader through his perhaps unwitting and reflex use of what T. S. Eliot has called the 'objective correlative'.[7] This is especially evident in recurring instances of fantasy-satire in the Irish Books.[8] Such instances tend to be non-discursive, having much in common with poetry; they evoke meaning and feeling in the reader, but as metaphors, images, and symbols are apt to do. Though they occasionally follow assertion, as lyrical exemplifications of ideas or convictions, fantasy-satire and extended revery contribute to the poetic content of *Pictures in the Hallway*, now and then as epic and drama.

Interspersed among the main sections of *Pictures in the*

Hallway are several episodes which are autonomous. Despite the presence of such largely disjointed elements, the book remains essentially a coherent account of O'Casey's earliest youth, a critical period in his development, during which he continues to react to the works and the thoughts of others while he makes his own preparations. O'Casey's reaction frequently takes the form of rebellion and still callow criticism. Nevertheless, his personal contributions toward the solutions of perplexing problems in life and art must come later, with heightened, more comprehensive vision and power to accomplish where others have failed to see or have failed to do – Shaw's, Joyce's, and O'Casey's fortunate transmutation of peculiarly Irish experience.

Autobiography proper is narrative fiction (*poesis* or *Dichtung*) of variable length characterized by the author's *expressed* or *implied* autobiographical intention. It is fundamentally different from reminiscence, mémoirs, diaries, collections of letters (edited), and so-called autobiographical fiction. Moreover, whether expressed or implied or merely suspected, autobiography usually functions best as a confederation of traditional literary forms – lyric, epic, and dramatic, each having more or less independent stasis as art once other requirements are satisfied.[9] Proceeding from this premise, 'I Strike a Blow for You, Dear Land,' 'All Heaven and Harmsworth Too,' and 'Pictures in the Hallway,' the last three chapters of *Pictures in the Hallway,* will be discussed as varied culminations of Johnny-Sean Casside's earliest youth, abstracted from the confederation of forms which is the second Irish Book.

I Strike a Blow for You, Dear Land

'Johnny's whole world was divided against himself. England was at war with the Boer Republics.' (*PITH*, 305). And Johnny's brother Tom, some time since called from the reserves to active duty with the Royal Dublin Fusiliers, is in South Africa serving with General Sir Redvers Buller.[10] Johnny is afraid that Tom might have been killed in the Battle of Tugela (January 18, 1900, into February),[11] or in its disastrous aftermath at Spion Kop, in the course of numerous defeats sustained by the British at the hands of heroic Boers – defeats cheered by the majority of Johnny's fellow-Dubliners.

This chapter is a continuation (after about a year and a half) of 'The Sword of Light,' immediately preceding it; yet it is antonomous, deriving from the previous attempt at reconciliation of opposing forces. It develops further Johnny-Sean Casside's espousal of Irish nationalism, which seems at times patriotic. However, the time has come for commitment and action – with accompanying pain and sacrifice. No longer can Johnny's love for Ireland be confined to learning the Irish language and to participating in ancient Irish sports, revived by the Gaelic Athletic Association. Dreams of the nation's past, which are largely of personal (lyrical) significance, must give way to projects for the future of Ireland affecting all Irishmen. Caught up in militant Republicanism, which advocates complete freedom from England, Johnny-Sean Casside joins most of his countrymen in siding with the Boers. But he remains loyal to his brother Tom, for whom he has genuine affection, who has promised to bring home 'a bunch of hair from Kruger's whiskers.' (*PITH*, 305) Still, as a Protestant in Dublin, Johnny still retains memories of his childhood, when loyalty to the Queen was an unexamined part of his life at home.

Johnny is charged with conflicting loyalties, a condition common among Dubliners in the course of modern British wars, which saw in action many gallant and renowned Irish regiments. Nevertheless, he separates his personal concern for Tom, a relatively private matter having nothing to do with nationality, from his condemnation of England, which is well-considered and absolute: 'Thousands of Irishmen were out there on the veldt, risking all for England; for her honour, and, Johnny thought bitterly, for the gold and diamond mines of Johannesburg.' (*PITH*, 305).

Today Johnny and Ayamonn O'Farrel (tram conductor, recalled from the previous chapter and elsewhere in the Irish Books) stand outside the office of the *Irish Independent*, watching flashing lights (red for a British victory, and green for a Boer success) and war bulletins posted on a screen before them: 'The news was flashed . . . that the British had lost ten guns, and a great cheer, thundering defiance, made the street tremble in an agony of joy.' (*PITH*, 306). And, presumably, the green light flashes amid the cheers of the crowd.

Not everyone supports the Boers, however; a woman speaks out for England and the British generals – Roberts, French, and Kitchener, all Irishmen. So Johnny's *other* loyalty finds a voice. This woman, 'striding towards middle age,' brings to mind Bessie Burgess, in *The Plough and the Stars*; this woman in the crowd is also outspoken in her loyalty to the Crown – and, in her fashion, to Ireland:

   – I don't care who hears me, she shouted, for we're full of life today, an' – Puff – we're gone tomorra. . . . Sayin' nothin' calculated to hurt a soul, I'll say yous are a lot o' starin' fools, watchin' and waitin' for somethin' you'll never be spared to see [Ireland's freedom]. I wonder, she went on, raising her voice to a screaming pitch, I wonder what all of yous, what any of yous 'ud do, if England went undher! (*PITH*, 303).

But Johnny is not in sympathy with the woman; he has seen a pretty girl in the crowd, to whom he is attracted not for purely patriotic reasons, despite her festive attire of military cut in blatant green.[12] The girl, also brave and outspoken, speaks against the supporter of the Empire, defying the menacing looks of a policeman nearby. Johnny and O'Farrel lead the girl away from a final outburst from the outraged loyalist: 'Whenever oul' England's in a quandary, up comes th' Irishman, tearin' up he comes, an' turbulent to pull her out of it – ah! me faithful, darlin' Dublin Fusiliers! ' (*PITH*, 311).The woman makes a point, which goes unheeded in the crowd : she alludes not only to Irish generals who serve the Queen, but to Irishmen recently called from their midst to defend England; notable is her reference to Tom's regiment. Thus O'Casey reinforces his earlier mention of Johnny-Sean Casside's conflict of loyalties. But Johnny himself is taken by the charms of a lissome, red-headed girl, whose name is Daisy Battles.

Johnny and Ayamonn O'Farrell, followed by the pretty girl, now hurry towards Dame Street, which leads westward to Dublin Castle, to investigate the reason for the excitement erupting nearby. A demonstration of some sort is in its early stages; and James Connolly, Arthur Griffith, and Maud Gonne ('a young woman with long yellow hair [*sic*], smiling happily, like a child on her first excursion') are observed in the midst of things. (*PITH*, 311–312).

Though this chapter of *Pictures in the Hallway* opens sometime in February, after the British reversals at Teluga (*PITH*, 305; cf. 310), it is now abruptly the first week of April, 1900. A protest has been organized against the planned Dublin visit of Queen Victoria,[13] who, ageing, wishes to pay tribute to the gallantry of her loyal Irish regiments in their fight against the Boers. It is one of her last public appearances before her death, next January. Members of the Celtic Literary Society, the Gaelic Athletic Association, and other nationalist groups have been mustered to overthrow the plans laid down by Irish Unionists for a gala welcome. But O'Casey is never explicit with respect to events or to dates in the Irish Books. There are merged into this episode actions which occurred during Dublin riots protesting Victoria's Diamond Jubilee, in June, 1897, not mentioned previously in *Pictures in the Hallway*. Thus what ensues is a generalized disturbance, devoid of specification or attempt at historical accuracy, which derives its components from O'Casey's memory of separate incidents through which he might have lived. Indeed, the scene described is imaginary; and its emotional impact on the youthful Johnny-Sean Casside alone seems to be autobiographical. Moreover, as the police charge the demonstrators (in Parliament Street), wielding batons and sabres, Johnny recalls 'when last he saw such a sight . . . safe on the top of a tram, warm and confident, close to his mighty mother's side.' (*PITH*, 313; cf. *IKATD*, 281–285). And O'Casey drops another thread tying the present with the past; furthermore, it was on the night of the illuminations honouring Victoria's Golden Jubilee (1887) when seven-year-old Johnny and his mother first encountered Ayamonn O'Farrell, the tram-conductor, who is now at his side.

Now neither safe nor confident, Johnny is, in fact, afraid. Despite his efforts to stand at a safe place in the crowd, he is in real physical danger for the first time in his life. (*PITH*, 311) He is in a battle, holding on to the hand of the girl and following O'Farrell's directions. Suddenly, Johnny and his friends are in the path of a charging mounted policeman, who is 'hacking away with a sabre gleaming sourly in the grey air'. (*PITH*, 315).

The scene becomes epic, sustained by emotion and vivid fantastic images; no longer, as autobiography, does it imply a factual correspondence to what might have happened that day in Dublin, or during many such days brought together. The method of exposition is conventional third-person narration, and the battle-scene suggests many in literature; notable, perhaps, is that of Henry Fleming's vindication at the close of *The Red Badge of Courage* (Chapter XXIII). Here, too, in Dublin's Parliament Street, bravery becomes a relative and random thing, the result of chance in a melée:

Back, inch by inch, came the crowd, melting before Johnny as the horseman advanced to where but a few yards separated them from the slash of his sabre. A man in front of them carrying a gaudy Boer flag, screamed when he saw the gleam circle over him, and then sank down without a murmur when the flash fell, letting the flag go from his grip, and as it toppled backwards, the staff came to rest on Johnny's shoulder. Now the horseman curvetted round to where they stood, and Johnny saw a pair of eyes, like flaming carbuncles, fixed on him from under the helmet's peak; saw the black mouth of the half-mad man opening nervously . . . as he roughly swung his horse round to where they stood. In the madness of fear, Johnny gripped the pole of the flag with both hands and blindly thrust it forward with all his might as the horse came prancing round on his hind legs. The hard, wooden spearhead of the flagpole caught the rider on the side of the neck under an ear, and Johnny caught a glimpse of an angry red tear where the spear had struck. . . . Johnny felt a horse's hoof grazing his leg, splitting his trouser-leg from knee to ankle; he saw Ayamonn running furiously over to the fallen rider; saw him stamp his heavy boot on the horseman's face, and though the hard rim of the helmet saved the face from being caved in, Johnny saw that the iron heel had left a bloody blob on the rider's chin. . . . (*PITH*, 315–316).

Johnny and his friends flee the street, to take refuge in a nearby public house. Later, when fear and excitement have abated, Ayamonn leaves; and Johnny accompanies the girl to her home in Ballybough, where Johnny enjoys further fruits of his victory in Parliament Street. Johnny is a hero; and he is taken as such, in spite of what he thinks to the contrary. (Cf. *PITH* 317).

All Heaven and Harmsworth Too

Internal evidence, which is sparse and remarkably inconclusive in the Irish Books, suggests that the nineteenth chapter of *Pictures in the Hallway* takes place in 'late spring,' probably at the end of the Lenten season, 1900, that is, about the time of the excitement of 'I Strike a Blow for You, Dear Land.' (See *PITH*, 246, 325, 333). Nevertheless, it is distinct from the previous chapter in both nature of content and emphasis; ostensibly, each of these chapters relates to a different period in the life of Johnny-Sean Casside, and no connection need be established between the two of them. Here as elsewhere in the Irish Books, dating must remain largely a matter of conjecture and, consistent with O'Casey's design, of limited value.

The method of exposition in the first half of 'All Heaven and

Harmsworth Too' is conventional third-person narration. It is devoted to a summary of events in Johnny-Sean Casside's life since early 1899, with emphasis on the deterioration of his relationship with his brother Archie. Archie has 'thrown up the stage as a bad and mad job,' following a disillusioning trip to the west of Ireland with a road company playing *Saved From the Sea.* (*PITH*, 324; cf. 246). Shortly thereafter, through a stroke of good fortune, he obtained a relatively well-paying position as confidential clerk for the Harmsworth Irish Agency, a large-scale distributor of Unionist and English publications in Ireland. In fact, recently Johnny himself has taken a quasi-temporary job with the same firm, five hours a day, five days a week, 'for five shillings a week, which paid the rent, provided two dinners in the week of threepence-worth of liver, or of scraps of meat for stew, and tuppence-worth of spuds, still leaving tuppence in hand for a possible emergency ' (*PITH*, 325).

Archie, 'flying high,' has married the plain daughter of a clergyman's 'son's son,' who might have drunk himself to death, leaving his family 'in the rough and rocky lap of poverty' (*PITH*, 325). There is irony of a familiar sort in O'Casey's mention of the remoteness of the respectability thus visited on the Casside family; he alludes to the middle-class pretensions of the very poor. However, Johnny's reaction to his brother's wife accords well with the present stage of his development; and as such, it is very different from O'Casey's at the time of writing (1939–1942). In this way, O'Casey maintains aesthetic distance from his material. Johnny dislikes his brother's wife, recently her air of social superiority, yet dimly recognizing her claim to status: 'Josephine Fairbeeley still remained a lady . . . a little, stumpy, plain, perky-faced lass, with an air that said to all she thought beneath her, I'm a lady born, a lady bred, an' when I die I'll be a lady dead.' (*PITH*, 325). Josephine Fairbeeley, though it was her great-grandfather who was the clergyman, has come down in the world with her marriage into the Casside family, Archie's position with Harmsworth's notwithstanding; and it is to this that Johnny responds. But the matter is of little lasting importance to him; his extensive self-education, in keeping most of the time with his espousal of causes, has brought about in him a different sense of alienation from that of his childhood. Johnny has grown secure and confident, almost arrogant; alienation has become integrity and self-assertion. He 'was building a house of his own in which there was no room for his brother or his brother's wife. And scornful thoughts of things outside were hardening his heart.

He knew that he was far and away his brother's superior, who never ventured to dispute an opinion of his, knowing, if the argument went too far, he'd but show an ignorance he was eager to hide.' (*PITH*, 326; cf. 351) As if to substantiate further Johnny's proclamation, which might appear to be extravagant – and a touch of *hybrus*, O'Casey adds immediately:

> At the moment, Johnny was trying his hand at German, but his funds allowed him to purchase only a second-hand tattered German grammar for threepence, that led him nowhere; and he was fain to wait for a better chance to get some better books to help him. Anyway, he was learning his own tongue gaily [*Gaelic*?]; and his already fine grasp of English gave him always a readiness, and sometimes put a sparkle into what he said to many who had been blessed with an everyday chance from the time they were born. Poor Archie was but small beer to him now. (*PITH*, 326)[14]

Still, there persists a hint of over-compensation for secret doubt, which agrees with the present stage of his development; it is perhaps his reaction to Archie's good fortune and to the relatively high social position of his wife: 'Johnny's broken-down appearance didn't look nice, and their home was no fit place to bring the daughter of a clergyman's son's son.' (*PITH*, 325) Irony apart, if this point is made intentionally by O'Casey, it is both overly subtle and obscure.

The second half of 'All Heaven and Harmsworth Too' differs from the first in tone, content, and technique; it assumes a lyricism and a pattern of allusion not found in the latter. Johnny-Sean Casside remains the centre of autobiographical focus; however, a state of mind or a mood evolves, not merely a summary of events to which his reactions are subordinated. In a sense, the second half of the chapter takes as its subject 'All Heaven,' in juxtaposition to 'Harmsworth,' the subject of the first.

It is a lovely evening in late spring; and Johnny toils pushing a ramshackle hand-cart down sunny streets on the fringe of the slums, near the North Wall and the Liffey quays. He thinks bitterly of his city:

> Rotten Dublin; lousy Dublin, what had it done for anyone? What had it for him? Poverty and pain and penance. They were the three castles. The gates of Dublin: poverty, pain, and penance. And the *Harmsworth Magazine,* giving, with the

aid of its kind, to Dublin the glory that was Greece and the grandeur that was Rome. Now he was a barrenut [baronet]. Thank God, the Gaelic League was doing all it could to turn the Irish people from a descent into a vulgar and idiotic Tophet; but, so far, with little success. (*PITH*, 333).

Johnny was doing Harmsworth's work (perhaps in harm's way), the work of a *baronet*, 'the Immanuhell of journalistic vulgarism, arraying the legitimate gets of King-Kong in the robes of glory once worn by the saints, sages, prophets, and poets of England.' (*PITH*, 330). That Irishmen, primitives as they are ('the gets of King-Kong'), should be anglicized, or legitimated, or both, goes against Johnny's sense of nationality. He scorns one, especially, of Harmsworth's magazines, which is called *Answers*. Arrayed in an orange cover (not *green!*), it is read avidly throughout Ireland, by priest, student, soldier, policeman, postman, and labourer; *Answers* is a purveyor of platitudes and half-truths, fashioned to lull the people into a state of ignorant complaisance, though it parades under the banner of knowledge and high-mindedness; it is England's costly gift to the Irish people, to insure their cooperation and, perhaps, to garner a decent profit in the transaction. (*PITH*, 331–332, 334–335).

Answers offers not only knowledge, but hope of the usual sort to its readers: a chance to overcome poverty, to become rich, without resorting to annoying attempts at political and social reform. 'Tomorrow would be the day for that joy journal; and [Johnny thinks] he'd be carrying a heavy cargo again, for there was a new competition on, offering as first prize a thousand pounds down, or two pounds a week for life. An' everybody would be stretching out a hand for it. Lousy, rotten, tiring Dublin, an ignorant perjury of life.' (*PITH*, 334).

It is now twilight, and the setting sun bathes the slums in ephemeral beauty; only the idea of ugliness subsists, glossed over by light and colour. O'Casey paints a picture; and his technique has become familiar:

> He saw golden arrows of the sun shooting up side streets, leading from the quay to God knows where. Here the hard, set, and leering faces of roughs leaning against a corner had changed into sturdy faces of bronze where the sun's shadow lingered, and became darkly golden where the sun's departing beams strayed towards them. . . . He left the cripped handcart by the side of the street, and went over to lean upon the river wall to

gaze at Dublin in the grip of God. The old tattered warehouses and shops, bespangled with the dirt of ages, had turned to glory. Children, born into a maze of dirt, their vagrant garments clinging wildly to their spattered bodies, put on a new raiment, satinised with the princely rays of the sun, as if she had winced at their ugliness and had thrown her own fair mantle over them all. . . . Johnny bowed his head and closed his eyes, for it was very beautiful, and he felt that his city could catch an hour of loveliness and hold it to her panting breast. (*PITH*, 335–336).

Johnny's curses are silenced; and he reaffirms his faith in God and in man: 'He resolved to be strong; to stand out among many; to quit himself like a man; he wouldn't give even a backward look at withering things that lived by currying favour with stronger things; no busy moving hand to hat for him. He would enlarge on a spare life, never pausing to pick up a prize that perished as soon as the hand grasped it. His treasures would be simple things.' (*PITH*, 337).

The beauty of twilight lingers; and the sunlight contributes, in effect, to a carnival. Johnny approaches a hurdy-gurdy player, who is 'robed with the sun as if for a religious festival'; in response to the music in the street, Johnny joins a young woman 'in the bonny madness of a sun-dance'. (*PITH*, 339). The young woman, who 'had laughingly beckoned to him with a golden hand,' is the sister of many young women in O'Casey's works: Jannice, in *Within the Gates*; the disappointed wife, in *The Star-Jazzer*; Irish Nannie, in *Nannie's Night Out*; and Mild Millie, in the Irish Books, are among them. They dance on, till the sun all but disappears and beauty begins to fade from the streets. Johnny kisses the girl goodbye, as no doubt he kissed Daisy Battles, and gives the hurdy-gurdy player his last sixpence. He goes his way, still praising God: 'But the glory of angels was departing; for the jubilant colours dimmed into darkness. . . .' (*PITH*, 340).

At this point in 'All Heaven and Harmsworth Too,' it comes as a surprise to learn that it is Good Friday, not actually nor consistently perhaps, but thematically. O'Casey proposes to compress the forty days of Lent into the interval between Johnny's sundance (carnival) and salvation, which will be realized tomorrow, with the distribution of *Answers* to those of faith. Johnny's protest is renewed, and it signals the beginning of Lent (Ash Wednesday postfigured): 'God's shadow was still there [echo: 'the sun's shadow,' above], for every church he passed had a flood of people flooding into them.' (*PITH*, 340–341). Now he stands outside a

Catholic church, listening to a Dominican preach on 'Hell and Many Roads that Lead There.' (*PITH*, 341). There is irony here, of course, in the spectacle of slum-dwellers, in the midst of earthly hell, flocking to church in fear of a Hell hereafter; but Johnny-Sean Casside continues to listen, frightened by what he hears. Like Dante, he visits Hell on Good Friday (thence to Paradise through Purgatory); and the Hell is Catholic, belonging jointly to Dante, to Stephen Dedalus[15], and to Johnny Casside – who is, after all, a 'pristine' Catholic. Johnny's descent into Hell was predicted earlier, in allusions to the danger to Irishmen of a 'descent into a vulgar and idiotic Tophet' (*PITH*, 333) and to Harmsworth as 'the Immanuhell of journalistic vulgarism.' (*PITH*, 330) But the allusion to Dante's Hell persists:

> Thoughts of frightful form and hue hurried through his [Johnny's] mind, and harried him, for he saw himself fixed in, and frozen fast in fire eternal [like Lucifer, whose sin of intellectual pride might be Johnny's]; fire keener in its thrust than tusks of steel, while whirlwinds of icy winds and smoky storms, suffocating the burning air, raged all around him, plunging his soul from the deepest misery to a misery deeper still; with senses tuned by immortality to their highest pitch, impaled [*sic*; impelled?] by justice to endure them all; buried in screaming pain, yet rushing pell-mell to a fiercer, biting woe; ever shrieking for a chance that died ten thousand years ago, to come to life again [Resurrection; Redemption]; a shriek, once uttered, sunk to silence by the malice-mongering laughter of hardened devils tossed into Hell in heaven's first battle with an evil power [faintly Milton's *pandemonium*, in *Paradise Lost*]. O Lord most mighty, O holy and most merciful Saviour, he murmured, deliver me not into the bitter pains of eternal death. (*PITH*, 341).

Johnny looks again into the church, and he is repelled by physical evidence of blind faith in God, which has nothing to do with his happiness on the Liffey quays a short while ago. At once his mood changes; he is coldly critical now, where he was emotional and fearful at the prospect of 'eternal death'; and he is cynical – perhaps because O'Casey himself once more intrudes at the time of writing:

> A holy city's our city of Dublin, thought Johnny; more ancient than Athens; more sacred than Rome; as holy as Zion. . . .

There are more saints in Ireland to the square inch than in any other country on the globe. All the people, at a penny a week, were preparing for a good death; all were enlisted in the army of prayer, praying for the holy souls prostrate in purgatory [Church Suffering]. . . . St. Dominic knew the streets of Dublin as well as those of Calahorra; his hand, that fell hot and heavy on the Albigenses, lies gently on the heads here; for of his three great rules, poverty and fasting are kept by crowds of people, though the third of silence has yet a long way to come; and St. Francis has gathered more pale and scarlet roses from the wretched wrecked streets of this city than he ever gathered from the grove outside of Portincula. (*PITH*, 342–343)

It is dark now, and Johnny has resumed his journey through the streets. Soon he overtakes an old man singing for stray pennies; there is an ironic suggestion of Christ or of a priest in the mournful figure, and the manner of his walking brings to mind the *Via Dolorosa* or the *Stations of the Cross*, being paced in churches everywhere. But O'Casey overrides this impression with expanded irony 'Moving with him [the old man], three steps, a pause, then three more steps, were a group of gaping children, a sad audience to a sadder song.' (*PITH*, 343)

The old man sings a traditional English hymn, heard in Catholic churches throughout the world, which is, however, not appropriate for Good Friday. Moreover, it is a joyous hymn, one that proclaims hope and trust in God's goodness; O'Casey's phrase, in the passage above, 'a sad audience to a sadder song,' suggests that the hymn is sad because it is untrue. Indeed, the old man is a sham, cursing the ragged children who follow him: 'Happily plaintive he made the hymn, and bitter the mutter he meant for the children.' (*PITH*, 344) With the cynicism, which is obvious, there is a touch of anti-clericalism, which is not obvious, in O'Casey's treatment of the old man – a protest against the meaningless formulas of churches in the face of widespread poverty and human waste. As the old man sings the hymn, its meaning becomes garbled and its sound cacophonous:

To Jesu's heart all burning with fervent love for man – G'way, little gaspers, keepin' me from doin' justice to meself! My heart with fondest yearning shall raise the joyful strain – Hell an' hot water to yous, for idle little ruts! While ages course along, blest be with loudest song, Th' Sacred Heart o' Jesus by every heart and tongue! (*PITH*, 344)

Johnny continues to push his cart, walking now beside two men who have been listening casually to the old hymn-singer. One of them has just made a discovery; he is certain that he has solved the puzzle in the competition featured in the current *Answers*. From the hymn, he has caught the word *heart* ('a kinda deer'), which he has combined with a letter (like a logogram or *crismon*) 'that's half an eff and half a dee'; and he has derived the word *Hartford* (*Hart + f + or + d*). The man is on his way toward winning 'two pounds a week for life,' though neither he nor his credulous companion has ever heard the word before.

O'Casey here seems to be playing a sort of game with his reader. Nevertheless, an analogy is at once apparent between this incident and what was expressed earlier in this section; and it serves to exemplify Johnny-Sean Casside's attitude toward blind faith and meaningless rituals. *God*, like *Hartford*, is merely a word culled by many from the stray, disjointed noises of life – including human speech. Too often it is the word, not the thing, that man invests with being. Indeed, reason (*a priori*) may derive the word and existence embodied in *God*, and blind faith may proclaim its human significance; but this is no substitute for life, feeling, and self-reliance. O'Casey and his reader know of the existence of Hartford (Connecticut, perhaps); but the two Dubliners, 'going in the same direction' as Johnny (*PITH,* 344), have never heard of it. 'Johnny began to hurry home, for an early rising lay before him. Answers, the Golden One, would be out tomorrow.' (*PITH,* 345).

Pictures in the Hallway

The last chapter of *Pictures in the Hallway* (which bears the same title and consummates the second Irish Book) opens several months after the departure of the Reverend Harry Fletcher[17] from the little parish of St. Burnupus, with announcements of the impending arrival of his successor, the Revered Edward Morgan Griffin. (*PITH,* 346). This indicates, in the course of the Irish Books, a return to sometime in the year 1899, that is, to a period *prior* to that of 'I Strike a Blow for You, Dear Land' and 'All Heaven and Harmsworth Too.' With respect to auto-biographical content and theme, the regression to 'The Sword of Light,' the seventeenth chapter of *Pictures in the Hallway*, is significant; it makes possible further delineation of Johnny-Sean Casside's 'pristine' Catholicism and green patriotism at a point in his youth where the previous delineation left off. However, the *need* for regression of this sort may be questioned: it is possibly a flaw in the organization of *Pictures in the Hallway*. Excepting the last paragraph, which effectively closes the second of the Irish Books, the material of this chapter could have been placed in a better position with respect to both content and theme, the idea of chronology notwithstanding. As implied above, the likely spot seems to be just before 'I Strike a Blow for You, Dear Land.' As it stands, the last chapter of *Pictures in the Hallway* appears to be largely an afterthought, despite the importance of its content.

The method of exposition in the introductory portion of 'Pictures in the Hallway' is conventional third-person narration. (*PITH*, 346–354). It is a summary of parish affairs and of experiences affecting Johnny-Sean Casside's spiritual growth since 'The Sword of Light.' (*PITH*, 283–304).

Johnny remains in communion with his faith, though the effects of Harry Fletcher's allegedly short, tempestuous stay at St. Burnupus's[18] have by now dissipated as far as other members of the congregation are concerned. Anticipating the arrival of the new rector was 'a tiny world of faint religion, vague, timid of anything a step away from a rare reading of a Bible verse; a happy or tearful belief that God made a call and left a card at baptism, marriage, or the burial of the dead. . . . Regular worshippers were few, for there was small chance of making a good thing out of Christ.' (*PITH*, 346).

Having successfully repulsed the ritualistic and 'Romish' overtures of the Reverend James S. Fletcher, the congregation had reverted to the old ways of dour Protestantism, which Johnny of the 'high-church'[19] was inclined to reject:

The people had an idea, in a dazed way, that somehow or other God had made a wonderful world, underfoot and overhead; though underfoot was rough, marred with dust, and stony. Their way to heaven was a lifelong journey through never-ending streets of dingy houses, some of the wayfarers stopping now and then for a drink in a gayer house, glass-framed, and painted a shining red or green, and gilded.' (*PITH*, 347; cf. 282).

Happily, this is not the case with Johnny-Sean Casside; secure in his faith, he has found a way of escaping the sordidness of his surroundings, from which God's good will seems absent, and of reinforcing his pristine Catholicism. which contrasts with the dour Protestantism of fellow-communicants, as a 'brighter and more musical conception of the Christian faith.' And the Lenten season of 1900, with its own resolution of forces during a Dublin Easter Week, is still a year or so to come. Johnny has discovered color and the spiritual implications of fine paintings. Moreover, 'he longed to be a painter, and his very bowels yearned for the power to buy tubes of cobalt blue, red lake, chrome yellow, Chinese white, emerald green, burnt sienna, and a deep black pigment.' (*PITH*, 348). Thus reinforced is the theme of color that runs through the previous chapter – where the sunset transformed the ugliness of the slums into a city of beauty and human dignity. And random colors, in tubes, are like random noise and scratches on paper, to be assembled in perception in just the right fashion to produce meaning, feeling, and blends of both. Additionally, fine painting freezes moments in all sense modalities as even the sun could not do in the ephemeral splendor of an evening on the quays remembered. Yet words are no longer quintessential, spoken or written, as they were and will be.

Though his ragged appearance and his shyness keep him away from the National Gallery, Johnny now pores over the paintings of Fra Angelico da Fiesole (1387–1455) and John Constable (1776–1837) in tattered second-hand portfolios purchased for a few pence at book barrows along the Liffey. He has discovered a new world of the spirit and of nature: 'With all he had learned from the Bible and the Prayer Book it was but an easy jump into the brightly-tinted world of Angelico.' (*PITH*, 349). Constable gives him landscapes far beyond the dingy confines of Dublin: 'under the green, sunlight, or dewy trees, planted by Constable's imagination, giving shade and gracefulness to an eager sun, he wandered afield; or looking down where the ripening corn was striding upward to a golden grandeur, he wandered down quiet paths rimmed with vivid green, touched in with lavish blossoms, shyly forcing forward to kiss a greeting to the careless passer-by. . . .' (*PITH*, 350). The allusion is to Constable's *The Cornfield*.

Constable gives Johnny nature in all its beauty[20]; but Fra Angelico gives him God, now personal and transcendent, to substantiate his faith in the purpose of life, which, paradoxically in Johnny-Sean Casside's grasp, can be *too* reasonable when it is denied empirical proof or demonstration. Indeed, the Renaissance painter asserts an earlier Christianity, more vivid and alive than the 'low-church' Protestantism which repels Johnny; what Fra Angelico has to say is in harmony with Johnny's own Catholicism, which owes more to emotion than to dogma and theology.

O'Casey's descriptions of two of Fra Angelico's paintings give evidence of the depth and lasting significance of his first experiences with painting, though he must have renewed his acquaintance with the artist since. Moreover, they reveal the emotional and spiritual content of his youthful Christian faith. Consistent with O'Casey's practice, the descriptions are designed to suggest his general experience with the work of the religious painter. Though they are accurate as far as they go, the first of these descriptions contains omissions and allusions to other paintings by Angelico. As autobiography, they are memories touched with imagination and present feeling – presumably at the time of writing. From the slums crowding the little church of St. Burnupus, 'Johnny ferried himself safely in the circle of delicate blue showing forth Angelico's golden-haired Saviour clad in a robe of shimmering creamy grey, a shining orb in a beautiful left hand, a halo of heavy gold transversed with a crimson cross, encircling His heavenly head. . . .' (*PITH*, 350).

In this way, O'Casey reacts to Fra Angelico's *Christ Scorned*,[21] presently in the Convent of San Marco, Florence. In the painting itself, Christ is seated on a red throne (a simple, rectangular block of stone, resting on a large block of white marble); He wears a crown of thorns and a white blindfold; in His left hand, He holds the orb (mentioned by O'Casey), and in His right a staff. Behind the seated figure is a rectangle of emerald green, serving as a screen on which are projected what appears to be the head and neck of a shepherd tipping his hat and whistling in the direction of the seated Christ, and four disembodied hands, one of which holds a stick pressing against the crown of thorns. At the foot of the enthroned Christ are the Virgin – seated, pensive and sorrowful, looking toward the lower left, out from the painting, and St. Dominic – also seated, turned in the same direction as the Virgin, poring over an open book. St. Dominic's halo is touched by a small crimson star, as it is invariably when the founder of Fra Angelico's order appears in his paintings. High in the semi-circular arch of the painting, the sky shows cobalt blue (not 'delicate blue'). The painting contains abstractions which are characteristic of Fra Angelico's work, in addition to details contributing to his allegorical naturalism. The painting is a wealth of varied strengths of color and delicate shadows. Christ's halo, heavy gold transversed by a crimson cross (mentioned by O'Casey), is one of Fra Angelico's signatures – as is his salute to the Dominicans. Christ is robed in white (not 'shimmering creamy grey'); and the theme of the painting is Christ's humiliation and suffering, not his triumph – as suggested by O'Casey's fragmentary description. O'Casey might have had in mind, with *Christ Scorned*, several other paintings by Fra Angelico, notably *The Last Judgment*.[22]

O'Casey's second description of a painting by Fra Angelico is precise, making possible identification of the work entitled *Christ Welcomed As A Pilgrim By Two Friars*[23]; here no significant details are omitted, nor are there any allusions to other paintings: 'There He was, standing in a purple arch of the heavens, staff in hand, looking with love on two Dominican brothers, one of whose hands timidly touched the Saviour's, the two of them dressed in robes, tenderly cream, covered with sombre black cloaks cunningly tinged with green, standing there gazing at Christ with a look that reverently called God their comrade.' (*PITH*, 349–350).

As a result of his experience with Fra Angelico, Johnny is transported into a different world – a world of medieval ecstasy and certitude, where there is no denial of God's good will, nor of human dignity. Sometimes he chanted hymns softly to himself, strolling towards heaven through a field of pinks and roses, meeting often on his way more lovely angels, blowing with flattened cheeks through golden trumpets over graceful psalteries or zithers, sounding in honour of the Blessed Virgin, while her Son fixed another gem in her crown of glories.' (*PITH*, 350) The last allusion seems to refer to Fra Angelico's *The Coronation of the Virgin*, also held at the Convent of San Marco, Florence, or to the painting on the same theme presently at the Louvre, Paris.[24]

Johnny begins to see beauty subsistent in the world about him 'so that the street he lived in was peopled with the sparkling saints and angels of Angelico, and jeweled with the serene loveliness Constable created out of the radiance of common clay.' (*PITH*, 351).

But predictably Johnny's happiness is lonely, another phase of his alienation while growing up: 'He tried to share these sights with his mother; but he saw they had but a timid and feebly whispered message for her, sending her more eagerly back to the motherly care of her crimson geranium, her gold musk, and her fuchia, with its purple bells and white waxy sepals drooping rayally over the sadness of the cracked and withering window.' (*PITH*, 351) Still, Johnny does share with his mother the impulse to clothe the sordidness of life with beauty; she nourishes beauty with her hands, Johnny with thought and emotion.

'Into this growing dwelling-place of Johnny's came the new

rector, to take up the pastorate of St. Burnupus.' (*PITH*, 351)
The Reverend E. M. Griffin is a learned, sensitive, and entirely
capable man, about forty-five, who soon awakens the parish from
its slumber. Like Harry Fletcher before him, he is 'high-church,'
tending toward ritual and close observance of the rubric; thus he
appeals to Johnny's 'pristine' Catholicism. Above all, the new
rector is tolerant of the desires of the majority of his congregation, which run often counter to his own inclinations with respect
to the conduct of services. Moreover, he does not confine his
efforts to matters of dogma or to Sunday or weekday fulfilment
of religious duties; he is forceful and productive in secular affairs
as well: 'the religious life of the parish became vigorous, homely,
orderly, under the direction and encouragement of the new
rector.' (*PITH*, 352).

The Reverend E. M. Griffin attracts the attention of several
organizations of Protestant men, who, at first, take him to be 'a
hale protestant after the Orangeman's pattern'. (*PITH*, 352) They
assume that he will aid them in their fraternal fight against Roman
Catholicism and, indeed, against Romish practices in their own
church. Members of these groups soon learn that the rector is his
own man,[25] who refuses to align himself with vested interests.
In reaction to his show of independence, these groups (composed
of small businessmen and petty public servants, opposed in many
ways to Irish nationalism) band together against Griffin's allegedly
'popish' tendencies. They strive to elect members of the Select
Vestry of St. Burnupus in order to force their policies and politics
on the new rector, hampering his efforts in the process.

Soon after his arrival, the new rector becomes the close friend
of Johnny-Sean Casside, gaining his support in various parish
activities. The Reverend E. M. Griffin appears as E. Clinton,
Rector of St. Burnupus, in *Red Roses for Me*.[26] Furthermore,
the fourth act of *Red Roses for Me* develops, in a minor key,
the theme of 'Buttle of the Boyne,' the main section in the
closing chapter of *Pictures in Hallway*, which recounts the dispute between Low-Church (Evangelical, or 'broad') and High
Church (Apostolic, or 'popish') factions in the parish of St.
Burnupus. Johnny-Sean Casside (like Ayamonn Breydon in the
play) sides with the rector against 'orange and blue' Protestantism;
in this way, too, he supports the cause of Irish nationalism
against secular Protestantism generally loyal to the British Crown
in Ireland.

'The Buttle of the Boyne,' the last section of *Pictures in the
Hallway*, chapter and Irish Book, is a fantasy-satire of a sort now

familiar, which incorporates a complex pattern of historical allusion. It differs both in method and technique of exposition from the first section of the chapter which serves as an introduction to it. As noted, the introduction delineates phases of Johnny's pristine Catholicism, bringing it into thematic – and dramatic – focus during the present situation in the parish of St. Burnupus. Johnny's reception of religion is reduced to emotion and a sense of beauty and personal values, with but passing notice of dogma or theology, a sort of mysticism; Johnny has discovered (before the arrival of the new rector) colour and subsistent purpose in the world, which render life even in the slums of North Dublin worthwhile and glorious. Conventional third-person narration now gives way to what verges on indirect stream-of-consciousness exposition. Johnny's thoughts are presented in the immediate context of his knowledge of history; his language is replete with multiple puns and portmanteau words, indicating throughout the influence of James Joyce. Perhaps, this is, as O'Casey claims, another tribute to his fellow-Dubliner.[27]

In a formal sense (making allowance for his individuality), Johnny-Sean Casside, at about nineteen years of age, is devoutly Protestant Episcopal; that is, he is a member of the Disestablished Church of Ireland.[28] Moreover, like the Reverend James S. Fletcher (Harry Fletcher and, earlier, the Reverend T. R. S. Hunter, in the Irish Books) and the Reverend E. M. Griffin, to whom he at this time owes his affiliation with the Church, as noted, Johnny is *high-church* in his practices and personal inclinations. He advocates the close adherence of the Church of Ireland to the early (pre-Reformation) standards – the persistent rubric – of the Catholic and Apostolic Church. (*See PITH,* 301). Denying out of hand the control and innovations of the Vatican, Johnny acknowledges the sole authority of the Protestant Bishops in Ireland; he is thus a Catholic, though Protestant and Reformed – like Henry VIII. Spiritually, at least Johnny shares more with his Roman Catholic comrades in the cause of Irish nationalism than he does with *low-church* Protestants, who would purge the Church of Ireland of ritual and the outward signs suggestive of Rome, and who tend to be loyal Unionists. For these reasons, and others suspected, in the ensuing fantasy-satire, Johnny fights on the side of James II, the deposed King of England, who represents the 'green' of Ireland, against Protestant William III (of the House of Orange), who represents the 'blue and orange' of English Protestantism and its ultimate Ascendancy in Ireland.

'The Battle of the Boyne' is an allegory, in which Johnny and the Rector, with their followers, oppose 'cordons of orange and blue and blue and purple' (*PITH*, 352), who are loyal Unionists coming against both Rome and Irish nationalism. The election of Select Vestrymen becomes the Battle of the Boyne (July 12, 1690); and it is fought again, this time (April, 1899) on the lawn of the Church of St. Burnupus, in North Lotts, Dublin. The outcome is startlingly different, however; the forces of James II win out over those of Protestant William of Orange: 'Not a single name of the Orange party's choice appeared on the list of elected members [of the Select Vestry], and a great clapping of hands sounded a *feu de joie* for the Orangemen, who stood up, and went out in silence and an angry shame.' (*PITH*, 371).Twelve good men and true were now available to help the Reverend E. M. Griffin in the work of the parish.

The chapter closes with Johnny-Sean Casside's resolution to move forward – earliest youth, in fact and fancy, was over:

By his help, the Orange banner had been replaced by the green [of St. Patrick, of Irish patriots, or of both], or the blue [of St. Lawrence O'Toole, of his city Dublin, or of both], with the sunburst awake in its centre. . . . He shook himself. He was staying too long in the Hallway looking at the pictures. All done by others. Very beautiful and strong, but all done by others. He'd have to start now doing things for himself. Create things out of his own life. He'd begin to make pictures himself; ay, pictures, too, that would be worth hanging in the Hallway for other people to see. (*PITH*, 373).

There is an echo here of Stephen Dedalus's proclamation at the end of *A Portrait of the Artist as a Young Man*, also in April: 'I go to encounter for the millionth time the reality of experience and to forge in the smithy of my soul the uncreated consciousness of my race.'[29] Johnny-Sean Casside, too, must emerge eventually as an artist shaping the stuff of his days; but first he will contribute to the present and the future of Ireland and of his fellow-man there and everywhere.

Notes

1 Sean O'Casey. *Mirror in My House: The Autobiographies of Sean O'Casey*. 2 vols. (New York: Macmillan, 1956). This handsome American edition contains the approximately one-half million words of the six autobiographies: *I Knock at the Door* (1939); *Pictures in the Hallway* (1942); *Drums Under the Windows* (1946); *Inishfallen, Fare Thee Well* (1949); *Rose and Crown* (1951); and *Sunset and Evening Star* (1954). These volumes were issued separately by Macmillan during the years indicated; bound together, they retain their original format and pagination. They will be cited by suitable short titles, as in note 3, below.

2 It is convenient to designate the first four volumes of O'Casey's autobiographies the *Irish Books*, as they encompass his first forty-six years, which were spent in Ireland and which close with his first successes as an Abbey playwright. The final two volumes become thus the *Books of Exile*. Indeed, only the Irish Books exemplify autobiography *per se*; the Books of Exile are blends of reminiscence and memoir differing in structure, point of view, and major theme from what precedes them. Moreover, there are signs in the fourth of the Irish Books which predict O'Casey's eventual abandonment of the genre.

3 The life-spans incorporated in *Mirror in My House* are as follows:

Volume		Period	Persona, of Central Character
IKATD	(1939)	1880–1890	Johnny Casside
PITH	(1942)	1891–1900	Johnny-Sean Casside
DUTW	(1946)	1905–1916	Sean-(Irish) Jack Casside
IFTW	(1949)	1916–1926	Sean O'Casside (O'Casey)
RAC	(1952)	1926–1934	Sean O'Casey (loss of persona)
SAES	(1954)	1934–1953	Sean O'Casey

4 In a letter to the present author (October 18, 1961), O'Casey observes, 'You yourself have unconsciously gathered me together in three words – I am a kinda trinitarian soul: Johnny, Jack, Sean – one in three and three in one, and it isn't easy not to divide the substance or confound the persons; for there is one person in Johnny, another in Jack, and another in Sean; yet these three persons make one man.' 'Lines from Torquary: Letters By and About Sean O'Casey,' *The Sean O'Casey Review, 3*, (2) (Spring 1977), 120.

5 The theme is alienation. See David Krause, *Sean O'Casey: The Man and His Work* (New York: Macmillan, 1960), p. 2, *passim*, for a discussion of O'Casey's Protestantism, itself an alienating factor in

the predominantly Catholic slums of North Dublin. See also Robert Kee, *The Green Flag: The Turbulent History of the Irish National Movement* (New York. Delacorte, 1972), especially p. 18, for a contrary view: 'To be Protestant, whatever one's status, and by no individual effort of one's own, is to be automatically superior.' Johnny-Sean Casside will reconcile these views, of course, somewhere on common ground.

6 See Susanne Howe [Nobbe], *Wilhelm Meister and His English Cousins* (New York: Columbia University Press, 1930), Chapters I and II, pp. 1–40, especially, where Professor Nobbe defines the apprenticeship novel, or *Bildungsroman*, in terms pertinent to the present discussion. Note p. 6: 'The *Bildungsroman* is distinct . . . from *Entwicklungsroman* which has more general scope and does not presuppose the more or less conscious attempt on the part of the hero to cultivate himself by his experience, which is essential to the *Bildungsroman*.'

7 T. S. Eliot, 'Hamlet,' in *Selected Essays*, New Edition (New York: Harcourt Brace, 1950), pp. 121–126.

8 See the present author's 'A Darwinian Garden of Eden: A Major Emphasis in O'Casey's Autobiographies,' *The Sean O'Casey Review*, 5, (2) (Spring 1979).

9 T. S. Eliot, 'The Three Voices of Poetry,' in *On Poetry and Poets* (New York: Farrar, Straus and Cudahy, 1957), 96–112, especially pp. 96, 104–105, and 109.

10 See Robert A. Huttenback, *The British Imperial Experience* (New York & London: Harper & Row, 1966), pp. 89, 99–104, *passim*; see also Kee, *op. cit.*, pp. 443–44.

11 On January 18, 1900, General Redvers Buller finally crossed the Tugela River and captured Spion Kop, a week later. However, he was forced to retreat with considerable losses. He failed in a third attempt February 6–7, 1900. Cf. *PITH*, 310, where Daisy Battles alludes to Buller's defeat at Colenso, December 15, 1899. Earlier in this year, Major John MacBride helped to form the Irish Brigade and became its second-in-command. It proved to be a small outfit, probably much less than its touted 1,000-man membership, of men in the Transvaal of Irish origin, mainly Americans. See Kee, *op. cit.*, p. 433 and p. 443n.

12 See Bernard Benstock, 'The O'Casey Touch,' *Sean O'Casey: A Collection of Essays*, ed. Thomas Kilroy (Englewood Cliffs, N.J.: Prentice-Hall, 1975), pp. 139–148, especially pp. 147–148.

13 See W. B. Yeats, Letter to *The Daily Express*, April 3, 1900, in *The Letters of W. B. Yeats*, ed. Allan Wade (New York: Macmillan, 1955), p. 338: The day before Victoria's visit to Dublin, Yeats described her as 'the official head and symbol of an empire that is robbing the South African Republics of their liberty, as it robbed Ireland of theirs. Whoever stands by the railway cheering for Queen Victoria cheers for that Empire, dishonours Ireland, and condones a crime.' Earlier, Maud Gonne had dubbed the tiny monarch 'Famine Queen'.

14 See Kurt Wittig, *Sean O'Casey Als Dramatiker: Ein Beitrag zum Nachkriegsdrama Irlands* (Inaugural-Dissertation, Martin-Luther-Universität Halle-Wittenberg; Leipzig: Fritz Scharf, 1937), especially a letter to the author, May 22, 1937, p. 13, n. 12: 'I know two

languages my own (Irish) and English.' It is interesting to note an earlier letter to Wittig, March 3, 1937, in the same study, p. 10, where O'Casey suggests, among other things, that he was born in 1884: 'I was born in Dublin about 54 years ago, worked as a labourer there, lived on very little, liked books, read as much as I could, and finally settled down to write plays.'

15 Compare James Joyce, 'A Portrait of the Artist as a Young Man,' in *The Portable James Joyce*, ed. Harry Levin (New York. Viking, 1949), pp. 382–397.

16 In a letter to the present author (May 12, 1961), O'Casey says with reference to projected studies of his autobiographies: 'Choose any ... phase you like; but, if on my attitude to 'Catholicism,' be sure to see the difference between the 'Faith once delivered to the Saints,' and the bloated blather of Cardinal, Bishop, Monsignor, & Canon.' 'Lines From Torquay,' *op. cit.*, p. 119.

17 See *Dublin: What's to be Seen, and How to See It.* New and Revised Edition (Dublin: Hodges, Figgis & Co., 1888), p. 5, where St. Barnabas' Protestant Episcopal Church is identified, in North Lotts, with the Reverend James S. Fletcher as its pastor. This suggests at once that O'Casey has mistakenly named the pastor *Harry* Fletcher. However, O'Casey states that the pastor is newly arrived (*PITH*, 228), in 1896–97; the Reverend Fletcher mentioned in the guide would have been in place eight or nine years. On the other hand, O'Casey having lived long in the neighbourhood (about twenty-two years) might now (at the time of writing) remember only dimly particulars concerning the pastor of St. Barnabas; indeed, it is also possible that the name Harry Fletcher is fictitious, and that coincidence accounts for the remarkable similarity in names. See also valuable biographical sketch and photograph of the Reverend James S. Fletcher in *The Sean O'Casey Review, 4,* (1) (Fall 1977), 75, where it is noted that he was Rector of St. Barnabas Dublin from 1872 to 1899 and that, incidentally, the Reverend James S. Fletcher is the 'Rev. T. R. S. Hunter' of O'Casey's autobiographies. (See *IKATD*, 135–138, *passim*). Again, thanks to Bill Young, Webb's Bookshop, Dublin.

18 See 'The Sword of Light,' the seventeenth chapter of *PITH*, 283–304; note especially 291–282: 'The poor man was having a harrying time with the true blue protestants because, they said, he was a ritualist, though he asserted he was only determined to carry out the rules of the rubric in decency and order. . . . The Orangemen loudly and defiantly spoke the creed when it was being intoned by the choir, shouting out Popery! when Mr. Harry and others turned toward the east as the creed was sung.'

19 Hence Johnny-Sean Casside is Protestant Episcopal or, in principle at least, 'pristine' Catholic – of a pre-Henry VIII sort.

20 Cf. Sir William Orpen (ed.), *Outline of Art*, rev. ed., ed. Horace Shipp (London: George Newnes, Ltd., 1953), p. 459, for a contemporary reproduction of John Constable's *The Cornfield*; the original is presently held by the National Gallery, London. See Orpen's comment, *ibid.*, p. 460: 'At a time when fashionable opinion held that 'a good picture, like a good fiddle, should be brown,' Constable dared to paint Nature truly in her own colours and became

the pioneer of "natural" landscape painting.' Somehow, there is a discernible accord here with O'Casey's earliest appreciation of Constable.

21 For a fine reproduction of *Christ Scorned*, see Giulio Carlo Argan, *Fra Angelico and His Times* (Lausanne, Switzerland: *SKIRA*, 1955), p. 95; for the original, visit the Convent of San Marco, Florence.

22 For a reproduction of *The Last Judgment*, see Argan, *op. cit.*, p. 112; the original can be seen at the Galleria Nazionale d'Arte, in Rome. *The Last Judgment* is the last panel of *The Ascension and Pentecost*.

23 For a (possibly) contemporary reproduction of *Christ Welcomed As A Pilgrim By Two Friars*, see Joseph Fattorusso (ed.), *Wonders of Italy*, 12th ed. (Florence & New York: W. S. Heinman, 1959), p. 249. The painting is held in the Convent of San Marco, Florence.

24 For reproductions of the two versions of *The Coronation of the Virgin*, see Argan, *op. cit.*, pp. 62 and 100.

25 See the caption to the frontispiece, a photograph of 'The Reverend E. M. Griffin, B.D., M.A.,' *Drums Under the Windows, op. cit. Pictures in the Hallway, op. cit.*, is dedicated to Griffin: 'A fine scholar; a man of many-branched kindness, whose sensitive hand was the first to give the clasp of friendship to the author.'

26 See Sean O'Casey, *Collected Plays*. 4 vols. (London: Macmillan, 1957–58), III, 123–232, especially 205–228. In his stage-setting for *Red Roses for Me*, O'Casey writes, 205: 'The grounds [surrounding the Protestant Church of St. Burnupus] aren't very beautiful, for they are in the midst of a poor and smoky district; but they are trim, and, considering the surroundings, they make a fair show. . . . It is a warm, sunny evening, the Vigil of Easter. . . .' The time within the play, 'a little while ago,' is probably April, 1914, at the end of the Great Lockout, not sometime in 1899.

27 O'Casey writes in a letter to the present author (April 9, 1962), 'Lines From Torquay,' *op. cit.*, 121: 'Joyce's influence was like a bugle-call, loud and clear first, fading away as it was being heard; or like heavy footsteps passing by an open window. . . .'

28 The Church of Ireland was disestablished in 1869; in 1870, a convention of Irish bishops, clergy, and laity was held; and its first act was to declare the adherence of the Church of Ireland to pre-Reformation standards and discipline of the Catholic and Apostolic Church, while accepting its status as Protestant and Reformed in opposition to the Vatican. See Edmund Curtis, *A History of Ireland*. 6th ed. (London: Methuen, 1961; originally 1950), pp. 373–374: 'The highly endowed State Church commanded the allegiance of only an eighth of the population, she had against her both the Romanist and Presbyterian elements, and though she claimed to be the ancient Church of Ireland with uninterrupted succession it had to be admitted that she had never been, nor could be the Church of anything but a minority, even though that minority was powerful in the upper classes.' See also Kee, *op. cit.*, p. 356: 'The Act disestablishing the Protestant Church over the whole of Ireland . . . was the first measure the Union Parliament had passed solely because the majority of the Irish people wanted it.'

29 'A Portrait of the Artist as a Young Man,' *op. cit.*, p. 526.

THE UNHOLY TRINITY:
A SIMPLE GUIDE TO HOLY
IRELAND c. 1880-1980

ALAN SIMPSON

In *Richard's Cork Leg*, Brendan Behan wrote: 'Other people have a nationality . . . The Irish and the Jews a psychosis.' The inevitable consequence of this profound truth is that we Irish love to tell people all about ourselves and how we became what we are. This can be tedious to others and, indeed, to ourselves. Both races can trace their complex histories back a very long time. Any method that can be devised to encapsulate these histories must be welcome. For the Irish, one such is the study of the works of their modern dramatists.

Few nationalities can boast such a comprehensive catalogue of readable and performable work embracing the recent social and political history of their race as can the Irish. Sean O'Casey forms the centrepiece of a triptych of modern Irish playwrights who have been widely read though less frequently performed outside their own country. J. M. Synge, O'Casey, and Behan in both their persons and in their plays form a bridge linking the Ireland of 1880 to that of 1980. They also, in their ethnic makeup, symbolise the emergence of the native Irish from the dominance of their conquerors.

Synge's first performable play, *The Shadow of the Glen*, was written in 1902. Behan's last play, *Richard's Cork Leg*, was drafted in the early nineteen-sixties. A thorough study of all the plays of Synge, O'Casey, and Behan would, without further research bring one a long way towards a full understanding of modern Ireland. It would also chart many of the changes in attitude that have taken place in most of the country since the closing years of the 19th century. In undertaking such a study, one should of course note that the plays (none of which deal with the more prosperous classes) fall into three separate catgories. The first, Synge's plays, are all rural in background. The second, O'Casey's early plays and all of Behan's, are urban and reflect the environs of Dublin and its working class. With one or two exceptions, O'Casey's later plays form the third category, and must be considered separately. Their setting is one of fantasy, sometimes located in a rural Ireland conceived in the author's imagination. Nonetheless, these plays, especially those written between World War II and his death are well worth considering in our context. In them, O'Casey deals with *public* issues and controversies, primarily involving the Catholic Church in Ireland. The main source of his information about these issues must inevitably have been the Dublin newspapers, for O'Casey was physically isolated in Devonshire during this period. This isolaton, as well as a deliberate change in dramatic technique, accounts for a certain lack of subtlety of comment in the dialogue. In turn, the lack of subtlety and his outspoken condemnation of the Irish Catholic Establishment accounts for the infrequent performances of the plays in Ireland.

The Behan plays, all of which were written between 1946 and 1964, are a more reliable guide to what the Dubliner in the street was thinking in private during those years. In them, Behan was frequently passing on to posterity the views of his father, Stephen Behan. Old Behan was as much an O'Casey character as any of those manufactured by Sean himself. Without his son Brendan to record them, the views of this archetypal Dubliner would have had for an audience but a few convivial cronies in a local pub. Behan's *The Big House*, a stunningly perspicacious retrospective view of the Irish Civil War of 1922-24 (which also forms the contemporaneously observed background to O'Casey's *Juno and the Paycock*) is important in this respect.

Synge and O'Casey differed from Behan in one important respect: their attitudes to playwriting. Synge and O'Casey were both conscious innovators. Behan was not. Nor was he a real revolutionary. O'Casey was actively and effectively engaged in revolutionary politics before he started playwriting. Synge could be described as a cultural rebel and patriot. In *Cork Leg*, Behan wrote:

The great majority of Irish people believe that if you become a priest or a nun you've a better chance of going to heaven. If it's a virtue to meditate in a monastery and get food and shelter for doing it – why then isn't it a virtue outside? I'm a lay contemplative – that's what I am.

He was right. He had a lively and creative mind. He lived an adventurous early life in politically extremist circles, but he made little conscious effort to *alter* his political or cultural environment. As the quotation suggests his role was of a reporter, witty and perspicacious though he may have been. He seemed also to be unaware of the nature of his technique and its development, even though *The Hostage* and *Richard's Cork Leg* foreshadowed world-wide stylistic changes and innovations in playwriting.

On the other hand, Synge was such an intrepid artistic explorer that in writing *The Shadow of the Glen* he chose the then virtually nonexistent Irish Theatre to push forward the frontiers of drama. Even Ibsen, who was working in an established theatrical tradition fifty years previously had hardly ventured into a more virgin territory. O'Casey's dramatic innovations are too numerous even to begin to list.

'No religion! No politics!' cried the Pakistani peddlar in the now-forgotten Abbey Theatre rural comedy of the nineteen-forties. I fear there can be no serious examination of any Irishman's social background without considerable involvement in these two forbidden subjects, especially the first. Just to remind readers that Synge and O'Casey were Protestants and that Behan was a Catholic is about as meaningful as noting that Shakespeare had a beard.

It was once the custom in paranoically nationalist Irish circles to exclude all but practicing Catholics of impeccably Hibernian Celtic descent from the title, True Irishman. Their most distinguished spokesman was Daniel Corkery. Nowadays such racist ideas are out of favour, even among political extremists. In the United States, where Ethnic Studies seem at least as popular as Ethics, it may not appear odd to have to define an Irishman. This is not the case in Britain where, possibly as a legacy of the Imperial frame of mind, it has been the practice to claim Protestant Irish writers like Shaw and Wilde as British, if not English. More recently, as a concession to progressive thinking, the term 'Irish-born' has come into use there. For our purposes, my countrymen can be broadly divided into Catholic native Irish and Protestant Anglo-Scots settlers. This goes back three hundred years or so which I feel sure is far enough. The violence which continues at the time of writing in North-east Ireland underlines the ethnic and religious division in that area. Synge, O'Casey and Behan were all born and brought up in Dublin and had little real contact with the North.

Behan, and O'Casey before him, liked to draw attention to anomalies in the generalisation that all Southers were Catholic and nationalist and that, conversely, the majority in the North-east were

Protestant and pro-British. The most notable example O'Casey provides is in *The Plough and the Stars*. Bessie Burgess is a working-class Unionist Protestant. The Dublin-ness of Bessie, combined with her outspoken loyalty to the British crown is subtly and accurately integrated into the writing. It seemed to me to seriously distort O'Casey's carefully detailed picture of Dublin slum life in 1916 when Belfast-born Siobhan McKenna chose to play Bessie with a Northern accent in the Abbey Theatre's 1976 revival.

O'Casey did not choose to include any Anglo-Irish gentry in his early writing. It was not that he was unacquainted wih the breed. He worked closely with the impeccably Anglo-Irish Countess Constance Markiewicz when he was secretary of the Irish Citizen Army in Liberty Hall just four years before submitting his first play to the Abbey. She was a theatrically patriotic revolutionary figure, but O'Casey disliked her intensely. He seems to have loved all the characters he put in his early plays, even when he disapproved of their behaviour. So 'The Countess' provided no copy.

Behan once described an Anglo-Irishman as "a Protestant with a horse". This is a generally accurate description and fitted the Countess nicely. It did not fit J. M. Synge so neatly. He was not sufficiently well-off to have a horse. He regularly travelled to and from his genteel Dublin suburb and what had once been the Synge's ancestral family seat in Co. Wicklow on a humble bicycle.

As I have implied, to describe Synge and O'Casey simply as 'Protestants' is not enough. Irish Protestants came from a mixed bag of genes. The Anglo-Irish form the best-known group, but they themselves evolved from two separate sources: Anglo-Scots colonial settlers and Gaelic nobility, who had changed their religion and Anglicised themselves in order to retain wealth and power. Some of the colonists did well over the generations, becoming less Anglo and more Irish in the process. Synge came from the latter stock, though his grandfather, by bad management had dissipated the family's wealth. His father was an only moderately successful lawyer who died when Synge was a baby. Throughout his life, except for periods he spent in Germany, France and on the West coast of Ireland, Synge lived frugally with his mother in modestly fashionable Dublin suburbs.

O'Casey's ancestral background is not as easy to establish, for the nineteenth-century 'lower orders' had neither the means nor the leisure to produce family trees. Those families, like the Synges who regarded themselves as gentry, took pains to publicise their

genealogy. O'Casey's grandfather has been identified by David
Krause as a poor farmer, a Catholic from Limerick. Krause offers no
information about O'Casey's paternal grandmother except that she
was staunchly Protestant. One might guess that her husband
dropped his 'O'' at the time of his marriage, even if he could not
go so far as to change his religion. It does not seem likely that Mrs
Casey (the grandmother) was of gentle birth. In addition to the
Anglo-Irish, there is a thin sprinkling of other Protestants in the
South who, like most of their co-religionists in the North-East, have
no social pretentions. Frequently they are the descendants of the
small traders and petty officials who sustained the British admini-
stration. When O'Casey's grandfather died, his grandmother, in
defiance of the rest of the family, raised her youngest son Michael
(O'Casey's father) as a Protestant. They fled to Dublin. Her other
children had been raised Catholics in Limerick, which to this day
has a reputation for religious intolerance. They remained in Dublin,
and when he grew up Sean's father became a clerk. He married
Susan Archer who, Krause has discovered, was a Protestant
auctioneer's daughter from Wicklow. By the time Sean was born,
though, his father was only a tenement caretaker, and he died
when Sean was six.

After Michael died, Susan struggled to bring up her sickly,
half-blind son and such of her large family as had survived infancy
In Innisfallen Parade, a small street of three-room workmen's
cottages near Mountjoy Prison on the unfashionable North Side of
Dublin. Later they moved to the East Wall, a small isolated area
cut off from the rest of Dublin by the sea, the docks and the
Great Northern Railway line.

Mrs. Casey of 9 Innisfallen Parade had one thing in common
with Mrs. Synge of 4 Orwell Park, Rathgar, apart from their
widowhood. They shared a profound and puritanical religious
conviction. The Church of Ireland, to which they both belonged,
embraced a very robust evangelical section. This section had more
in common with American Bible Belt Christianity than with the
Middle and High Churchmanship of the Church of England with
which it is in communion. In the Casey household Biblical fervour
must have been heightened by the fact that Michael Casey had
served his religious cause in the bigoted atmosphere of the Irish
Church Missions, a proselytising organisation dedicated to saving
Papist souls by fair means or foul. All through the nineteenth
century the Irish struggle for souls between Protestants and
Catholics had swayed first one way and then another. There must
have been the occasional conversion from conviction. However,

after Catholic Emancipation in 1829, the main Protestant weapon was economic. They gave soup and other handouts to starving peasants in the country and to the urban poor in the city slums in exchange for defection to their ranks. The Caholics for their part used intermarriage in retaliation. The Catholic Hierarchy promulgated stringent regulations (some still effectually in force) to ensure that the children of a mixed marriage would be brought up Catholics. It seems likely that O'Casey's grandfather's marriage was the subject of such an interdiction. In *Richard's Cork Leg*, Behan adroitly sums up the Catholic attitude to the struggle:

Bawd I: A pervert is when a Catholic becomes a Protestant.
The Hero: Not a pervert. A convert.
Bawd I: A convert is when a Protestant becomes a Catholic.

Throughout his life O'Casey seemed fated to exist in the no-man's-land of this sectarian war. His lack of detachment in matters relating to the Catholic Church frequently blunted the edge of his wit, a tendency that became more marked as he got older. The rarely-produced *Behind the Green Curtains*, written shortly before his death, is fatally flawed in this respect.

While Mrs. Synge was no less concerned than Mrs. Casey to pass on to her son her own puritanical zeal, she was apparently less successful. On the surface at any rate, there is no evidence in Synge's plays of any great concern with overtly religious matters. O'Casey's later plays are diminished by a sectarian approach. But his writing technique was enriched by his youthful familiarity with Holy Scripture. Notable examples are *The Silver Tassie, Red Roses for Me,* and *The Star Turns Red*. If Synge emerges as less interested in sectarian division than O'Casey, he was equally successful at arousing the disapproval of Irish Catholic orthodoxy. As recently as the nineteen-fifties it was thought quite daring to present *The Shadow of the Glen* or *The Tinker's Wedding* in Ireland, even in Dublin.

Both Protestant writers were to fall in love with Catholic women. Synge's family were saved embarrassment by the playwright's untimely death. He was engaged to be married to the Abbey actress, Maire O'Neill, who created the part of Pegeen Mike in *Playboy*. Eighteen years later O'Casey married Eileen Reynolds who, in her own words, was 'Irish, though educated in England by nuns who had taught her a lady-like accent.' It was fortunate for both of them that Eileen moved in the atmosphere of upper middle-class sophistication for which English Catholicism is noted. They were married in the Church of the Holy Redeemer in Chelsea. Had circumstances demanded that they be married in Dublin, Sean would have been subject to intolerable humiliations to which it is hard to imagine a man of his temperament submitting. O'Casey was at that time on the crest of a wave of success. The prospects must have seemed good. In his terms he was now well-off. Eileen, though on her own assessment a modest performer, had been by Sean's standards earning a good living in the theatrical profession. She introduced him to comforts unknown to Irish writers dependent on their earnings in their own country. They rented a house in St. John's Wood which was comparable to the Synge family residence in suburban Dublin. Viewed in retrospect their optimism was gravely misplaced. Within a few months Yeats rejected *The Silver Tassie*. From that point O'Casey's earnings began to decline and did not recover until the American royalties from his prose diaries began to accumulate. The author was then in his sixties.

Death saved Synge, and years later Behan, from this most embittering syndrome. Because Synge, by intellectual choice, and O'Casey and Behan involuntarily wrote dialogue in the idiom of their native country it was and is difficult for their plays to succeed financially outside it. In the rest of the English-speaking world their work has been admired in literary circles but infrequently financially rewarding in the theatre where it belongs. An exception was *The Hostage* to which by her production and cast Joan Littlewood gave an Anglo-Saxon framework, making it more acceptable in London and New York.

Eileen O'Casey blames Yeats's jealousy for the *Tassie* rejection. She may well be right. Dublin is a small city. In London and New York such emotions get absorbed in frenzied activity. There is always another theatre, another publisher to try. Should O'Casey have gone back to fight? Synge died before his literary reputation was established enough to threaten Yeats. Yeats's own plays never received any sort of popular acclaim.

O'Casey would have found it extremely difficult to stand up to Yeats on his own ground. Also, Dublin in the late twenties and thirties would have been an especially difficult place for someone of O'Casey's views on socialism and more especially where the Irish brand of Catholicism was concerned. After a century of playing a subservient role to the minority Protestant Ascendancy, the leaders of the Catholic Church in the Irish Free State of the twenties found that they were the new Establishment. Being only human they soon started to make a public show of the fact, and to flex their authoritarian muscles. Religious statues were put up all over the place. In many towns the Catholic parish churches and cathedrals were located in side streets. Now the clergy started to acquire prime sites in central positions for large and ostentatious buildings. In the thirties O'Casey would have seen as a more serious development the formation of the Catholic, fascist Blue Shirts, ridiculed in hindsight by Behan in *Richard's Cork Leg.* Predictably O'Casey depicted them in a sinister light when writing *The Star Turns Red* in Devon at the end of the decade.

About the time that *Tassie* was rejected the Legion of Mary had gone on a rampage in the North Side and cleaned up 'Monto,' Dublin's red light district. Perhaps the model for Rosie Redmond was packed off to some Magdalen Laundry with the rest of her profession. In nearby Russell Street, Behan had just turned five years old. Apart from closing the brothels and sweeping the prostitutes from the streets, the Catholic puritans of the Legion had done little to alter the lives of the poor in the Dublin slums. In fact things had not changed much in that respect since the eighteen-seventies, when Bernard Shaw was a young man around the South Circular Road across the Liffey. For was not Doolittle, in *Pygmalion,* based on a Dublin model too? In any event, I cannot think of a better description of the Behans than 'undeserving poor' in contrast to the respectable circumstances of the church-going Susan Casey and her half-blind, scripture-quoting son.

By all accounts the young Brendan spent more time sipping Guinness at the bedside of his dissolute Granny English than Sean had spent at Sunday School at St. Barnabas' Church in East Wall. Brendan's mother was an average Mass-going Catholic. She taught her son not Bible stories but popular and Republican songs and ballads, some of which had been written by her brother, Peadar Peadar Kearney, author of *The Soldier's Song,* the Irish national anthem. Though Brendan's father, Stephen, was a housepainter like his father before him, he had briefly studied for the priesthood. He had a wide-ranging taste in literature as well as a sturdy left-wing trade unionism, tempered with a witty cynicism and a cheerful agnosticism. Larkin, Connolly and O'Casey himself featured among the Behan family heroes. However, their enthusiasm for any cause was always liable, like Fluther Good's, to be diverted by the prospect of a few 'balls of malt' or pints of porter. In a sense, the Behans were walking O'Casey characters who created their own dialogue as they went along. Stephen Behan, like Johnny Boyle in *Juno,* had fought on the Republican side in the Irish Civil War. But fate had dealt kindly with him and he was not embittered in the process.

With such a background the young Behan was in no sense an outsider among his social class and co-religionists as Synge and O'Casey had been among theirs. The only features in Behan's young life to distinguish him from his classmates in the local Christian Brothers' School were his lively wit and an early interest in writing. The family tradition of Republican activism was unremarkable at that time and in that place. It was a boyish spirit of adventure which landed him in a British juvenile prison, Mountjoy Gaol, and political internment, and which provided him with material for *The Quare Fellow* and *Borstal Boy* especially. Behan could not exactly be described as a typical Irish Catholic of his time. He was nevertheless much more typical than Synge and O'Casey were of their backgrounds. By the time of Behan's death in 1964 Dublin was beginning to change radically. Such of Brendan's ideas as can be deduced from a careful reading of all his writing are not untypical of the views of a large section of the *present* generation of younger Dubliners. What distinguishes Behan's work from that of his contemporaries and successors is the economic, sharp and penetrating quality of the wit with which his thoughts are expressed.

It can, I hope, be seen from the foregoing summary that, in regard to his antecedents and background, O'Casey was, in essence, a sort of middleman between Synge and Behan. I will examine the plays of the three writers to see if O'Casey's dramatic output holds the same position.

Synge wrote only six plays, three of them very short. The most famous, *The Playboy of the Western World,* is not lengthy, but no one will question its acceptance as a major contribution to modern drama in the English language. *The Well of the Saints* is even shorter, and is usually performed with a curtain raiser. *Deirdre of the Sorrows* was only a draft script which the author never lived to complete. In making a comparison between Synge and O'Casey one must bear in mind that O'Casey wrote some twenty plays of widely varying lengths as against Synge's small output. However, the generally accepted merits common to both playwrights seem to be their joint ability to integrate the comic with the tragic, and to write dialogue which integrates a poetic element with realistic prose. These gifts had rarely been successfully deployed together in the English language before.

O'Casey wrote no unrelieved tragedies, but he did write a few purely farcical pieces, the most obvious being *A Pound on Demand*, which is little more than a well-written music-hall sketch. Of Synge's plays, two were unrelieved tragedy, *Riders to the Sea* and the draft, *Deidre of the Sorrows*. Even the draft contains one very small piece of comedy. It is so small and subtle that it could easily be missed. Naisi is looking for Deirdre, 'the young girl who told us we might shelter here'. In her reply Lavercham says, 'I wouldn't put you tracking a young girl, not if you gave me the gold clasp you have handing on your coat.' Synge's draft text continues: 'NAISI (giving it to her). Where is she? Lavercham then gives him precise instructions as to where he can find Deirdre.' This little joke could easily be overlooked or deliberately ignored in production. But it is precisely in the spirit of much of the best comedy of O'Casey and Behan. It could even be construed as an indication of the possibility that Synge might have put some humour in a later draft of the play had he lived to write one.

The Well of the Saints has rarely received productions worthy of its power, but although its harsh, tragic element is very strong, particularly in Act II, the play is well laced with both broad and subtle comedy throughout. *The Shadow of the Glen* is hard to define, although it is usually loosely classified as farce. Nevertheless the character of the young wife married to an old man (who pretends to be dead to catch out her shenanigans with a younger) is, in many ways quite as tragic as those of the wives in Ibsen's *Hedda Gabler* or *A Doll's House*. Indeed, they quite possibly inspired her creator.

We are left, then, with the brief *Riders to the Sea* as Synge's only completely unrelieved tragedy. This form is not, and never has been, popular in Ireland. It was, perhaps for the same reasons, foreign to Synge's nature too, even though *Riders* is a minor masterpiece. *Deirdre*, after all, is not typical of Synge. He was dying, and probably sensed it when he wrote the draft. And he was, without melodramatising the situation, tragically in love with Molly O'Neill at the time.

It was in *The Playboy of the Western World* that all Synge's talents are deployed most typically, and to the greatest effect. One must, therefore, examine it carefully and relate it to O'Casey's best major works. In his preface to *Playboy*, Synge wrote: 'in countries where the imagination of the people, and the language they use is rich and living it is possible for a writer to be rich and copious in his words, and at the same time to give the reality, which is the root of all poetry, in a comprehensive and a natural form.' He goes on, of course, and it was left to O'Casey (and, later, Behan) to disprove him 'in the modern literature of towns, richness is found only in sonnets, or prose poems, or in one or two elaborate books that are far away from the profound and common interest of life.' Synge, though a Dubliner, had apparently not kept his ears open when walking or cycling about the town.

The Playboy of the Western World is generally accepted as a classic. It is more than that. Many classic plays are flawed in some respect, and are difficult to perform. Director and actors may have to work hard indeed to make some classics acceptable to a modern audience. This is not the case with *Playboy*, in Ireland at least, where the rich Gaelic-derived dialogue is still easily comprehensible. Its only limitations are the availability of good leading actors and reasonably competent direction. In fact, like Wilde's *The Importance of Being Ernest* it will even stand up to quite an amount of poor acting and incompetent direction. *The Playboy* can still entertain and move under conditions that would reduce many accepted classics to an agony of boredom.

Some of the elements necessary to the creation of a work of this sort are a good story, rich or 'poetic' language, that is a joy in itself, actability, and directability. The story can be an emotional narrative, like *Waiting for Godot*, and need not be literal. *The Playboy* has it both ways, so to speak. Anglo-Saxon actors have one problem with *Playboy* (apart from dialect) which they do not share with Irish members of their profession. They find difficulty in comprehending Christy Mahon's (and other characters') attitude to the truth or otherwise of Christy's statement that he has killed his father. Did he believe he had done so, or was he consciously lying? In my view, it is not necessary to answer this question. The correct attitude to the question is to ignore it as do Philly Cullen and Jimmy Farrell at the beginning of Act III:

> PHILLY: . . . and he not able to say ten words without making a brag of the way he killed his father . . .
> JIMMY: A man can't hang by his own informing, and his father should be rotten by now.

With the exception of this non-Irish problem concerning the nature of truth, the actability of the play is both evident to the reader and proven in performance over the years. There are no over-written or mawkish passages which the actor has to camouflage with his professional technique. From the point of view of the director, too, there are remarkably few difficulties in staging. The off-stage horse race sequence in Act III used to present some problems, but several recent directors have solved them by bringing the actors out of the cottage and causing them to play the commentary direct to the audience.

As I have implied, Synge, in writing *The Playboy of the Western World*, unveiled to the new Irish theatre and to the English-speaking world the art of integrating the poetic, the tragic, the dramatic, and the comic in theatrical dialogue and action. This art, never fully exploited in the theatre before in English, even by Shakespeare, had lain dormant since Elizabethan times. The fact that Synge's plays were written in Gaelic-derived dialect must be the only obvious reason why it took fifty years for his methods to find general acceptance by English and American dramatists. I hope readers will agree with my suggestion, to be expounded later in this thesis, that O'Casey brought Synge's techniques a stage further when he was creating his own greatest works a dozen or so years after Synge's death.

Synge's gifts were very well proportioned. In the *Playboy* he created rounded and acceptable characters of both sexes, and the writing supplied the precise amount of information that is required about each one that is necessary for audience or reader to become involved in the emotional or physical action. No more, no less. Despite the uproar that *Playboy* caused in 1907, Synge had injected the appropriate proportionate amounts of sex and religion into his rural history with great delicacy. Given the emotional state of the country of the time, an outcry was inevitable. I have mentioned that *The Tinker's Wedding* was the only Synge play to portray an Irish priest on stage. The off-stage priest in *Playboy* says, through the mouth of Shawn Keogh, all that is needed to be said about the part played by the clergy in Irish rural life of that time. Likewise, Synge's detached acceptance of the status quo of religious practices and belief in his characters, revealed through their dialogue, expresses no personal bias, or even opinion.

The *Playboy* is essentially about love, the love of a man for a woman and a woman for a man. Beckett's *Waiting for Godot* is essentially about the *equilibrium* of love. The play begins and ends with the tramps in a state of loving equilibrum. Pozzo and his servant also reach a different sort of equilibrium. In *Playboy*, equilibrium is not reached. Pegeen is left distraught. Therefore *Playboy* is tragedy where *Godot* is not. The tragic ending of *Playboy* is reached briefly over a few pages in Act III. It is none the less tragic because of the brevity of the sequence. Surely one could claim that the line, 'Oh my grief, I've lost him surely. I've lost the only Playboy of the Western World,' is not merely one of the best curtain lines ever written, but also illustrates Synge's economy of phraseology. Tragedy does not demand that the stage be littered with corpses at curtain-fall.

Up to the point when Pegeen turns against Christy with the line, 'And it's lies you told, letting on you had him slitted, and you nothing at all,' the Pegeen/Christy relationship is balanced with first one on top and then the other. Tragically (in the dramatic sense) equilibrium is never reached, as it must be for lasting human love. Synge's insight into human nature was prodigious, but his sense of economy and proportion was such that it never led him into overwriting. It would be possible to write a treatise on the subject of how in fact a marriage between the couple would have failed. Synge completely resists the temptation, and writes an Ibsenite play about a woman in marriage without ever getting as far as the wedding. At the same time, he had such a highly developed *theatrical* sense that he created in Christy a male role quite as challenging as that of his female lead.

Synge's life was as economical and well proportioned as *The Playboy of the Western World*. It was tragic in that it was brief, but within that brief span he seems to have packed a full complement of emotional experience.

O'Casey's eighty-four years were as spendthrift and unsymmetrical as Synge's were well ordered, and this was reflected in his writing. O'Casey's twenty-odd plays vary from the sublime (*Juno*) to the ridiculous (*Behind the Green Curtains*), and within most of his plays the quality of the writing varies within the same gamut. Three of Synge's plays, *The Shadow of the Glen*, *The Well of the Saints*, and *The Playboy of the Western World* are each as near perfect, within their class, as one can conceive possible. Without in any way belittling the dynamic sweep of O'Casey's output, only one major play, *Juno*, emerges, to me, as completely satisfying in comparison with *Playboy*.

When not laying about him in one of his many wordy battles with those with whom he disagreed, O'Casey was well aware of his shortcomings as a person and as a playwright. He wrote *Red Roses for Me* in maturity, happily married to Eileen O'Casey, and living in as much peace as he was ever to attain. He must have known what he was about when he put into the mouth of the autobiographical hero, Ayamonn, this honest and penetrating self-analysis:

I tell you life is not one thing, but many things, a wide branching flame grand and good to see and feel, dazzling to the eye of no-one living it. I was not one to carry fear about with me as a priest carries the Host. Let the timid tiptoe through the way where the redder roses grow, though they bear thorns, sharp and piercing thick among them!

It is not surprising that someone who felt like that should sometimes overstep the bounds of literary prudence. *Red Roses for Me* could well have been his best play had the Abbey Theatre (as several have lamented) not been denied to him as a workshop. However, writing in isolation he was cut of from sympathetic and detached criticism of a sort that Augusta Gregory might have provided in the old days.

Unlike Synge, O'Casey was a romantic and even a sentimentalist at heart. One gets the impression that he had little conception of mature man-woman love until he met Eileen. By then, perhaps it was too late to incorporate the experience into his dramatic writings, though he made a small attempt in *Within the Gates*. His emotional knowledge was only used to full advantage in writing about mothers. In *Red Roses* he does not make use of this knowledge as he does in *Juno* and neither Mrs. Breydon nor the girl friend, Shiela, provides the audience with a satisfying partner for Ayamonn's emotional core. Juno Boyle was complete in herself and needed no emotional companion. O'Casey's remembered relationship with the Rector of East Wall is valid, and is represented in *Red Roses* by Ayamonns' relationship with the Rector of 'St. Burnupus,' but it is inadequately developed.

Where the play comes nearest to excellence is in its use of non-realistic techniques. The style is that which had excited him when he first saw expressionist dramas in the London Gate Theatre in 1926. He deploys it to good effect, and *Red Roses* is more of a whole than *The Silver Tassie*. (*Tassie* has defeated, and will defeat all directorial attempts to give it artistic unity.) Even if skilled modern direction could make it structurally complete, *Red Roses* is sentimental at heart and over-written by the standards set by J. M. Synge in *Playboy*.

Among the later O'Casey plays, the short *Hall of Healing* does succeed in capturing some Synge-like detachment and mingles the real tragedy of lives broken by conditions in the Dublin slums with the hilarious comedy based on truthful characterisation. Unfortunately the playwright refrained from or was unable to develop the themes suggested by the interesting roles he created in that play.

Among O'Casey's farcical works, *Purple Dust* is the best, but they all require directorial assistance far above the normal calls of duty to achieve successful production, and cannot be in any aspect regarded as comparable with Synge at his best. We are left with *The Shadow of a Gunman*, *Juno*, and *The Plough* as being the only O'Casey plays individually comparable to *The Playboy* on what might be described as equal terms.

All three plays were written over a period of less than four years, but there is a marked development in O'Casey's technique between the first, *Gunman,* and the last, *Plough. The Shadow of a Gunman* is a very simple play, as simple in its way as *The Shadow of the Glen.* If it seems a little over-melodramatic it must be remembered that it was written in, and depicted, a time and a place when such melodrama was part of everyday life. The dialogue is unheightened, realistic, Dublin working-class speech of the period. Davoren and Seumas are no more nor less than two aspects of the playwright. If O'Casey was trying to be, as Synge put it, 'rich and copious in his words', he contrived it by making Davoren a poet, as he considered himself to be. On its own terms there are minor faults in the play. O'Casey was always to have problems in mixing the down-to-earth documentary back-grounds of much of his work with the need for appropriate dramatic action to suit his epic ambitions. *Juno* is entirely free from blemishes of this sort. For example, in *Gunman* a tiny irritant, to some directors at least, would be the fact that O'Casey allows so little time to lapse between Maguire's departure for Knocksedan and the newspaper report of his death. It is the kind of detail that one cannot imagine Synge leaving uncorrected in any of his finished work. The small, rather sentimental, core of the plot which involves Minnie Powell is not enough to put *Gunman* into the same epic class as *Juno* and the *Plough.*

If one is to make a selection between the *Plough* and *Juno* as O'Casey's 'best play,' there is little to choose from between them. The epic background of the 1916 Insurrection, the four different realistic settings, Uncle Peter's Forresters regalia, and the British soldiers in Act IV all give the *Plough* a colourful and even 'show-biz' quality that has instant audience appeal. It is when one comes to examine the internal structure and details of the characterisation that signs of some of O'Casey's basic weaknesses begin to show themselves. None of these weaknesses are so marked that they cannot be camouflaged by a first-rate director and cast, but they exist, and for the purposes of comparison with Synge, they make *Juno* a more satisfactory sampling of O'Casey at his best.

If one starts with the structure, it would be reasonable to expect that the Clitheroes, husband and wife, would be the central figures in the story. This is not the case. Jack is killed off-stage and for the moving final act the audience's sympathies are totally engaged by Bessie Burgess. I have stated earlier that O'Casey loved all his characters. I think, however, that this is not the case where the Clitheroes are concerned. Directors and actors must be fully stretched to make either character acceptable. C. Desmond Greaves's book, *Sean O'Casey: Politics and Art*, suggests that O'Casey had a guilt complex about not having fought in 1916. The author implies that, because his mother had sacrificed so much for him when he was a child, O'Casey could not bring himself to desert her for Connolly and the Citizens Army when she was frail and in her 79th year. This could indeed be so. It could explain why Jack and Nora are such unsatisfactory people, and why the old Protestant woman, Bessie Burgess, turns out to be the real hero at the end of all, as Synge might have put it. In *Red Roses for Me*, O'Casey romanticises the 1913 Strike and has his autobiographical hero slaughtered by the brutal soldiery, while his mother is comforted by the saintly rector of the East Wall Church of Ireland church. In this way, suggests Greaves, O'Casey sought to exorcise the ghost of 1916.

There are lesser problems in the *Plough*, all of which can usually be camouflaged by very good acting and directing. There are signs of O'Casey' facination with alliteration which, in his plays, was to become an obsession. In the *Plough*, the alliteration is sometimes acceptable, sometimes not. A certain amount of rhetoric, alliteration, and so forth is still part of the general usage of Dublin speech. Also, it should be noted that the malapropism flourishes as happily in Dublin today as it did when Richard Sheridan heard it in the environs of Dorset Street (his and O'Casey's birthplace) in the eighteenth century. Nevertheless, speech patterns in a creative patois such as Dublinese do not stand still. It is difficult even for the native Dubliner to say what phraseology is completely authentic sixty years after the supposed utterance. However, whether authentic or created by the author, some phrases are acceptable to my ears, at least, and some are not, even granting poetic licence. Moments of high emotion or drunkenness justify a more florid vocabulary. For instance, when the Covey says 'your mind is the mind of a mummy,' I find it acceptable. Where he says (before the row with Fluther in Act II) 'but when you start luscious lies,' it jars slightly, for according to O'Casey's stage directions, the Covey has not yet lost his temper. Some of Nora's lines are self-consciously 'poetic' and diminish the credibility of the role. 'Make a companion of the loneliness of the night' is a phrase which I feel no average actress should be asked to utter. Likewise, a sober Bessie in Act IV should find difficulty with 'madly mingling memories of the past'.

If the alliterative or consciously poetic phraseology sometimes is a little overdone in the *Plough*, so are the insertions of non-realistic sequences in otherwise completely realistic scenes. As I have mentioned, good direction can smooth out any built-in jerkiness from one style to the other (some modern directors might prefer to *emphasise* the stylisation by means of a sort of theatrical 'jump-cut'), but to my mind the best written plays do not make undue demands on either directors or actors.

The pub scene in Act II contains most of the directorial head-aches of this particular sort. The *Figure in the Window* is hard to handle, and of course the 'Ireland is greater than a mother' sequence is an obvious pitfall. The second duologue of the act, between Uncle Peter and Fluther, while one of the author's most scintillating comic passages, is also quite different from the overall realism of the play. It would have been more stylistically in context if it had been written by Samuel Beckett in the nineteen-fifties. To me, it indicates that O'Casey, having attained a degree of perfection in *Juno*, had already started on a stylistic journey towards a goal he would never reach.

It could be argued that the various moments of dramatic excellence in the *Plough* (such as the section leading up to the final section) add up to something greater than that which was achieved by Synge in *Playboy* or by O'Casey himself in *Juno*. I submit that the total artistic unity of the latter two works sets them jointly apart from and above most of modern playwriting in English, including the *Plough*, if artistic unity and all around perfection is what is sought. If any serious criticism is to be levelled at either Synge's *Playboy* or O'Casey's *Juno*, it will be by people who regard the 'well-made play' as a term of abuse. Such people are less numerous in 1980 than they were in the 1950s and 1960s.

O'Casey had strong opinions about the Civil War, extreme patriotism and labour politics among other things. He never shoves these opinions down the audience's throats in *Juno*, but allows them to emerge unobtrusively, but powerfully, through the mouths of less-than-perfect characters. For instance, he uses Mary Boyle, a sweet, but not very bright girl, to expound some of the O'Casey trade-union principles. The melodrama of the Civil War situation is never allowed to overstep the bounds of credibility, but is carefully woven into the story through the circumstances in which Johhny finds himself. The schoolteacher, Bentham, allows O'Casey to indulge briefly but amusingly in the Shavian game of baiting the middle classes, but he doesn't permit himself to let this amusing irrelevancy to get out of hand. Likewise, he keeps the Dublinese dialogue firmly rooted in the overall realism and never (as he does in the *Plough*) allows the poetic or the alliterative tail to wag the naturalistic dog.

Perhaps the most satisfying positive feature of *Juno* is the firm structure, held together by the well-defined character of Juno herself. It is surely one of the best female leading roles in the English language. If, as I have surmised, O'Casey was, at the time of writing *Juno*, without knowledge of mature man-woman relationships, it did not matter. With Juno, the mother, he was working in an area he understood in depth. Juno's ups and downs are followed in great detail and at no point in the play does the heroine became mawkish or self-pitying in the way Nora does, and which automatically denies the latter woman the audience's sympathy. With Juno as his heroine, O'Casey supplies an epic quality rare in modern playwriting.

All the lesser characters, from the Captain down, are drawn with precision, and actors and audience are supplied with the exact amount of detail necessary for balance, proportion and sympathy. In this respect alone, *Juno* can be said to attain equal stature with *Playboy*. Synge's stated ambition, 'to be rich and copious in his words and at the same time to give [the] reality,' is fully achieved in *Juno*. O'Casey brought Synge's ideas further than their originator. He was genuinely closer to the people he was writing about, only distanced from them by his mother's religious denomination and ancestry. In *Juno* he avoided all reference to religious differences and attained Synge's detachment, while at the same time achieving greater intimacy with his characters.

Brendan Behan's intimacy with his characters was complete. Such artistic detachment as he achieved, and which is fairly consistent throughout his work, was born in him. It was sharpened by his experiences in jail, which occurred at exactly the right moment in his mental development. In contrast, East Wall, where O'Casey spent his formative years was and is a small village within Dublin City. It is a very closed community which perhaps explains the almost parochial quality that remained with O'Casey throughout his life and coloured a great deal of his work. Behan was very urban, as Synge was, despite the subject matter of the latter's plays. Behan's output was similar to Synge's except that Behan, like O'Casey, never attempted an unrelieved tragedy. Two short farces, written for the radio; two full-length tragic comedies; one medium radio comedy; and one unfinished draft play.

Behan's farces are lightweight, and have more in common with *A Pound on Demand* or *The End of the Beginning* than with *The Shadow of the Glen* or *Tinker's Wedding*. The radio comedy, *The*

Big House, though a bit wordy has been successfully staged in Dublin and London, where it was well received. *The Shadow of the Glen* and *Tinker's Wedding* were on the same bill. It is of interest that, of the two Synge plays, only the *Shadow's* reception matched that of Behan's play. I also completed and edited the draft play, *Richard's Cork Leg*; staged it at the Abbey and elsewhere in Ireland, and at the Royal Court Theatre in London, where it received high critical praise. However, it is *The Quare Fellow* and *The Hostage* which must provide the basic material for comparison with Synge's *Playboy* and O'Casey's *Juno*.

Like O'Casey, but unlike Synge, Behan was emotionally immature regarding women at the time he wrote his two major works. In *The Quare Fellow* he got round this problem, if one can put it that way, by including no women in his cast. In *The Hostage*, the little puppy-love affair which forms the beautiful centre-piece to the play appears to be based on an adolescent attraction for a young English conscript sailor which Behan describes in fair detail in his autobiographical prose work, *Borstal Boy*. In *The Hostage* the writing is economical and moving without being sentimental, and I think more successful by far than the Davoren-Minnie Powell relationship in O'Casey's *Gunman* with which it could loosely be compared. It proved quite strong enough to stand up to Joan Littlewood's hilariously decorative production of the premiere and many other robust revivals over the last twenty-two years.

The Quare Fellow and *The Hostage* are so widely different in style that it is difficult to select one or the other as the most representative of Behan's talents. Broadly speaking, *The Quare Fellow* is comparable to O'Casey's early work, and *The Hostage* represents what I think O'Casey was aiming for in the plays written after *Red Roses for Me*.

The Quare Fellow, like *Juno*, expresses the author's opinions through the mouths of appropriate, but not necessarily worthy, characters. It is, like *Juno*, so naturalistic as to be almost documentary. The ostensible hero, Warder Regan, is a satisfyingly rounded character about whom the author preserves an uncritical detachment, as O'Casey did with Mrs. Boyle. The lesser characters are well-drawn and carefully woven into the plot. The disappointment, for those looking for dramatic symmetry, is that Dunlavin and Neighbor (who broadly correspond to the roles filled by the Captain and Joxer in *Juno*) are neglected by the author at the end of the play. This arises, I suspect, from Behan's laziness. There was no emotional reason, such as I have suggested in relation to the Clitheroes at the end of the *Plough*.

The most original feature of *The Quare Fellow* is the fact that the real hero (or anti-hero) of the play, the condemned man, is never seen or heard. The play is about the effect of a hanging on warders and prisoners in Mountjoy Gaol. It powerfully condemns, by implication, the use of capital punishment, but this condemnation is never put into words anywhere in the text. This artistic *tour-de-force* was never matched by either Synge or O'Casey, although it can hardly be grounds for granting Behan the same stature as either of his illustrious predecessors in the Irish theatre.

What Behan does achieve, gloriously, however, is to be 'rich and copious in his words, and at the sametime give [the] reality'. The language of Behan's contemporary Dublin is recorded in quite as satisfying a manner as by O'Casey in *Juno*. There are no phrases or sequences (as there are in *Plough*) which create any problems for actors or directors familiar with the idiom. The play, however, was carelessly written and in a naturalistic, documentary manner which is verbose in spots. All successful productions have been subject to stringent editing by their directors. O'Casey was too touchy ever to have permitted such editing.

When considering *The Hostage*, it is interesting to note that, while all three of these Irish playwrights learned their native language in adulthood, Behan was the only one to write a play in it. *The Hostage* was written on commission, under the title of *An Giall*, for Gael Linn, an organisation dedicated to the preservation and promotion of the use of the Irish language. A literal translation of the young heroine's speech, when her boyfriend is accidentally killed, reads: 'Leslie, there was none of your people there to mourn you, love. I will be your little mother, your little sister, your lover and I will never forget you (crying) never. Oh, Leslie . . . Leslie . . . Leslie . . . Leslie.' It is moving, direct and I think it offers some grounds for comparison with the curtain line of *Playboy*. In the published version of the play, which the author translated for Joan Littlewood's London première of the play in English, after its smash Dublin première in Irish, this speech is reduced to: 'He died in a strange land, and at home he had no one. I'll never forget you, Leslie, till the end of time.' By submitting his work to the creative direction of Littlewood, Behan may have lost some of the 'richness and copiousness of his words' here and there, but the play gained immeasurably in other ways. When editing *Richard's Cork Leg,* I discovered that the author had learned a lot from Littlewood about contemporary theatrical technique. Had he lived, he might have written several more important plays in a style which was ideally suited to the latter end of this century.

O'Casey, on the other hand, was an auto-didact. He was determined to be his own man whatever the consequences, even, presumably, if he got pricked by the long thorns 'where the redder roses grow'. In a letter to me in 1961, he wrote: 'if one is to be proficient in that art [playwriting] what he does or tries to do must be his own and not the work of anyone else be his work good or bad.' O'Casey wrote these words having matched the perfection of *The Playboy of the Western World*. Sadly, Behan never did that.

A number of things have happened in Ireland since 1964. One of the effects of the Second Vatican Council (unwelcome to conservatives among the Catholic hierarchy, clergy and lay zealots) has been a change in the attitudes of younger Irish people. Censorship has been greatly reduced, though not abolished. A number of emigrants of the 1950s have returned. Many Irish people have travelled abroad, not as emigrants, but as U.N. officials, business entrepreneurs and tourists. The country is more prosperous than ever before, though this has brought new problems undreamed of by Synge, O'Casey and Behan, some of which are shared by fellow members of the European Community. The tension in Northern Ireland remains. Behan wrote of it in *The Hostage*, but that was before the escalation of violence since 1969. Anyway, neither he nor O'Casey had any direct, intimate contact with Northern Protestants. *Purple Dust, Cock-a-Doodle Dandy*, and even *The Star Turns Red* have been performed in the Abbey with, alas, barely a frisson. *Richard's Cork Leg* drew a pulpit protest from the Bishop of Cork in 1972. Brendan would have been pleased.

In *Richard's Cork Leg*, Behan wrote: 'The English and Americans dislike only SOME Irish – the same Irish that the Irish themselves detest, Irish writers – the ones that THINK. But then, they hate their own people who think. I just like to think, and in this city I'm hated and despised.' This was not quite true. Perhaps it was wishful thinking. He had, to me, a disarming wish to be considered in the same bracket as O'Casey without having to experience the real pain and misery that O'Casey was fated to endure. Behan's funeral which took place a short time after the above passage was written, was, in a city that loves funerals, reputedly the biggest since that of Jim Larkin, the labour leader. What more could a Dubliner wish for?

Brendan was a very transparent, human person, and like many of us he wished to be liked, despite his frequent outrageous and boorish behaviour. Synge was a very private person. Out of a sense of delicacy, he seems to have been genuinely concerned not to give offence to anyone. He took great pains to avoid upsetting family and neighbors, Catholic and Protestant when, having ceased to believe in orthodox Christianity, he wished to avoid attending church services. At the same time he was in no way a hypocrite. He was like the musician he once aspired to be, and was genuinely pure *artist*. Unfortunately, his gift was in an art form notoriously prone to controversy. He was really taken by surprise by the violent reaction to his plays. At the same time, artist that he was, he could see no compromise.

O'Casey revelled in polemic. He expended much of his later life and energy in conducting controversies when he would have been better and more lucratively employed in writing more plays or improving those he had written. I never met O'Casey; I only once spoke to him on the telephone. To judge by the affection with which he is regarded by those who were close to him, despite the spikey image he often projected, he must have been both a loving and lovable man.

Synge, O'Casey and Behan all served their craft, their art and their country well in their very different ways.

SHAW'S OTHER KEEGAN: O'CASEY AND G.B.S.

STANLEY WEINTRAUB

In November 1919 Bernard Shaw received yet another request to write a preface to someone else's manuscript. His policy on such appeals from aspiring authors was clear, and he would eventually prepare a printed postcard which would inform disappointed applicants that they could not count upon an introduction by G.B.S. to boom their work. The newest entreaty came from an unknown writer in Dublin who was aware of Shaw's wartime writings on Irish questions and had put together a book of his own – *Three Shouts on a Hill*, on Irish labour, nationalism, and the Gaelic language – from articles he had produced for the *Irish Worker* and *Irish Opinion*.

Shaw had no idea that the 'Shaun O'Casey' who signed the letter was an impecunious, self-taught union organizer and journalist already nearly forty. His kind response, nevertheless declining to write still another preface, suggested that he thought he was dealing with an earnest young man.

'I like the foreword and afterword much better,' Shaw began, 'than the shouts, which are prodigiously overwritten.' Like other writers who wanted a Shavian preface to help get a book published, O'Casey received instead more questions than answers, Shaw wondering why O'Casey appeared ambivalent on labour issues and was impractical enough a nationalist to come out against the English language. 'You ought to work out your position positively & definitely,' he advised. 'This objecting to everyone else is Irish, but useless.' Besides, it was 'out of the question' for O'Casey to assume that a preface by an established author would advance him as a writer. 'You must go through the mill like the rest and get published for your own sake, not for mine.'[1]

Although O'Casey would carry the letter in his wallet for years, until it was frayed and cracked at the creases, the relationship appeared unlikely to prosper.

212

Shaw went on to produce *Heartbreak House*, which he had completed during the war, and to write his play-cycle *Back to Methuselah* as well as *Saint Joan* before he would hear of O'Casey again. Meanwhile O'Casey had been reading Shaw's plays as they were published, and was now writing some of his own, offering them to a cautious Abbey Theatre management which nevertheless had produced three of them, *Kathleen Listens In, Shadow of a Gunman* and *Juno and the Paycock*, by 1924. He hoped, O'Casey wrote Lady Gregory, with whom he discussed Shaw's and Mark Twain's versions of *Saint Joan* (Mark Twain's was a 'supplement'), that Eamon de Valera would read *Back to Methuselah* and acquire broader vision. It was already clear from the published text of *Shadow of a Gunman* that year that O'Casey had also been reading the earlier Shaw. The self-styled 'poet and poltroon' Donal Davoren, the first page of stage directions declared, has been 'handicapped by an inherited self-developed devotion to "the might of design, the mystery of colour, and the redemption of all things by beauty everlasting." ' O'Casey was quoting from the deathbed credo of Shaw's rogue-artist Louis Dubedat in *The Doctor's Dilemma*, and Davoren's romantic idealism is an ironic contrast to the amoral, courageous Dubedat. G.B.S., O'Casey confided to Mrs. Shaw years later, had been his 'anamchara – soul-friend – as we say in Ireland,' for many years before he 'met him in the flesh'.

That March, when *Juno and the Paycock* had opened at the Abbey, gripping its audiences and turning O'Casey into a local hero, veteran playgoer Joseph Holloway had a chat with the new playwright in the theatre vestibule. 'He told me,' Holloway noted in his diary, 'that when he started to write plays he thought he was a second Shaw sent to express his views through his characters, and was conceited enough to think that his opinions were the only ones that mattered. It was Lady Gregory who advised him to cut out all expressions of self, and develop his peculiar aptness for character drawing.'[2] O'Casey was rarely able to eliminate himself from the dialogue of his characters. The indebtedness to Shaw would be emerging in more ways than this misunderstanding of Shavian dialogue (based so much on debating technique), where even the Devil in *Don Juan in Hell* – or Inquisitor in *Joan* – has to be given persuasive lines.

O'Casey's intentions may have been otherwise, but Juno herself is, in a number of her appeals, reading an O'Casey editorial, however eloquent. Yet echoes from Shaw were more apparent in *Juno and the Paycock* in the 'paycock' figure of Captain Boyle,

who may be O'Casey's genial parody of *Heartbreak House's*
Captain Shotover, the aged and philosophic retired seaman who
warns mankind of impending apocalypse. In *Juno* the dark
vision is reduced to absurdity in Boyle's repeated declarations that
'the worl's in a state o' chassis!' And Shotover's nostalgic recol-
lections of living to the fullest demands of body and spirit as
opposed to the softness he sees in the younger generation are
again turned to absurdity by the lazy and unemployable Jacky
Boyle and Joxer Daly, his parasite. 'I was ten times happier on
the bridge in the typhoon, or frozen into Arctic ice for months in
darkness. . . .' Shaw's seafaring patriarch tells young Ellie Dunn.
'At your age I looked for hardship, danger, horror, and death,
that I might feel the life in me more intensely. I did not let the
fear of death govern my life; and my reward was, I had my life.'[3]
Boyle, his wife Juno observes, had earned his 'Captain' designation
the easier way. He was only in the water 'in an oul' collier from
here to Liverpool, when anybody, to listen or look at you, ud
take you for a second Christo For Columbus!' The sarcasm is
quickly forgotten by Joxer and Boyle. Joxer recalls 'the young
days when you were steppin' the deck of a manly ship, with the
win' blowin' a hurricane through the masts, an' the only sound
you'd hear was "Port your helm!" and the answer, "Port it is,
sir!"'

'Them was days, Joxer,' says the Captain. '. . . Nothin' was too
hot or heavy for me then. Sailin' from the Gulf of Mexico to the
Antanartic Ocean. . . . Often, an' often, when I was fixed to the
wheel with a marlin-spike, an' the win's blowin' fierce an' the
waves lashin' an' lashin', till you'd think every minute was goin'
to be your last, an' it blowed, an' blowed – blow is the right word,
Joxer, but blowed is what the sailors use. . . .'

For an audience familiar with *Heartbreak House*, the shiftless
braggart Captain Boyle may have been meant to have special
irony, reinforced when we recall that Shotover's 'seventh degree
of concentration' can only be reached at his age with the aid of
rum. Jacky Boyle prefers to induce forgetfulness (rather than
perception) with whiskey, and in the last scene, drunk, he
mumbles something about 'Irelan' sober . . . is Irelan' free,' and
recalls only that the world remains 'in a terr . . . ible state o' . . .
chassis!' The desolated flat which Juno and Boyle have occupied
is O'Casey's first Irish version of Heartbreak House.*

---

* Later O'Casey would insist that *Heartbreak House* was Shaw's finest
play, once arguing the point with Charlotte Shaw, who stood by *Saint Joan*
(*Autobiographies*, VI, 248).

In Boyle's romanticizing of tawdry reality – his philosophy as
well as his religion come for him in a bottle – can be seen the
symptoms identified in Larry Doyle's lament in *John Bull's Other
Island*, that gentle satire of Irish ways apparently interpreted more
harshly by O'Casey in play after play. 'Oh, the dreaming! the
dreaming!' Doyle observes,

> the torturing, heart-scalding, never satisfying dreaming, dream-
> ing, dreaming, dreaming! No debauchery that ever coarsened
> and brutalized an Englishman can take the worth and usefulness
> out of him like that dreaming. An Irishman's imagination never
> lets him alone, never convinces him, never satisfies him; but
> it makes him [so] that he cant face reality nor deal with it
> nor handle it nor conquer it; he can only sneer at them that do,
> and be 'agreeable to strangers,' like a good-for-nothing woman
> of the streets. It's all dreaming, all imagination. He cant be
> religious. The inspired Churchman that teaches him the sanctity
> of life and the importance of conduct is sent away empty;
> while the poor village priest that gives him a miracle of a
> sentimental story of a saint, has cathedrals built for him out of
> the pennies of the poor. He cant be intelligently political; he
> dreams of what the Shan Van Vocht said in ninetyeight. If you
> want to interest him in Ireland you've got to call the unfortu-
> nate island Kathleen ni Houlihan and pretend she's a little old
> woman. It saves thinking. It saves working. It saves everything
> except imagination, imagination, imagination; and imagination's
> such a torture that you cant bear it without whisky.

In his *The Plough and the Stars*, produced at the Abbey in 1926,
we are reminded of the sardonic thrusts of *Major Barbara*. 'I am
rather interested in the Salvation Army,' says Barbara's father,
the armaments manufacturer Andrew Undershaft. 'Its motto
might be my own: Blood and Fire.' Shocked, one of his prospec-
tive sons-in-law insists that it could not be 'your sort of blood
and fire, you know'.

'My sort of blood cleanses,' insists Undershaft: 'my sort of
fire purifies.'

O'Casey's play invokes the Irish Citizen Army, not the
Salvation Army, when the shadowy figure of one of its ruthless
officers is silhouetted and heard through the pub window. 'It is a
glorious thing to see arms in the hands of Irishmen,' he exhorts

the unseen crowd. '. . . Bloodshed is a cleansing and sanctifying thing, and the nation that regards it as the final horror has lost its manhood. . . .'

Fluther's sentiments in the play, says critic Saros Cowasjee, have the ring of Shaw. 'Fight fair!' Fluther asks about the Easter rising. 'A few hundreds scrawls o' chaps with a couple of guns an' Rosary beads, again' a hundhred thousand trained men with horse, fut, an' artillery . . . an' he wants us to fight fair! [*To Sergeant*] D'ye want us to come out in our skins an' throw stones?' Shaw, Cowasjee reminds us, had published a protest against the British executions in May 1916, observing that the rebellion 'was a fair fight in everything except the enormous odds my countrymen had to face.'[4]

Although it would have been poor strategy for O'Casey to point to these apparent echoes of Shaw – even if he recognized them himself – he would, nevertheless, call in G.B.S. when precedents or examples were useful. When Lennox Robinson, then running the Abbey, objected, on behalf of actress Eileen Crowe, to allegedly indelicate language in *The Plough and the Stars*, O'Casey pointed out that Shaw had used *bastard* in *The Devil's Disciple*, which the Abbey had produced six years earlier. It was not Miss Crowe's only objection, and when she refused to speak her lines as written she was replaced. O'Casey would have increasing difficulty with Irish prudes as well as with Irish patriots. The patriots, of course, objected to everything in *The Plough*, and in a letter to the *Irish Independent* the playwright again invoked the name of Shaw, who, he said, hated patriotic sham, pointing to the description of the supposedly heroic cavalry charge in *Arms and the Man* as 'slinging a handful of peas against a window-pane'.[5]

The author of *Gunman*, *Juno* and *Plough* had read and seen all of Shaw he could encounter in Dublin, but almost certainly thought that the only indebtedness to Shaw in his plays was his deliberate quotation from *The Doctor's Dilemma*. Irish productions of Shaw in the mid-1920s included *Saint Joan* and *Man and Superman*, both of which O'Casey attended. The *Man and Superman* presentation, he thought, was bad indeed, 'a helter-skelter performance' in which 'all the actors were subdued by the relentless enthusiasm' of F. J. McCormick, who played John Tanner. Thinking innocently that, with the successes of his plays at the Abbey, he was 'among old friends,' he spoke his mind. The reaction was a choked hush. Then McCormick, who had overheard, pushed close to O'Casey and warned, 'I hear you've been criticising our rendering of Shaw's play. You've got a bit of a name now, and you must not say these things about an Abbey production. If you do, we'll have to report it to the directors; so try to keep your mouth shut.'

O'Casey was bewildered by the crude blast, but went home and naively wrote a long letter to the play's director, Michael J. Dolan, pointing out the flaws he thought he saw in the production, adding that the letter might be utilized in any way it could be helpful. 'It's just like Sean,' said Lennox Robinson. When the letter was posted on the Abbey's notice-board, it ended O'Casey's access backstage. The next time he came by, Sean Barlow, a property man, asked what he was doing there. He was on his way to the Green Room, O'Casey explained. 'There's none but the actors and officials allowed on the stage,' said Barlow, 'and we'd be glad if you came this way no more.'

By the time O'Casey's next dispute with the Abbey and its public erupted, he was living in London, deliberately keeping his distance; and he had met Shaw, whose aid he soon needed in person. In the dispute over *The Silver Tassie*, Shaw would put in more writing time than any preface for another author would ever cost him.

To recount O'Casey's struggle with the Abbey management over *The Silver Tassie* in 1928 is unnecessary here. It permanently embittered the playwright's relations with the theatre which most needed him, confirmed his estrangement from the soil which had inspired him, and left him without a regular audience or theatre for his work thereafter. Shaw would not only come to his defense but help him find a producer in London.

O'Casey had sent a copy of the play to Shaw, who answered via Charlotte that both had read *The Silver Tassie* with '*deep interest*' and enthusiasm, and wanted to have both Sean and Eileen to lunch to talk about it. As Shaw himself put it to O'Casey in a separate letter before the luncheon at Whitehall Court, 'What a hell of a play! I wonder how it will hit the public.' By then he knew how it had hit the directors of the Abbey. W. B. Yeats, Shaw explained, was 'not a man of this world; and when you hurl an enormous smashing chunk of it at him he dodges it. . . .' Yeats had hectored O'Casey on writing about the Great War (in which neither had participated) rather than the Irish struggle, 'You never stood on its battlefields or walked its hospitals, and so write [entirely] out of your opinions.' 'Was Shakespeare at Actium or Philippi?' O'Casey had countered. 'Was G. B. Shaw in the boats with the French, or in the forts with the British when St. Joan and Dunois made the attack that relieved Orleans?'

To Lady Gregory, with whom Shaw interceded, the author of *Saint Joan* wrote that Yeats 'should have submitted' to *The Silver Tassie* 'as a calamity imposed on him by the Act of God, if he could not welcome it as another *Juno*.' But the elderly Lady Gregory, who, Shaw told O'Casey, was really on his side, was in no position to countermand Yeats, Walter Starkie and Lennox Robinson. 'Playwriting,' Shaw explained in a note on the back of another of O'Casey's letters, 'is a desperate trade.'

Despite the uproar, which had resulted in newspaper editorials and letters-to-the-editor, Macmillan was willing to take its chances on publishing the play, and O'Casey secured Shaw's permission to use portions of his 'hell of a play' letter on the jacket of the book – an unusual gesture for G.B.S. O'Casey then attempted to use the quote further, for a critic in *The Irish News* of Belfast had attacked the play he had not seen by observing, confidently, 'Bernard Shaw would never have put his name to *The Silver Tassie*.' But in effect Shaw had, came the O'Casey rejoinder, and he quoted the 'hell of a play' paragraph from Shaw's letter. On 7 July the paper, staunchly Roman Catholic and Nationalist, reported receipt of the letter and its inability to print it 'unamended'. There was a censorable word in the quotation from G.B.S., which the *News* took as another example of O'Casey's bad taste.

Hearing softened words from Yeats and Robinson, who needed a palatable O'Casey, Shaw urged conciliation, which O'Casey saw as impossible. The Abbey management, he insisted, had 'turned a Playhouse into a silly little temple, darkened with figures past vitality. . . .' By this time Eileen was in contact with Charlotte Shaw, who agreed with her that it was a period when Sean 'wants a lot of looking after,' and offered G.B.S. as intermediary wherever useful. But Shaw's advice was not always heeded. After C. B. Cochran had lost money on a splendidly mounted production of *The Silver Tassie*, and warned O'Casey in Shavian fashion that he needed to write things which were not only fine but which had some expectation of 'material reward,' O'Casey turned to political plays with no chance of commercial success, and a story which the English printer considered too immoral to set in type.

To Cochran, Shaw suggested that he had earned a place in a producer's Valhalla. The play would pass 'into the classical repertory,' he wrote, 'and it was a magnificent gesture of yours to produce it. The Highbrows *should* have produced it: you, the Unpretentious Showman, *did*, as you have done so many other noble and rash things. . . . If only someone would build you a huge Woolworth theatre (all seats sixpence) to start with O'Casey and O'Neill, and no plays by men who have ever seen a five-pound note before they were thirty or been inside a school after they were thirteen, you would be buried in Westminster Abbey.' The criteria didn't quite fit G.B.S. himself, yet came close.

In 1932 Yeats decided that Ireland needed its own Academy of Letters, and induced Shaw to become its first president (with Yeats himself as vice-president). The first thirty-five writers invited to become founding members included O'Casey. But they also included, obviously, Yeats as well as the Abbey's impresario, Lennox Robinson. Bitter at the Abbey's treatment of him, for which he blamed Yeats, O'Casey found reasons to refuse admission, pointing to the dangers of implicit censorship through the approval or disapproval of the Academy. Besides, he added in a letter to the *Irish Times*, the whole idea was a 'literary cocktail' rather than anything truly useful for Ireland. That Yeats was clearly the evil genius behind the Academy, he made no attempt to hide. That the invitation to join came over Shaw's signature made it, O'Casey later wrote in his memoirs, 'the hardest refusal he had to face,' the 'one favour' Shaw had ever asked him. A letter of refusal was sent to Shaw, O'Casey recalled, 'but no answer came back'. No such letter has turned up. Perhaps O'Casey had let his public statements stand for him, and only imagined the letter later. In any case, Shaw knew what it would have cost O'Casey's pride to join something which had been Yeats's brainchild.

That year O'Casey was slipping deeper into debt. His income from minor journalism was not supplementing his meagre royalties enough to arrest the slide. While preparing the prompt copies of his plays for Samuel French he received an offer from the publisher to purchase half the amateur rights to *Gunman, Juno* and *Plough* for £300. He consulted Shaw, who warned him against the 'absurdly bad bargain,' and enclosed a 'loan' of £100. 'My advice,' Shaw added, 'is to let wife and child perish, and lay bricks for your last crust, sooner than part with an iota of your rights.' O'Casey needed more than that, but was reluctant to ask Shaw, who at about the same time was extricating his old friends Sidney and Beatrice Webb from assorted difficulties with a check for £1,000. O'Casey signed away his rights to French, only to discover later that the publisher was holding £300 in

royalties for him, claiming that they had been unable at the time
to locate his address.

A rare opportunity for reciprocity came to O'Casey in the
1930s. To Charlotte he had described Shaw's *Too True to Be Good*
as a 'rare title' and a 'terrible [meaning terrifying] philosophy,'
and in *The Listener* he wrote a long review of *Too True* and
On the Rocks, Shaw's next political-prophetic play. *Saint Joan*,
he wrote, was easier to take, 'like an illuminated Book of Hours
that one can finger and fondle, and be amused by the quaint
pictures, thanking God all the time that we are not as other men
were.' On the other hand, Shaw's apocalyptic plays set in the
near-present were 'flames of courageous thought which some day,
sooner or later, will burn to ashes the hay, straw, and stubble
of cod mercy and truth and righteousness and peace that find their
vent in the singing of hymns, piling of law upon law, and the
pampering of the useless and the unfit.'[6] But O'Casey was not
merely championing Shaw: he was pointing implicitly to his own
increasingly uncommercial playwriting perspectives – visions of
apocalypse in the present.

Within the Gates, an example of O'Casey's current method, had
opened a month before his essay had appeared, and the playwright
had brought Bernard Shaw to sit with him at the Royalty Theatre
on opening night. The play, however, needed more than that.
An essentially plotless, poetic, sentimental denunciation of
hypocrisy and misery, it was Strindberg's *Dream Play* set in Hyde
Park and peopled with contemporary types. What the public
wanted was another *Juno* or *Plough* – Hibernian poetic realism
rather than Strindbergian dream visions. He was not about to
turn back, instead telling Shaw that *he* should write a play about
the rebellion of Jack Cade. Shaw 'could make a Communist
St. Joan of him'. O'Casey, rather, would begin a new symbolic
play, *The Star Turns Red*, which would have no chance of either
critical or commercial success.

With little hope of burgeoning play royalties, and work on his
'semi-autobiography' going slowly, O'Casey lived frugally and in
debt. With his children growing into school age, he and Eileen[7]
warmed to Shaw's suggestion that living away from the London
area could be both inexpensive and valuable for schooling,
especially if the O'Caseys could find a place near the modern
Dartington School in Devon. A spacious Victorian house in
Totnes was available at £85 a year, very little by London
standards, but the landlord (a dentist), seeing O'Casey and his
brood, asked for a co-signer of the lease, to guarantee his rent.

Not wanting to bother G.B.S. directly, O'Casey asked Charlotte, who invited him to the Whitehall Court flat to talk about it over lunch. Businesslike, she asked about the house, the rates, and if O'Casey was working on anything remunerative. O'Casey flushed at the means test and G.B.S. barked, 'Oh, give it to him!' The questioning halted, and everything seemed settled, but the landlord refused to accept a woman – even a millionairess – as guarantor. G.B.S. quickly obliged, writing O'Casey on 17 October 1938, 'Your landlord, being a dentist, has developed an extraction complex. He proposed a lease in which I was not only to guarantee all your convenants, but indemnify him for all consequences.' Since Shaw loved haggling over contracts, and vetting other people's legal documents, nothing could have made him happier. 'I said,' Shaw told O'Casey, '[that] I did not know his character but knew enough of yours to know that the consequences might include anything from murder to a European war; so I re-drafted the agreement. The lawyers, knowing that their man was only too lucky to get a gilt-edged (so they thought) security, and that his demands were absurd, made no resistance.'

To Charlotte Shaw (G.B.S. was difficult to thank so directly) O'Casey wrote that he indeed needed the financial guarantee but – he took Shaw's joking remark literally – 'I'm not going to anyone to guarantee my morals.' Then he added, documenting what must have been the beginning of the Shavian impact upon him, 'I have always had to fight like the devil for life; but you must blame your husband, G.B.S., for whatever sharpness and wit that have come into my fighting qualities; and [as well] my young Dublin comrade, member of the Fourth Order of Saint Francis, who first put the green-covered copy of *John Bull's Other Island* in my then reluctant hand.'

'Read *John Bull's Other Island*,' Kevin O'Loughlin had promised, 'and the Ireland you think you know and love will vanish before your eyes.'

'Well, that's a damn fine recommendation!' O'Casey had said sceptically, but when payday came he had gone to Jason's bookshop and purchased the sixpenny paper edition. By the time of his letter to Charlotte, *John Bull* had taken on an almost metaphorical quality to him.

By then, too, O'Casey was again a father (Shaw sent the infant Shivaun fifty pounds), and now working on a play which he hoped would combine what he wanted to do with what he hoped the public would accept. The result was the comic fantasy *Purple*

Dust, a try at social criticism through a symbolic decaying country house and characters who might have come out of *Heartbreak House*. Saros Cowasjee, rather, sees a bond between *Purple Dust* and the play which had first turned O'Casey to Shaw a generation earlier. Still, as Cowasjee observes, Shaw had probed deeply into both Irish and English psyches, while O'Casey, who lived largely self-insulated from his surroundings, was unable to see profoundly into the English milieu. Shaw's characters can be absurd without being puppets or fools. In *Purple Dust*, O'Casey did not get beyond being cantankerous and colourful, but whether or not his inspiration had been *John Bull* or *Heartbreak House*, the result was one of his rare later plays which had some box-office success in his lifetime.

There are close resemblances in structure as well as theme to *John Bull's Other Island,* as Ronald Rollins notes. Both comedies utilize the device of English expeditions to a backward Ireland, a portion of which they propose to rehabilitate, and both expose fraudulent sentiment, spiritual torpidity, paralyzing class antagonisms, and consequent economic stagnation. 'Excessive, neurotic fascination with imaginative splendours and/or glories of the past makes people, so Shaw and O'Casey suggest, inept participants in the present, rendering them victims and enemies of change, innovation, and progress.'[8]

John Bull's Other Island reverberates through O'Casey's plays, although perhaps nowhere so much as in *Purple Dust*. Larry Doyle's penetrating analysis in *John Bull* of the Irishman's dreaming imagination, which 'never lets him alone,' permeates O'Casey's characters from Davoren to the Irish dreamers of *Purple Dust*; and Cowasjee sees in both *John Bull* and *Purple Dust* the same portrayal of the 'irresponsibility of the Irish, their sense of humor, their pride, their flattery of the English, the poetic brilliance of their speech and their queer love-making. . . .' The apocalyptic ending, however – a flood rather than a bombing – echoes *Heartbreak House*, and the warnings of imminent catastrophe are reminiscent of the prophecies of Shotover and Hector (and even echo the spoof of English respectability in *Caesar and Cleopatra*, about the dying of their bodies blue by Britannus and his confreres, so that even when stripped of their clothes they could not be robbed of their respectability). Says Philib of the English interlopers for whom he must work, reclaiming a dilapidated mansion on the edge of a river which regularly overflows its banks, 'Hammerin' out handsome golden ornaments for flowin'

cloak and tidy tunic we were, while you were busy gatherin'
dhried grass, and dyin' it blue, to hide the consternation of your
middle parts; decoratin' eminent books with glowin' color an'
audacious beauty were we . . . when you were still hundred
score o' years away from even hearin' of the alphabet. Fool? It's
yourself's the fool, I'm sayin', settlin' down in a place that's only
fit for the housin' o' dead men! . . . Wait till God sends the heavy
rain, and the floods come! '

Later O'Casey would describe *Purple Dust* in *Heartbreak House*
terms as without partisan politics – not an attack on England,
'not even on any particular class in the country. . . . It is to some
extent, a symbolic play, and unconsciously, a prophetic one too.
The auld hoose, beloved by so many for so long, is in a bad
way; old things are passing away, and new things are appearing
in the sky, on the horizon, and right here in the middle of us.
The house is falling, and we hardly know where to pick up the
bits.'

The move to Devon, prompted by Shaw, would prove to have
the drawback for O'Casey that he was no longer in easy visiting
distance of 'Shaw's Corner' at Ayot St. Lawrence. 'Sean missed
him exceedingly,' Eileen O'Casey remembered, as the war years,
then beginning, were years of decreased mobility, both because of
wartime restrictions and O'Casey's increasingly failing eyesight.
It would have been such a help, Eileen thought, if her husband
'could have talked to somebody who really loved the theatre and
who was in harmony with him.' It was time, Shaw wrote O'Casey
in 1943, that he produced a 'money-spinner'; but written exhorta-
tions were the best that Shaw could do at 87, worn down himself
with age and with care for Charlotte, who had died that year
of a crippling bone ailment.

Several times after that Eileen managed visits to Ayot without
Sean, Shaw in his ninety-fourth year greeting her with 'Well,
Eileen, you've still got your good looks.' In a note about the visit
to O'Casey, Irish diplomat John Dulanty, the mutual friend who
had driven Eileen there, added, 'I wandered out of the room to
give them the opportunity of a mild flirtation.'

The corespondence with O'Casey continued until almost the
end Shaw writing him several months later, in May 1950, that
Irish Catholics were still sending him 'medals of the Blessed
Virgin, guaranteeing, if I say a novena, that she will give me
anything I ask from her, to which I reply that the B V needs
helpers and not beggars.' While over the years Shaw had been
generous in many ways to the O'Casey family, Sean himself had

never begged anything, after the abortive request for a preface, but the lease guarantee which cost G.B.S. nothing more than his signature. The genteel poverty in which the O'Caseys were surviving in Devon was something he never realized, and in the immediate postwar years, when the self-styled Green Crow seemed to be turning out plays and polemics with regularity, Shaw had assumed the best, although O'Casey's cranky new comedies made little money. He would never find out otherwise.

After Shaw's fall at Ayot in July 1950, in which he broke a hip and became bedridden in his final months, Dulanty and Eileen returned at their first opportunity to see Shaw. It was October, and Shaw was frail and clearly failing, 'caged now,' as O'Casey would write, 'in his own home'. Privately, to Dulanty Shaw asked how the O'Caseys were doing, and Dulanty confided that he did not think they were 'all that good'. When Shaw told him that he had heard, rather, that they were 'in clover,' Dulanty felt that Eileen should tell him the truth. Afterwards, as Shaw and Eileen talked of the children, and the daily lives of the family, Shaw suddenly asked, 'And how is Sean financially?' Unwilling to be a supplicant she replied, 'Of course, we are perfectly all right.' Shaw 'said he had heard we were in clover, and was relieved about it.' He went on to talk of his loneliness after the passing of so many friends and contemporaries, and Eileen felt that it was time to return to London, where she had been staying. It was the O'Caseys' last chance to be remembered in his will, and it had passed by.*

A few days later Shaw asked to see her. He opened his eyes when she walked in and said faintly, 'I really think I am going to die.' Sean, he told her, would have to carry on for him. 'No,' she said frankly, realizing that O'Casey was 70 and nearly sightless, 'Sean is too old.' At his request she kissed him goodbye, and he sank back into sleep. He died two days later, on 2 November 1950. O'Casey's tribute 'to a Fighting Idealist' appeared in the first *New York Times Book Review* issue to be printed after Shaw's death.

In *Sunset and Evening Star* (1954), the sixth and last volume of his autobiographies, O'Casey would publish a long chapter, 'Shaw's Corner,' lovingly detailing his relationship with G.B.S.

---

* Later, O'Casey, on his own deathbed in 1964, wept to Eileen that he was leaving her nearly penniless. 'You could have married a millionaire,' he said, remembering what a beauty she had been when he, at forty-seven, had married her thirty-seven years earlier. 'If you hurry up,' said Eileen gently, 'I still can.'

No one has been more eloquent or more persuasive about the
poetic element in Shaw's plays (so often labelled as non-existent).
Not only did O'Casey see poetry in Shaw's prose but in the
Shavian theatrical imagination:

> Some critics say there is no poetry in Shaw's plays (how often
> have the Dublin bravos signed this in the air with a sawing
> hand!); and no emotion. There is poetry in the very description
> of the Syrian sky at the opening of *Caesar and Cleopatra*, in the
> way the Bucina calls, in the two great figures dwarfed between
> the paws of the Sphinx, in the rush of the Roman Legion into
> the Palace, halting to cry Hail, Caesar, when they see him
> sitting alone with the Queen of Egypt; poetry, and emotion, too.
> There is poetry and fine emotion in the scene on the banks of
> the Loire in the play of *Saint Joan*, and in the Saint's sorrow
> when she sees that while the world venerates her at a safe
> distance, the same world wants her no nearer; here is ironical
> emotion, shot with sadness stretching out to the day that is
> with us, for, with Christians now, it is not, Get thee behind me,
> Satan, but Get thee behind me, God. . . . There is poetry and
> emotion in *Candida*; poetry of a minor key in the way the
> doctors regard the thoughtlessness of the artist, Dubedat, rising
> into a major key at the death of the artist when the play is
> ending; it flashes through every scene of *Heartbreak House*;
> and stands dignified and alone in the character of Keegan in
> *John Bull's Other Island*; the poetry and emotion gleams out
> in the revelation that God is close to Feemy Evans, the fallen
> woman of the camp, though the respectable humbugs wouldn't
> let her finger-tip touch the bible. The English critics are afraid
> to feel: Eton and Harrow seem to have groomed them against
> the destitute dignity of tears. . . .

O'Casey had been writing his memoirs since the early 1930s,
and the third, *Drums under the Windows* (for which he had
designed his own jacket, with the figure on the left, looking over
a toy-town Dublin, meant to be Shaw) had included nearly a
dozen pages on the epiphany that was his encounter with *John
Bull's Other Island*. 'Near naked, Ireland stood, with the one
jewel of [Father] Keegan's Dream occasionally seen sparkling in
her tousled hair, attaching poverty to pride; a shameful figure,
but noble still, though her story was hidden and her song unsung.'
The spurned O'Casey could identify readily with the reputedly
mad, unfrocked Keegan, in O'Casey's words 'banished from the

altar, hinging himself more closely to his breviary than ever, torturing himself delightfully with the vision of a country where the state is the church and the church the people; three in one and one in three; where work is play and play is life; where the priest is the worshipper, and the worshipper the worshipped; three in one and one in three; carrying the vision around with him to pour it into the loneliness of a round tower: the dream of a madman, but the dream of an Irishman, too.' In the mirror in Casey's house he could always confront the face of Father Keegan.

Notes

1 Shaw's letters are quoted from the notes to David Krause, ed., *The Letters of Sean O'Casey*, I, 1910–1941 (London and New York, 1975), and from Eileen O'Casey. *Sean* (New York, 1972).

2 Robert Hogan and Michael J. O'Neill, *Joseph Holloway's Abbey Theatre* (Carbondale. Ill., 1967). entry for March 18, 1924. p. 227.

3 Shaw's plays are quoted from the *Bodley Head Bernard Shaw* (London, 7 vols., 1971–74).

4 Saros Cowasjee, Sean O'Casey, *The Man Behind the Plays* (London, 1963), pp. 77–78.

5 O'Casey's letters are quoted from Krause.

6 'G.B.S. Speaks Out of the Whirlwind,' *The Listener*, 7 March 1934, Supplement III–IV.

7 Eileen's memories hereafter supplement the *Letters* and O'Casey's own autobiographies. *Mirror in My House* (New York, 1956).

8 Ronald G. Rollins. 'Shaw and O'Casey: John Bull and His Other Island,' *Shaw Review*, X (1967), 60–69.

9 Ronald Ayling and Michael J. Durkan, *Sean O'Casey. A Bibliography* (London, 1978), pp. 71–72.

SEAN O'CASEY AT THE ABBEY THEATRE

ROBERT G. LOWERY

Sean O'Casey's record at the Abbey Theatre leaves no doubt that he is Ireland's national playwright. His three Dublin plays rank 1-2-3 in the number of performances in the history of the Abbey (followed by Lady Gregory's *The Rising of the Moon* which was often on the same bill as *The Shadow of a Gunman*), and, in terms of quantity, he is the most popular of all Irish playwrights. What is remarkable about this record is that the first of O'Casey's plays was not performed until almost twenty years after the founding of the Abbey, and that for several years the dramatist imposed a ban on all professional productions in Ireland of his plays.

What follows is a chronological record of the productions of O'Casey's plays at the Abbey. Each run is presented in weekly dates, followed by the number of performances that week, and the producer/director of the play. A cumulative total through 1978 appears at the end of the account.

I am grateful to the staff of the Abbey Theatre, especially Tomas MacAnna and Deirdre McQuillan, for their assistance, for their patience, and for letting me roam unhindered through their hallways and closets.

* – World premiere
** – Irish premiere

1923

The Shadow of a Gunman (1)	*April 12 – 14	(4)	Lennox Robinson
The Shadow of a Gunman (2)	August 6 – 11	(7)	Lennox Robinson
The Shadow of a Gunman (2)	August 15	(1)	Lennox Robinson
Cathleen Listens In (3)	*October 1 – 6	(7)	Lennox Robinson
The Shadow of a Gunman (4)	October 15 – 20	(7)	Lennox Robinson

(1) With *Sovereign Love* by T. C. Murray.
(2) With *Crabbed Youth and Age* by Lennox Robinson.
(3) With *Man of Destiny* by George Bernard Shaw and *Riders to the Sea* by J. M. Synge.
(4) With *The Jackdaw* by Lady Gregory

1924

The Shadow of a Gunman (1)	Jan. 28 – Feb. 2	(7)	Michael J. Dolan
The Shadow of a Gunman (2)	February 7 – 9	(4)	Michael J. Dolan
Juno and the Paycock	*March 3 – 8	(5)	Michael J. Dolan
	March 11 – 15	(6)	
The Shadow of a Gunman (3)	April 8 – 12	(6)	Michael J. Dolan
Juno and the Paycock	April 29 – May 3	(6)	Michael J. Dolan
	May 6 – 10	(6)	
The Shadow of a Gunman (3)	August 11 – 13	(3)	Michael J. Dolan
The Shadow of a Gunman (4)	August 18 – 23	(7)	Michael J. Dolan
Juno and the Paycock	September 15 – 20	(7)	Michael J. Dolan
Nannie's Night Out (5)	*Sept. 29 – Oct. 4	(7)	Michael J. Dolan

1924 Continued

Play	Date		Director
The Shadow of a Gunman (6)	Oct. 27 – Nov. 1	(7)	Michael J. Dolan
Juno and the Paycock	November 11 – 15	(6)	Michael J. Dolan

(1) With *Queer Ones* by Con O'Leary
(2) With *Meadowsweet* by Seumas O'Kelly
(3) With *Never the Time and the Place* by Lennox Robinson
(4) With *In the Shadow of the Glen* by J. M. Synge
(5) With *Arms and the Man* by George Bernard Shaw
(6) With *Riders to the Sea* by J. M. Synge

1925

Play	Date		Director
Juno and the Paycock	January 12 – 17	(7)	Michael J. Dolan
Cathleen Listens In (Revised) (1)	March 3 – 7	(6)	Michael J. Dolan
The Shadow of a Gunman (2)	March 24 – 28	(6)	Michael J. Dolan
Juno and the Paycock	August 17 – 22	(7)	Michael J. Dolan
	August 24 – 29	(7)	
The Shadow of a Gunman (3)	September 7 – 12	(7)	Michael J. Dolan
The Shadow of a Gunman (4)	November 23 – 28	(7)	Michael J. Dolan

(1) With *The Whiteheaded Boy* by Lennox Robinson
(2) With *Spreading the News* by Lady Gregory
(3) With *The Proposal* by Anton Chekov
(4) With *Portrait* by Lennox Robinson

1926

Play	Date		Director
The Plough and the Stars	*February 8 – 14	(8)	Lennox Robinson

1926 Continued

Juno and the Paycock	March 22 – 27	(7)	Lennox Robinson
The Plough and the Stars	May 3 – 8	(7)	Lennox Robinson
Juno and the Paycock	July 5 – 10	(7)	Lennox Robinson
The Shadow of a Gunman (1)	August 5 – 7	(7)	Lennox Robinson
Juno and the Paycock	September 13 – 18	(7)	Lennox Robinson
Juno and the Paycock	Dec. 27 – Jan. 1	(8)	Lennox Robinson

(1) With *Meadowsweet* by Seumas O'Kelly

1927

The Plough and the Stars	January 18 – 22	(6)	Lennox Robinson
The Shadow of a Gunman (1)	March 8 – 12	(6)	Lennox Robinson
The Shadow of a Gunman (2)	July 4 – 9	(7)	Lennox Robinson
	July 11 – 16	(7)	
Juno and the Paycock	August 4 – 6	(4)	Lennox Robinson
The Shadow of a Gunman (3)	October 11 – 16	(7)	Lennox Robinson
Juno and the Paycock	November 21 – 26	(7)	Lennox Robinson

(1) With *The Rising of the Moon* by Lady Gregory
(2) With *Parted* by M. C. Madden
(3) With *Meadowsweet* by Seumas O'Kelly

1928

The Shadow of a Gunman (1)	February 20 – 25	(7)	Lennox Robinson
Juno and the Paycock	April 23 – 28	(7)	Lennox Robinson
The Plough and the Stars	May 9 – 12	(5)	Lennox Robinson

1928 *Continued*

Juno and the Paycock	August 20 – 25	(7) Lennox Robinson
The Shadow of a Gunman (2)	September 17 – 22	(7) Lennox Robinson
The Plough and the Stars	Oct. 29 – Nov. 3	(7) Lennox Robinson
	November 6 – 8	(3) Lennox Robinson

(1) With *Spring* by T. C. Murray
(2) With *The Gaol Gate* by Lady Gregory

1929

Juno and the Paycock	January 21 – 26	(7) Lennox Robinson
The Shadow of a Gunman (1)	Feb. 25 – Mar. 2	(7) Lennox Robinson
The Plough and the Stars	May 20 – 25	(7) Lennox Robinson
The Shadow of a Gunman (2)	November 12 – 17	(7) Lennox Robinson
Juno and the Paycock	December 26 – 29	(9) Lennox Robinson

(1) With *Crabbed Youth and Age* by Lennox Robinson
(2) With *Hyacinth Halvey* by Lady Gregory

1930

The Shadow of a Gunman (1)	Feb. 25 – Mar. 2	(7) Lennox Robinson
The Plough and the Stars	April 1 – 6	(7) Lennox Robinson
The Plough and the Stars	July 14 – 19	(7) Arthur Shields
The Shadow of a Gunman. (2)	August 18 – 23	(7) Arthur Shields
Juno and the Paycock	Dec. 26 – Jan. 3	(10) Lennox Robinson

(1) With *The Countess Cathleen* by W. B. Yeats
(2) With *The Pipe in the Fields* by T. C. Murray

1931

The Plough and the Stars	January 26 – 31	(7)	Lennox Robinson
The Shadow of a Gunman (1)	June 2 – 6	(6)	Lennox Robinson
The Plough and the Stars	July 13 – 18	(7)	Lennox Robinson
Juno and the Paycock	August 4, 6, 8	(4)	Lennox Robinson

(1) With *The Words Upon the Window Pane* by W. B. Yeats

1932

Juno and the Paycock	July 12 – 17	(7)	Lennox Robinson
The Plough and the Stars	August 1, 3, 5	(3)	Lennox Robinson
The Shadow of a Gunman (1)	August 24, 26, 27	(4)	Lennox Robinson

(1) With *Crabbed Youth and Age* by Lennox Robinson

1933

Juno and the Paycock	June 26 – July 1	(7)	Lennox Robinson
The Shadow of a Gunman (1)	August 21 – 26	(6)	Lennox Robinson
The Plough and the Stars	September 18 – 23	(7)	Lennox Robinson

(1) With the first productions of *The Jezebel* by J. K. Montgomery

1934

The Shadow of a Gunman (1)	Jan. 29 – Feb. 3	(7)	Lennox Robinson
Juno and the Paycock	April 9 – 14	(7)	Lennox Robinson
The Plough and the Stars	May 28 – June 6	(7)	Lennox Robinson
Juno and the Paycock	August 7, 9, 11	(4)	Lennox Robinson

1934 *Continued*

The Plough and the Stars	September 3 – 8	(7)	Lennox Robinson

(1) With *Spreading the News* by Lady Gregory

1935

The Plough and the Stars	August 8 – 10	(3)	Lennox Robinson
The Silver Tassie	**August 12 – 17	(6)	Arthur Shields
Juno and the Paycock	Oct. 28 – Nov. 6	(6)	Lennox Robinson
The Shadow of a Gunman	December 16 – 21	(6)	Lennox Robinson

1936

The Plough and the Stars	February 17 – 22	(6)	Hugh Hunt
The Shadow of a Gunman (1)	May 18 – 23	(6)	Hugh Hunt
The Plough and the Stars	September 21 – 26	(6)	Michael J. Dolan
The Shadow of a Gunman (2)	October 5 – 10	(6)	Hugh Hunt

(1) With *The Shadowy Waters* by W. B. Yeats
(2) With *Kathleen ni Houlihan* by W. B. Yeats

1937

The End of the Beginning (1)	*February 8 – 13	(5)	Arthur Shields
The Plough and the Stars	March 1 – 6	(6)	Arthur Shields
Juno and the Paycock	May 10 – 15	(6)	Arthur Shields
The Shadow of a Gunman (2)	May 31 – June 6	(6)	Hugh Hunt

(1) With *The Silver Jubilee* by Cormac O'Daly. No performance 10 February, Ash Wednesday
(2) With the first production of *In the Train*, dramatised by Hugh Hunt

1938

Play	Date		Director
The Plough and the Stars	April 18 – 23	(6)	Hugh Hunt
The Plough and the Stars (1)	April 25 – 30	(6)	Hugh Hunt
The Plough and the Stars	August 16, 18	(2)	Hugh Hunt
Juno and the Paycock	August 29 – Sept. 3	(8)	Hugh Hunt
The Shadow of a Gunman (2)	Oct. 31 – Nov. 5	(6)	Arthur Shields
	December 12 – 17	(6)	Michael J. Dolan

(1) Abbey Theatre Festival
(2) With the first production of *Baintighearna an Ghorta* by Seamus De Bhilmot

1939

Play	Date		Director
The Plough and the Stars	January 2 – 7	(6)	Michael J. Dolan
The Plough and the Stars	May 18 – 20	(4)	Michael J. Dolan
Juno and the Paycock	May 22 – 27	(6)	Michael J. Dolan
The Plough and the Stars (1)	August 14 – 19	(6)	Michael J. Dolan
The Shadow of a Gunman (1) (2)	September 4 – 9	(6)	Michael J. Dolan
The Plough and the Stars (1)	October 2 – 7	(6)	Michael J. Dolan

(1) Abbey Experimental Theatre
(2) With *The King of Spain's Daughter* by Teresa Deevy

1940

Play	Date		Director
Juno and the Paycock	January 15 – 20	(6)	Michael J. Dolan

1941
None

	1942		
The Plough and the Stars	January 26 – 31	(6)	Frank Dermody*
	February 2 – 7	(6)	
	February 9 – 14	(6)	
	February 16 – 21	(6)	
	February 23 – 28	(6)	
	March 2 – 7	(6)	
Juno and the Paycock	November 9 – 14	(6)	Frank Dermody
	November 16 – 21	(6)	
	November 23 – 28	(6)	
	December 1 – 6	(6)	
*Sometimes under the name Proinnsias MacDiarmida (see the years 1964–66)			
	1943		
	None		
	1944		
The Plough and the Stars	March 13 – 18	(6)	Frank Dermody
	March 20 – 25	(6)	
	Mar. 28 – Apr. 4	(5)	
The Shadow of a Gunman (1)	April 8 – 15	(7)	Frank Dermody
	April 17 – 22	(6)	
The Plough and the Stars	May 1 – 6	(6)	Frank Dermody

(1) With *Lost Light* by Roibeard O Farachain

Play	Year / Dates		Director
Juno and the Paycock	*1945*		
	Feb. 26 – Mar. 3	(6)	Frank Dermody
	March 5 – 10	(6)	
	March 12 – 17	(6)	
	March 20 – 24	(5)	
The Plough and the Stars	October 2 – 6	(6)	Frank Dermody
	October 8 – 13	(5)	
	October 15 – 20	(6)	
	October 22 – 27	(6)	
	Oct. 29 – Nov. 3	(6)	
	November 5 – 10	(6)	
The Shadow of a Gunman (1)	*1946*		
	March 11 – 16	(6)	Frank Dermody
	March 18 – 23	(6)	
The Plough and the Stars	*1947*		
	October 13 – 18	(6)	Michael J. Dolan
	October 20 – 25	(6)	
	Oct. 27 – Nov. 1	(6)	
	November 10 – 12	(3)	Michael J. Dolan
The Plough and the Stars	*1948* None		
	1949 None		

(1) With *The Rising of the Moon* by Lady Gregory

1950

The Shadow of a Gunman (1)	May 26 – 27	(2)	Ria Mooney
The Shadow of a Gunman (1)	May 29 – June 3	(6)	Ria Mooney
	July 3 – 8	(6)	
	July 10 – 15	(6)	
	July 17 – 22	(6)	
	July 24 – 29	(6)	
	July 31 – Aug. 5	(6)	
	August 7 – 9	(3)	

(1) With *Village Wooing* by George Bernard Shaw

1951

Juno and the Paycock	February 12 – 17	(6)	Ria Mooney
	February 19 – 24	(6)	
	Feb. 26 – March 3	(6)	
	March 5 – 10	(6)	
	March 12 – 17	(6)	
	March 19 – 20	(2)	
The Plough and the Stars	May 14 – 19	(6)	Ria Mooney
The Plough and the Stars	May 22 – 26	(5)	Ria Mooney
The Plough and the Stars	June 25 – 30	(6)	Ria Mooney
	July 2 – 7	(6)	Ria Mooney
	July 9 – 14	(6)	
	July 16 – 21	(6)	
	July 23 – 28	(6)	
	July 30 – Aug. 4	(6)	

1951 *Continued*

	(1)			
The Silver Tassie (2)	August 6 – 11	(6)	Ria Mooney	
	September 24 – 29	(6)		
	October 1 – 6	(6)		
The Shadow of a Gunman (3)	Oct. 29 – Nov. 3	(6)	Ria Mooney	
	November 5 – 10	(6)		
	November 12 – 17	(6)		

(1) At The Rupert Guinness Hall, Dublin
(2) At the Queen's Theatre until 1966
(3) With *Village Wooing* by George Bernard Shaw

1952

Juno and the Paycock (1)	May 19 – 24	(6)	Ria Mooney
(2)	May 26 – 31	(6)	
Juno and the Paycock	June 30 – July 5	(6)	Ria Mooney
	July 7 – 12	(6)	

(1) With *An Imaginary Conversation* by Conal O'Riordan
(2) With *An Crann Ubhall* by Harold Brighouse

1953

The Shadow of a Gunman (1)	September 5	(1)	Ria Mooney
The Shadow of a Gunman (2)	September 12	(1)	Eamon O Guailli
The Shadow of a Gunman (2)	October 26 – 27	(2)	Eamon O Guailli

(1) With *The Paddy Pedlar* by Michael J. Molloy
(2) With *In the Shadow of the Glen* by J. M. Synge

	1954		
	None		
	1955		
The Plough and the Stars	April 25 – 30	(6)	Ria Mooney
	May 2 – 7	(6)	
	May 9 – 14	(6)	
The Plough and the Stars	June 13 – 18	(6)	Ria Mooney
	June 20 – 25	(6)	
The Plough and the Stars	June 27, 29	(2)	Ria Mooney
The Plough and the Stars	July 1, 4, 6, 8, 11	(5)	Ria Mooney
The Plough and the Stars	July 13, 15	(2)	Ria Mooney
The Plough and the Stars	July 18 – 23	(6)	Ria Mooney
The Plough and the Stars	August 1, 3, 5	(3)	Ria Mooney
The Plough and the Stars	August 29, 31	(2)	Ria Mooney
The Plough and the Stars	September 2	(1)	Ria Mooney
	1956		
The Shadow of a Gunman	February 13 – 18	(6)	Ria Mooney
Juno and the Paycock	May 14 – 19	(6)	Ria Mooney
	May 21 – 26	(6)	
Juno and the Paycock (1)	June 25 – 30	(6)	Ria Mooney
	July 2 – 7	(6)	
	July 9 – 14	(6)	
Juno and the Paycock	August 7, 9, 11	(3)	Ria Mooney

1956 Continued

| Juno and the Paycock | August 14, 16, 18 | (3) | Ria Mooney |

(1) With *Ull Glas Oiche Shamhna* by Maired Ni Ghrada

1957

The Plough and the Stars	January 8 – 12	(5)	Ria Mooney
	January 14 – 19	(6)	
The Plough and the Stars	February 4 – 9	(6)	Ria Mooney
	February 11 – 16	(6)	
	February 18 – 23	(6)	
The Plough and the Stars	May 6 – 11	(6)	Ria Mooney
Juno and the Paycock (1)	May 13 – 18	(6)	Ria Mooney
Juno and the Paycock	July 1 – 6	(6)	Ria Mooney
	July 8 – 13	(6)	
	July 15 – 20	(6)	
The Plough and the Stars	October 28, 29, 30	(3)	Ria Mooney

1958
None

1959
None

1960
None

(1) Festival production

1961
None

1962
None

1963
None

1964

Play	Dates		Director
The Plough and the Stars	February 11 – 15	(5)	Proinnsias MacDiarmada*
	February 17 – 22	(6)	
	February 24 – 29	(6)	
	March 2 – 7	(6)	
	March 9 – 14	(6)	
Juno and the Paycock	March 17 – 21	(5)	Proinnsias MacDiarmada
	Mar. 23 – 25	(3)	
	Mar. 30 – Apr. 4	(6)	
	April 6 – 11	(6)	
	April 13 – 18	(6)	
Juno and the Paycock	July 6 – 11	(6)	Proinnsias MacDiarmada
The Plough and the Stars	July 20 – 25	(6)	Proinnsias MacDiarmada
	July 27 – Aug. 1	(6)	
The Shadow of a Gunman (1)	August 17 – 22	(6)	Proinnsias MacDiarmada
	August 24 – 29	(6)	
	Aug. 31 – Sept. 5	(6)	
Juno and the Paycock (2)	October 26 – 31	(6)	Proinnsias MacDiarmada

(1) With *Sovereign Love* by T. C. Murray
(2) Program note: 'On this, the first occasion on which there have been performances of an O'Casey play since the death of the author, the Directors of the Abbey Theatre salute his memory and pay tribute to his genius, which shed lustre on the Theatre and added to the renown of Ireland.'
*   Sometimes under the name Frank Dermody (see the years 1942–46).

1965

Play	Date		Director
The Plough and the Stars	September 6 – 11	(6)	Proinnsias MacDiarmada
	September 13 – 17	(6)	Proinnsias MacDiarmada
The Shadow of a Gunman (1)	October 4	(1)	

(1) With *Cathleen ni Houlihan* by W. B. Yeats

1966

Play	Date		Director
Hall of Healing (1)	Feb. 28 – Mar. 5	(6)	Tomas MacAnna
	March 7 – 12	(6)	Tomas MacAnna
Hall of Healing	April 25 – 30	(6)	Proinnsias MacDiarmada
The Shadow of a Gunman	May 2 – 7	(6)	
	May 9 – 14	(6)	
The Plough and the Stars (2)	August 15 – 20	(6)	Proinnsias MacDiarmada
	August 22 – 27	(8)	
	Aug. 29 – Sept. 3	(6)	
	September 5 – 10	(6)	
	September 12 – 17	(6)	
	September 19 – 24	(6)	
	Sept. 26 – Oct. 1	(6)	
The Plough and the Stars	November 14 – 19	(6)	Frank Dermody

(1) With *Yerma* by Federico Garcia Lorca
(2) At New Abbey Theatre

1967
None

1968
The Shadow of a Gunman (1)

May 13 – 18	(5)	
May 20 – 25	(6)	
May 27 – June 1	(6)	
June 3 – 8	(6)	
June 10 – 15	(6)	Vincent Dowling

(1) With *In the Shadow of the Glen* by J. M. Synge

1969
Juno and the Paycock

October 6 – 11	(6)	
October 13 – 18	(6)	
October 20 – 25	(6)	
Oct. 27 – Nov. 1	(6)	
November 3 – 8	(6)	Vincent Dowling

1970
The Plough and the Stars

December 1 – 5	(5)	
December 7 – 12	(6)	
December 14 – 19	(6)	
December 21 – 23	(3)	
Dec. 28 – Jan. 2	(5)	Shelah Richards

1971

Play	Date		Director
The Plough and the Stars	January 4 – 10	(6)	Shelah Richards
	January 12 – 16	(6)	
The Plough and the Stars	February 15 – 20	(6)	Shelah Richards
	February 22 – 27	(6)	
The Plough and the Stars	May 20 – 22	(3)	Shelah Richards
The Plough and the Stars	May 27 – 29	(3)	Shelah Richards
Hall of Healing	June 22	(1)	Peader Lamb
The Shadow of a Gunman (1)	June 28 – July 3	(6)	Shelah Richards
The Plough and the Stars	July 5 – 10	(6)	
The Shadow of a Gunman (2)	November 8 – 13	(6)	Vincent Dowling
	November 15 – 20	(6)	
	November 22 – 27	(6)	
The Shadow of a Gunman	December 13 – 18	(6)	Vincent Dowling
	December 20 – 22	(3)	
	Dec. 27 – Jan. 1	(6)	

(1) At the Peacock Theatre, Students from the Abbey Theatre Workshop
(2) With *The Gaol Gate* by Lady Gregory

1972

Play	Date		Director
Bedtime Story			
The End of the Beginning (1)	May 23 – 27	(5)	John Lynch
Bedtime Story			
The End of the Beginning (1)	June 27 – July 1	(5)	John Lynch
The End of the Beginning (1)	July 20 – 22	(3)	John Lynch

1972 Continued

Play	Date		Director
The Silver Tassie (2)	July 24 – 26	(3)	
	September 27 – 30	(4)	Hugh Hunt
	October 2 – 7	(6)	
	October 9 – 14	(6)	
	October 16 – 21	(6)	
	October 23 – 28	(8)	
The Silver Tassie	December 26 – 30	(5)	Hugh Hunt

(1) At the Peacock Theatre with *Splinters from a Glass* by Edward Rowe
(2) One preview September 26

Play	Date		Director
1973			
The Silver Tassie	January 1 – 6	(6)	Hugh Hunt
	January 8 – 13	(6)	
The Silver Tassie	Apr. 30 – May 5	(6)	Hugh Hunt
The Silver Tassie	July 30 – Aug. 4	(6)	Hugh Hunt
	August 6 – 11	(6)	
1974			
None			
1975			
Purple Dust	Jan. 30 – Feb. 1	(5)	Tomas MacAnna
	February 3 – 8	(6)	
	February 9	(1)	
	February 10 – 15	(6)	

1975 Continued

Play		Dates		Director
Purple Dust	(1)	February 17 – 22	(6)	
		Feb. 24 – Mar. 1	(5)	Tomas MacAnna
		April 8 – 12	(5)	
		April 14 – 19	(6)	
		April 21 – 26	(6)	
		April 28 – May 3	(6)	
Purple Dust		July 8 – 12	(5)	Tomas MacAnna
		July 14 – 19	(6)	
		July 21 – 26	(6)	
Figuro in the Night				
The Moon Shines on Kylenamoe	(2)	August 12 – 16	(5)	Tomas MacAnna
		August 19 – 23	(5)	
		August 25 – 30	(6)	
	(3)	September 1 – 6	(5)	

(1) No performance February 25, death of Ernest Blythe
(2) At the Peacock Theatre
(3) No performance September 2, day of mourning for Eamonn de Valera

1976

Play	Dates		Director
The Plough and the Stars (1)	May 14 – 15	(4)	Tomas MacAnna
	May 17 – 22	(6)	
	May 24 – 29	(6)	
The Plough and the Stars	August 2 – 7	(6)	Tomas MacAnna
	August 9 – 14	(6)	

1976 Continued

The Plough and the Stars (2)

August 16 – 21   (6)
August 23 – 28   (6)
September 27 – 29   (3)   Tomas MacAnna

(1) Fiftieth Anniversary performances. Includes two previews May 12 and 13
(2) Dublin Theatre Festival

1977

Cock-a-Doodle Dandy (1)

August 11 – 13   (5)   Tomas MacAnna
August 15 – 20   (6)
August 22 – 27   (6)
Aug. 29 – Sept. 3   (6)
September 5 – 10   (6)

Cock-a-Doodle Dandy (2)

October 6 – 8   (3)   Tomas MacAnna

(1) Includes two previews August 9 and 10
(2) Dublin Theatre Festival

1978

The Star Turns Red** (1)

February 2 – 4   (7)   Tomas MacAnna
February 6 – 11   (6)
February 13 – 15   (3)
February 23 – 25   (3)
Feb. 27 – Mar. 1   (3)

(1) Includes two previews January 31 and February 1

TOTALS	
The Plough and the Stars	637
Juno and the Paycock	420
The Shadow of a Gunman	403
The Silver Tassie	84
Purple Dust	69
Cock-a-Doodle Dandy	32
Hall of Healing	31
The Star Turns Red	22
The End of the Beginning	21
Figuro in the Night	21
The Moon Shines on Kylenamoe	21
Cathleen Listens In	13
Bedtime Story	10
Nannie's Night Out	7
	1791 Performances

NOTES ON CONTRIBUTORS

RONALD F. AYLING is an associate professor of English at the University of Alberta in Canada. Dr Ayling acted as literary executor to the O'Casey Estate, and catalogued the extensive O'Casey papers in the Berg Collection, New York Public Library. His books include *Blasts and Benedictions*, a posthumous selection of O'Casey's writings; *Sean O'Casey*, an anthology of O'Casey criticism for the Modern Judgements series; and *Continuity and Innovation in Sean O'Casey's Drama*. With Michael Durkan, he is the author of *Sean O'Casey: A Bibliography*.

BERNARD BENSTOCK is professor of English and Comparative Literature at the University of Illinois. His books include *James Joyce: The Undiscovered Country; Paycocks and Others: Sean O'Casey's World; Sean O'Casey; Approaches to James Joyce's 'A Portrait': Ten Essays,* co-edited with Thomas F. Staley; and *Who's He When He's at Home: A James Joyce Directory,* with Shari Benstock. He is the author of many articles for several scholarly journals and has served as president of the James Joyce Foundation Ltd.

MARY FITZGERALD gained her Ph.D. from Princeton University for work on Lady Gregory and W. B. Yeats, and taught at Fordham University before taking up her present appointment at the University of New Orleans. She is specialising in contemporary Irish poetry and the Abbey Theatre, and is Reviews Editor of *Yeats Annual*.

DAVID KRAUSE is professor of English at Brown University. He is editor of *The Letters of Sean O'Casey* and *The Dolmen Boucicault*, and author of *Sean O'Casey, The Man and His Work, Sean O'Casey and His World*, and *A Self-Portrait of the Artist as a Man*. He is the author of the O'Casey chapter for *Anglo-Irish Literature* for the MLA Review of Research series, and of many articles on Yeats, Synge, O'Casey, and Irish comedy for several scholarly journals.

ROBERT G. LOWERY was born in 1941, is married, and holds a M.A. degree in European history from Hofstra University, from which he received a Graduate Fellowship. He is the publisher of the *Sean O'Casey Review*, an international journal of O'Casey studies, and the editor of *Ais Eiri, The Magazine of Irish-America*, which is published by the Irish Arts Center, New York City.

WILLIAM J. MAROLDO is professor of English at Texas Lutheran College. He has professed English and comparative literatures, philosophy, and government and political science at New York University, Maryland, Colorado, and the U.S. Air Force Academy.

ALAN SIMPSON (1920–1980) had a long and distinguished career in drama. He was co-founder of the Dublin Pike Theatre, artistic director of the Abbey Theatre, and a frequent lecturer on Irish theatre. He directed over 100 productions including the world première of several Brendan Behan plays and the British premières of Samuel Beckett's *Waiting for Godot* and Tennessee William's *Rose Tattoo*.

STANLEY WEINTRAUB, director of the Institute for the Arts and Humanistic Studies, is a Research Professor at the Pennsylvania State University and editor of *The Shaw Review*. He is the author or editor of over thirty books, including *Private Shaw and Public Shaw, Journey to Heartbreak, Beardsley, Whistler*, and his most recent, *The London Yankees* and *The Portable Oscar Wilde*.

INDEX